Property of: LAR

D0223973

MAKE THE SALE!

How To Sell Media With Marketing.

BY MARY ALICE SHAVER

©1995 M.A. Shaver

First Edition

Published by The Copy Workshop

Division of Bruce Bendinger Creative Communications, Inc.

2144 N. Hudson • Chicago, IL 60614

312-871-1179 FX: 312-281-4643

ISBN: 0-9621415-6-9

Make The Sale!
How To Sell Media
With Marketing.

©1995 Mary Alice Shaver
First Edition
Second Printing

Published by The Copy Workshop
Division of Bruce Bendinger Creative Communications, Inc.
2144 N. Hudson • Chicago, IL 60614
312-871-1179 FX: 312-281-4643

ISBN: 0-9621415-6-9

Editor: Bruce Bendinger
Cover & Typographic Design: Alvin Blick

No part of this publication may be reproduced or transmitted in any form or by any means, electronic or mechanical, including photocopy, recording or any information storage and retrieval system now known or to be invented, without permission in writing from the publisher, except by a reviewer who wishes to quote brief passages in connection with a review written for inclusion in a magazine, newspaper or broadcast.

Advertising examples are copyrighted materials reproduced for educational purposes under "fair use" provisions of U.S. Copyright law. They are selected at the discretion of the author as they represent principles discussed in the text.

Property of
LAkota Journal

To Dan.

AUTHOR'S NOTES.

CHAPEL HILL, NC. This book has literally been written on the road as I moved from Chapel Hill to Charlotte to Miami and back again to my beloved Chapel Hill.

Perhaps that's appropriate since the information comes from many areas as well. This book brings together selling, marketing, media techniques, research, pricing, presentations, writing and design.

All these areas are part of today's job of using the media for advertising and for marketing. To do the job – whether it's selling space or time, planning advertising for your own business or working in an agency – you'll use the information and ideas every day with continually shifting priorities.

The media today operates in a constantly changing environment. The traditional local media – newspapers, radio and television – are challenged by an array of new media vehicles.

All media – no matter the format for delivery – must provide the customer with increasingly greater amounts of audience-specific data. Customer service and indivdually targeted advertising plans and campaigns are essential in today's competitive environment.

Using the media for marketing involves problem solving at many levels, and this book is designed to give you the tools to do just that. It gives you the basic facts and provides examples of real client situations. I hope you find it helpful in your demanding profession.

The ideas for the book came from my own experience in the business, from classes I have taught, from innumerable conversations and interviews, and from what I learned from my own students.

If you're a student, this book gives you the basic information and insight into a career in media sales. If you're already working on the job, it can serve as a reference and idea book.

However you use it, it's intended to be a working book to use in whatever ways you need to build success for you, your clients and your business.

A career in media sales is demanding, rewarding, discouraging, exciting, and challenging. I hope this book prepares you for all of these.

Recognition and thanks must go to ...

My editor, Bruce Bendinger, who hung in through all my moving about and helped make a book out of what began as class notes. Mairee Ryan, Sara VanCleef, Melissa Davis, and Lorelei Davis Bendinger at The Copy Workshop who helped proof and produce and cheer me on.

Tom Bowers, colleague and friend, who let me teach this course at UNC and whose first version of the course was the inspiration for all that followed.

Jim Avery, who talked me into actually writing the book and has remained a friend throughout. John Sweeney, who always knows when to listen, when to give a confidence boost, and when to send me back to my computer.

Ten years worth of good students who taught me how to talk about the material in the book.

Gene Williams of *The Charlotte Observer*, Chris Lytle of The AdVisory Board, Jeanne Sentman, and all the others who read and commented and gave professional feedback on the book.

R.B. Fitch of Fearrington and the National Association of Broadcasters for letting me incorporate their material into the book.

Special thanks must go to Dan for all the many hours of reading, commenting, developing graphs, and sending FedEx materials back to Bruce at the book's home base.

Finally, my family – Dan, Jeanne, Charles, Erica, Janet, and Joe – who I know are resigned to the fact that they'll be receiving copies of the book as Christmas presents – your love is the greatest gift.

Mary Alice Shaver
Summer 1995

EDITOR'S NOTES.

CHICAGO, IL. When this book was first suggested to us, we understood the strength of the concept right away.

The problem

In schools across the country, students learn the basics of advertising and marketing. Yet, for many, the real job opportunities lie in a related area for which little real training is currently offered – media sales.

Meanwhile, at newspapers, radio stations, and other local media companies across the country, management has to deal with the results – potentially qualified people who are untrained and unfamiliar with the field.

The opportunity

Then we were told about the innovative course that Prof. Mary Alice Shaver was teaching at the University of North Carolina.

Here was a sound, disciplined approach to the basics of media selling within an academic setting.

Better yet, the result was a book that makes as much sense in the tough competitive world of media marketing as it does in the classroom.

It really is the best of both worlds.

The challenge

As we worked to turn the course into a text, we developed even more appreciation for the difficulty of this profession.

- It demands skills in marketing.
- It demands skills in media.
- It demands creative skills.
- It demands salesmanship skills.

But, difficult as the field of media sales may be, developing this book with Prof. Shaver has been a wonderful experience – because we realized how many young men and women this book will help.

The result

We like the fact that media sales is presented as creative, challenging and satisfying work for intelligent people.

It is not "something to fall back on," but an excellent career option for many. Media sales is a field with good opportunities for qualified people.

We like the fact that this book combines academic tradition and discipline with real-world reality.

Professor Shaver calls it, "street smarts."

Professor Shaver knows the subject she teaches – as a graduate student, she paid for tuition by selling ad space.

In fact, media runs in the family – her husband Dan is with the Charlotte Observer and her daughter Jeanne is building a career in radio sales.

As we see the increasing need for better pre-job education in all fields of marketing, we are pleased to present this important book.

Bruce Bendinger
The Copy Workshop

ABOUT THE AUTHOR

Professor Mary Alice Shaver teaches Advertising at the University of North Carolina in Chapel Hill.

Her innovative course in Media Sales was one of the first college programs to focus on this important area of career opportunity.

Before entering the academic world, she worked in promotions, advertising sales and newspapers.

While working on her degree at the University of Illinois, she was Sales Director of a small local magazine.

She is former Head of the AEJMC Advertising and Media Management Divisions and former Chair of the Department of Journalism and Broadcasting at Florida International University.

She is active in consulting with media organizations on issues related to media placement, sales and revenue generation.

CONTENTS:

MAKE THE SALE. Contents:

III. GETTING STARTED.

Homework and Fieldwork
Local market knowledge – the foundation for success

IV. MAKING MESSAGES.

Getting the Message
How this section is organized

V. FROM PROSPECT TO PRESENTATION.

Process and Progress...
A business-building approach – from Hitting the Streets to Closing the Sale

MAKE THE SALE. Contents:

VI. STAYING ON THE JOB.

Earning and Learning

How to up your salary and your Learning Curve

I.
SPACE
&
TIME.

"In simple times, advertising people had
two concerns: what to say
and how to say it.
Now the issue is where, when and how
can advertising people reach
receptive prospects...
Today's toughest question is how to find
your customers at the most strategic time
- that's why media is
the new creative frontier."

Keith Reinhard, Chairman DDB/Needham

When you sell media, you sell a product like no other in the world.
Your "product" is space and time.

When you sell media, you sell potential and opportunity.

In many industries, your job is done once you make the sale. In the world of media, your job is just beginning.

When you're a Media Person, you're more than a sales person. *You become a marketing partner!*

Your job is helping your client's business succeed – and, of course, building repeat business.

And when you sell space and time, you often help develop the message that fills that space and time.

You literally make the product you sell – a product that sells what your client sells.

That's one more reason that media may be one of the most creative sales jobs anywhere. Because you will find yourself in many different businesses – you'll be in the car business, the bar business, the banking business and more.

Two roads to success

In tomorrow's economy, two types will be successful:
- Those who know how to make things people want.
- Those who know how to sell things.

This book is about how to sell space and time.

It's about how to turn space and time into things that people want. It's about how to turn space and time into things that sell things – advertising messages.

Space and time is a "product" like no other in the world.

THE MEDIA AGE

As Alvin Toffler notes in *Power Shift*, the value of information in our society is becoming equal to the value of things.

Multi-million dollar movies, the music industry and virtually everything related to computers are part of this growing world of information. So is media – the channels that carry so much of our information – from your local newspaper to the latest cable channel bouncing off a satellite.

Today, there are more media channels than ever.

In a world where we often read about job cutbacks, the world of media is one that is still growing.

Everywhere you turn, there are new media forms and new media options. And the traditional media formats of newspaper and broadcast are still going strong.

And each one of those media companies, from the daily newspaper to the latest piece of on-line technology, depends on smart hard-working people to help them succeed in the marketplace.

Furthermore, with more media choices than ever, it is more critical than ever that marketers make the right decisions with their media-driven marketing programs – to connect with their markets.

They need someone like you to help make those connections – they need a Media Person.

BECOMING A MEDIA PERSON

This is a point we'll be making repeatedly throughout this book – *media sales is more than selling.*

Today, media sales demands substantial amounts of marketing and creativity as well as selling ability.

But if you have what it takes, becoming a media person can be an excellent career decision.

The Good News

Selling media is a job for people who want to work with people, learn an incredible amount about local business, help other people make money and, just maybe, make a lot of money themselves.

As a former student – now an ad director – told one of my classes: *"I give myself a raise every year. And that's beyond what my company gives me on my salary. I decide what I want to make and then I work to earn the commissions to meet my goals. It's good for my clients, it's good for my employer – and it's very good for me."*

It can be very good for you, too. Here's a job that lets you get out of the office and meet people, lets you earn more money if you're willing to put in more work, teaches you new skills all the time and provides a challenge every day.

That's the good news.

The Bad News

The bad news is that it can be tough.

And, if you're with the wrong medium, at the wrong time, in the wrong market – it can be impossible.

But, most times it's not that bad. It's just... tough.

A good Media Person can meet the challenge.

A good Media Person can find the right marketers for their media channel and develop a program that works.

This book will show you how to do that.

It will also show you how to do something else... sell.

A SUCCESSFUL SALESPERSON

You already know a lot about selling

You learned about selling every time you talked a friend into doing something you wanted to do for the evening.

You figured out how to talk about the benefits to the other person or the group. You listened to objections, answered them and pointed out additional benefits. You connected with people and you helped them connect with your message.

You were selling – even if you didn't call it that. The critical component is making the right connections.

Chris Lytle, of The AdVisory Board, points out, "As long as you're in business, you're in sales. An attorney who can sell is called a 'partner'."

THE CRITICAL CONNECTION

As a media person, your job is to help create that critical connection between marketers and markets and help match (or help create) the right message for your medium – a message that connects marketers with customers.

The 4M's of Media Sales:

That's our "secret formula" for selling media with marketing – The 4M's of Media Sales: Market/Marketer/Message/Media.

The objective of this book is to help you learn how to make those connections.

We'll learn about it piece by piece, and then we'll learn about how to put the pieces together and make the connections you need to complete the sales process.

The 4 M's of Media Sales:

The Media Marketplace

First, we'll learn about the media marketplace. You'll see the strengths of various media forms – so you can sell their strengths if you work for one of them and so you can sell against them if you work for a different media company.

Your Local Market

Then, we'll help you learn about the market – your market – its size, its shape, and its opportunities.

Then, we'll talk about developing messages.

TWO TYPES OF MESSAGES

You'll be developing two types of messages – the client's advertising message and your own sales presentation.

1. The Ad itself

In local media markets, the sales person is often a critical part of helping to develop the message.

Message development is also often a necessary part of a successful sales call.

This book will help you with the basics of message development and the basics of putting together "spec ads."

2. Your Sales Presentation

Here you put all the elements together in a 20 minute drama that leads to the sale.

We'll talk about making messages that make connections. We'll talk about asking the right questions, meeting objections, and how to do it again if you don't make the sale the first time.

WHAT THIS BOOK WILL DO FOR YOU

This book will teach you to channel all the selling skills you already have and to develop new ones.

It will give you the background you need to know about your local media market.

It will try to teach you how to think like a marketer as well as a salesperson – so that you'll sell answers to marketing problems as you sell space and time.

It will give you a start in the creative side of marketing – showing you how to develop messages that connect with both customers and clients.

It will show you how to analyze, develop, and present media packages for clients.

Together, all of that will help you build a successful career in media sales.

You may even be able to *"give yourself a raise"* every year – year after year – by selling space and time.

1. TARGET AUDIENCE.

*"Your target audience is
your advertiser's prospect.
Spend at least part of every call
focusing on your customer's customer –
or your prospect's prospect."*

Chris Lytle – The AdVisory Board

There are several audiences for this book.
Primarily, they fall into two categories:
* Those who sell or would like to sell media.
* Those who buy media.
Taking a look at your audience is always a good way
to start – whether it's selling media or writing a book.
So let's take a look at the audiences for this book.

ONE. Target Audience.

PEOPLE WHO SELL MEDIA

In this first category are:

1. Beginning Media Sales Reps and Media Sales Management with training responsibilities

2. Students in Sales and Media classes

3. Students who work for a campus publication

There's something in this book for each of you.

1. Beginning Media Sales Reps & Sales Managers

This book is particularly useful for training people new to the world of media. There are many good advanced sales training courses – this is for beginners.

It will provide you with the basic information every Media Sales Person should know – from Market Analysis to Final Presentation.

If you're a beginning sales rep who wasn't fortunate enough to have this class in school, you'll find this book is a handy reference tool.

It's a good source book for understanding what is going on in your job and what is expected of you.

First, we'll show you how to look at media vehicles – yours and that of the competition.

Next, in the part of the book called "Getting Started," we'll show you how to look at your market.

Then, we'll show you how to begin crafting messages.

Finally, we'll show you how to put it all together into a Sales Presentation that will help you "Make The Sale!"

If you're already working, we assume you'll be too busy to do the exercises, but we think you'll see that many of them have practical application as you learn your job.

They'll provide you with a solid framework to put together your own Local Market Profiles, your own Media Plans, and your own Sales Presentations.

Local Market Emphasis

Since media selling, particularly for beginners, most often takes place at the local or regional level, most of the book will approach selling from that angle.

But you should realize that most areas we'll cover also have broader applications – such as: getting to know the local market, developing rate packages and plans, and working with the client.

Whether you make a local or a national sales call, they'll help you prepare before you call on the client and help you serve the client better.

You'll get help in thinking about client and sales problems in your local market. And you'll learn to think about and work against competition more effectively.

A Note to Sales Managers

You already know a lot of what's in this book.

So while the book will provide a good review, the real value to you will be in helping you help your new sales reps to understand what they don't know – but need.

If you're a Sales Manager, this book will help you help your staff. We think you'll find it a useful tool for sales meetings and a framework for training your reps.

This book will help you to teach your sales force the basics.

2. Students in Sales and Media classes

This book is designed to teach you how to perform in a challenging and demanding field.

The Good News

Media sales is an excellent way to get into the advertising and sales business. Media sales is one of the best "first job" opportunities for those who want to go into marketing and advertising.

Whether it becomes your career, or it's the stepping stone to another area, learning to do it well will help you develop skills that will help in any marketing job.

There are probably more opportunities for beginners in this area than any other. This book will give you a good grasp of what's involved in a media sales career.

It will not only provide basic information, but through a series of exercises, it will help you develop the skills you need to succeed.

It will show you how to find the information you need to know about your market. It will show you how to turn that into an initial presentation that matches your media with marketers who will benefit from reaching your audience.

It will even show you how to craft a message that will build your client's business – as part of a presentation that makes the sale for you.

In each area, this book will provide specific examples of client needs and problems and teach you how to work with those clients to solve them.

You'll learn how to work up packages for clients and the terms and jargon for what you deal with every business day.

This book will give you a good look at how local media are bought and sold, the knowledge, skills and attitudes you need to succeed, how to work against competition, as well as the major issues and trends in local media today.

We hope it will teach you how to assess your potential for a sales career and help you to improve in areas where you may not be as strong as you'd like.

The Bad News

The bad news is that one of the reasons all those new jobs open up in media sales is that a lot of people don't have what it takes.

But when you're finished with this book – *if you learned the lessons* – you'll be in good shape to know what you're getting into. And you'll be ready to make the most of that first sales job.

3. Students who are selling space or time for a campus paper or other local publication

A campus newspaper is one of the best places for students to get "real world" training and see if they have an aptitude for media sales.

You'll represent a real media vehicle that delivers a specific audience to clients – usually your fellow students.

If you're already working for the campus newspaper or broadcast station, this book can help you sharpen your skills and show you how to make the most of this special experience.

You'll find ways to increase your efficiency and your sales. You can use the worksheets to assess your own clients' problems and come up with solutions.

PEOPLE WHO BUY MEDIA

The second category of users will be:
1. **Small Business Owners**
2. **Small Local Agencies**
3. **Large Agency Media Departments**

People who buy media on a local or national level may also find this book useful, particularly for training.

For the most part, this book will provide you with a helpful picture of what you should look for in the people who come to see you with their media proposals.

1. Small Business Owners

If you have a small business, here's the information you need to put your ad dollars where they'll count the most for you.

This book will help you choose between the media programs that are best for your company and those that will probably not be money well spent.

One of the critical concerns for all marketers is getting cost-effectiveness from their advertising expenditures – if you have to make those decisions for your company, you may find that this book pays for itself rather quickly.

It will show you how to compare media for different advertising needs and problems.

It'll teach you to figure out rate plans and packages.

As a result, you'll learn to ask the right questions and to evaluate options. You'll be able to work better with your rep – or directly with the media.

2. Small Local Agencies

If you're in a small agency, this book can be a handy reference for all media. The checklists will help you to think of areas your clients might need and to assess your market plans for them.

You'll be better able to think of options and formulate better rate packages for your accounts.

Best of all, the relationships with your media contacts should be more effective. You might even be able to help them do their job better.

3. Large Agency Media Departments

If you're in a large agency, this book will give you a better picture of how things work at the "grass roots" level.

It will help you do a better job developing your own localized media plans for larger regional and national accounts.

Sales In A Changing World

One more important point for those of you in this target group. The advertising agency world is changing at all levels – local, regional, and national.

Even in the large agencies, the lines are blurring.

Many of the large multi-media deals crafted by Time, Inc. Meredith, and many of the TV network product promotions involve selling ideas contributed from the media side of the equation.

Meanwhile, many marketers are shifting budget emphasis from advertising to *promotion.*

New Problems and New Opportunities

This creates both additional problems and additional opportunities for those on both sides of the relationship.

The advertising budget is cut back. Problem.

A promotion needs advertising support. Opportunity.

The regular advertising agency doesn't have the assignment. Problem. (Particularly if it's your agency.)

There's a new breed of "Integrated Marketing Communications" company that has a special project. Opportunity. (Particularly if no one else is calling on them.)

The agency world is changing dramatically.

This book will help you make the most of those changes – whichever part you work in.

The Importance of Local Markets

Even if you work at a large agency with national accounts, knowing how to understand local markets can pay off.

As more and more marketers are concerned with "micromarketing" and "event marketing," execution at the local level is becoming more important.

As they say, "Think global. Act local."

Whatever audience you're in, for the rest of this book we will talk to you as though you had one job.

What is that job?

We'll talk to you as a Media Person – a Media "Rep."

You're someone who knows how to connect marketers with their markets – with media.

2.
THE ROLE OF THE MEDIA REP.

*"Advertisements contain the only truths
to be relied on in a newspaper."*

Thomas Jefferson

TWO. *The Role of The Media Rep.*

Rep stands for Representative.
You represent your medium to advertisers and potential advertisers.
Sales is part of your job, but only part of it.

The Media Rep works with clients on a regular basis – planning, making presentations, placing ad orders, developing new campaigns, researching what's working elsewhere, solving problems, and coordinating long-term plans.

Three Key Components of Success

While it's a varied job, three key components add up to selling as a marketing partner. They are:

1. Setting Goals
2. Making Connections
3. Building Relationships

Let's take them one by one.

1. SETTING GOALS

A key to this process is goal-setting

Translating customer needs into marketing goals and then selling the space or time to meet those goals is a major part of a Media Rep's job.

Goals help you keep client needs foremost and provide a good reason to bring clients new ideas and opportunities on a regular basis.

Setting goals is the basis of establishing that long-term relationship – which is key to repeat sales.

When it works the way it should, the client will come to view the rep as a valued marketing professional who can help make his or her business more successful.

A key to that success is setting goals – and meeting them.

2. MAKING CONNECTIONS

Connecting with good ideas

We've already mentioned the critical connections in *"The 4M's of Media Sales."* Other connections are also important.

Solving problems often involves making connections.

M Market
Marketer
Message
Media

A creative idea, like a solution to a problem, is *"a new combination of two previously existing elements."* (From James Webb Young's, *A Technique for Producing Ideas.*)

– 25 –

Each idea, each relationship, is a new connection.

And it's one of the exciting aspects of media – when you can connect a marketer with a market and help a business grow.

One of the first skills a Media Rep must develop is making the right connections between marketers and media with the right plan and the right message.

Finding the right match is key to success

The days of the sales rep as an "order taker" have been over for quite a while. These days, the sales rep is a professional who solves marketing problems daily.

And you have to solve the right problem – a rep who sells the client more than he needs and pushes for quick gain cannot win over time. It's the wrong match and doomed to fail.

A rep who avoids addressing the hard issues on any aspect of this process – such as letting the right plan run with an inadequate message – will soon see why media sales can be such a difficult job.

Connections and Combinations

On the other hand, assessing the client problem and suggesting other media in combination with the one you sell can both help clients build the best marketing plan and build confidence in you as a professional.

Demonstrating concern that the message is right – and taking the time to get it right – can make the difference between a successful program that builds traffic and relationships and an unsuccessful program that only makes it more difficult to sell your medium.

Making the right connections is critical to your success.

3. BUILDING RELATIONSHIPS

Helping businesses succeed builds your business

Today, "Relationship Marketing" is a hot new concept. Media Sales Reps have known this for years.

The best reps build good relationships with their clients and view the job as being in for the long haul.

Listening and understanding the clients' needs is part of that. The better your understanding, the better you can translate those needs into workable plans that can help both of you succeed.

By paying attention and listening to what the client is really saying, you'll be able to help that client in ways that will pay off for you both.

Be a problem-solver and a problem-<u>finder</u>

The Media Rep must be an involved and creative problem-solver – not someone who knows all the answers.

Each problem – no matter how minor it may seem – is important to the client who has it.

Knowing the right questions to ask can often be as important as knowing the answers. At least in the beginning.

Many people can solve problems, few can find the right problem to solve.

Sales trainer Bill Gove's advice is *"be a problem finder."*

You will see that successful problem identification is key to strategic marketing thinking.

Many reps view clients as friends (and vice versa) and find helping others to succeed a rewarding part of the job.

But the initial basis of the relationship is helping clients meet their marketing goals.

THE CHALLENGE OF COMPETITION

You will learn very quickly that you're not the only smart, hard-working person out there. That's one of the challenges.

There are lots of other reps on the beat – even for small stores, you often have to get in line. This means your pitch has to be the best and your product has to be right for the client.

There are only so many ad dollars around. Your job is to get some of those dollars away from the other guys at the same time you serve the client in the best way possible.

This book should help you to do just that - by setting goals, making connections and building the relationships that will help you achieve those goals.

As a marketing partner.

II.
THE MEDIA
TODAY.

"'The Medium is the Message' because it is the medium that shapes and controls the search and form of human associations and action."

Marshall McLuhan

More media, more opportunities – and more competition.

The fact is, there are more media choices today than ever before – for the retail and service businesses and for the audience as well.

Options and Opportunities

More challenge – and more choices – work to make local media more customer-service oriented.

Today's increased range of media options means increased flexibility with customer-specific options:

• Sales reps get a chance to serve clients better.

• Advertisers can choose from a wider variety of media options and audiences.

• Agency campaigns can be targeted more specifically than ever. They can incorporate and test new kinds of media for client effectiveness.

And, for all these reasons, the battle for advertising dollars has never been tougher.

An Overview and more...

That's why today's media plans need to be more audience-directed, customized for specific needs, and more cost efficient.

In this section, we'll give you an overview of the opportunities in today's local media world and then provide you with some tools for making comparisons – one of the first steps to building an effective media plan.

First, we'll examine specific mediums, from the traditional daily newspaper to new media formats.

Then, we'll take a look at the Local Media Mix, to see how they all work together and how different markets evolve different media solutions to meet marketer's needs.

3. LOCAL MEDIA.

Even as the media universe is evolving and expanding, it is still fairly stable on the local level. Let's take a look at the primary media options in your local marketplace.

NEWSPAPERS

The traditional metropolitan daily newspaper reaches a large and diverse audience with large and diverse content that ranges from national and international to local news and features.

It covers politics, crime and schools, opinion and reader letters, sports of all kinds, entertainment, comics and features on subjects from local people to child rearing to food, arts, travel, decorating, homes and more.

Two Products

In reality, a newspaper is selling two products:
1. **News and information to readers**
2. **Audience access to advertisers**

Local news and information is a primary reason for readership. Advertising is also an important component to readers – it's product news, the type of commercial information that can help people know about special shopping opportunities or where to go see that new movie.

Two Types of Advertising

Newspapers offer both display and classified advertising to large and small businesses.

Display advertising gives advertisers a chance to tell a message in detail, provide both text and illustrations, and distribute coupons.

Classified advertising is another fascinating example of the marketplace at work. In this case, the audience seeks out the item. And those interested in a new puppy, a used car or an apartment near the campus will wade through the listings to find what they're looking for.

Circulation – Who Reads the Paper?

Who reads the paper? While newspapers are read by many differing kinds of audiences, the typical newspaper reader is slightly older (over 35), more educated and with more income and more likely to own his own house or condo than a non-reader.

While newspaper *circulation* is up in many regions of the country, *penetration* (the percentage of households getting the paper) is down.

Penetration has dropped from over 100 percent after WWII – when many households received two papers – to an average of 62 percent today.

Naturally, individual markets vary. In some markets, newspapers enjoy a 90 percent penetration rate. Other markets have a penetration rate of only around 40 percent.

While direct metropolitan daily competition exists in only a few markets today, there are many other kinds of media that have cut into newspaper readership and market penetration.

This is a problem for papers, as advertisers have traditionally bought papers for the large mass audience.

Newspapers have responded to this challenge.

Today, newspapers try to offer two kinds of audiences for advertisers: the traditional large audience and more narrowly defined audiences reached by niche market publications.

For example, young people (18-35) are a low-reader group. Newspapers are working continually to attract more readers in this demographic category. A special program for school-age children, Newspapers in Education, puts newspapers into classrooms and provides instructional materials in an effort to make reading a habit for this future audience.

Newspapers are also working to get more women readers, as research shows they are less likely to read than men. Many papers conduct research to find out the interests of their female readers – and try to provide content that will attract them.

Lack of time is a major reason many women give for not reading – or for not reading regularly. Working women with children find it particularly hard to find time to read.

Home Delivery and Street Sales

Many readers subscribe to newspapers and receive home delivery. This ensures that the paper is in the home, and advertising sales reps use the fact that readers choose the paper, pay for it and have it in their homes every day as a strong selling point.

Other papers are sold in what is called "single copy sales" which means the papers are sold from racks at locations in town such as stores, gas stations and other locations. This type of selling is also called "street sales."

Single copy sales are very strong in large cities where there is a lot of activity in the downtown area and where there is a lot of commuter traffic. These kind of sales mean that people see the advertising when they are in shopping areas – this is a selling point for advertising reps.

Beyond the regular readers (both subscribers and single copy buyers) and non-readers, there are "at-risk" readers who are only marginally loyal to newspapers.

These people may be single copy buyers or subscribers. What distinguishes them from regular readers is their low involvement with the paper. They may only buy a few days of the week or, if they subscribe, they read only a few days of the week. Newspapers feel these readers may be more likely than others to drop the paper and become non-readers.

Placement – Selling the Whole Paper

One common problem that sales reps have to overcome is that Section A (the front page and its section) is generally perceived as the most desirable placement in the newspaper.

While it is true that most readers do look at the front page and through the entire front section, other sections of the paper are read as frequently and – depending on the target audience – with more time and more care.

Research figures from the paper will show both frequency and type of audience for the different sections.

The "A" section is most valuable for the largest and most general advertisers, such as department stores.

For smaller or specialized product advertisers, other sections may be a better placement and return more readership for the dollars spent. Advertisers may ask for placement within sections. Some of the largest advertisers have the same placement day after day. For department stores, this is often facing pages or the back page in the "A" section; for some other kinds of stores, it may be the back page of other sections. One "perk" that advertisers may request is this kind of special and consistent positioning.

Readers like to find the same kinds of news and features in the same place every day. Sectionalization – placing the same kind of material in individual sections daily, weekly or whenever it appears – makes finding the information easier. It also gives a special content section for advertisers whose target audience is likely to be made up of readers.

Typical sections include:

Local news
Business
Sports
Living
Features
Travel
Arts
Entertainment

Zoned Editions

Zoned editions offer special geographically-based content for different sections of the newspaper market.

Certain pages – or a section – are devoted to this material, offering readers an opportunity to find material of real local interest to them while offering advertisers a chance to reach a market close to their businesses.

Because the market areas are only a portion of the entire circulation, ad rates in zoned editions are less expensive, allowing small advertisers to reach their own neighborhood markets.

Many papers zone the city region itself into four or five zones; others zone both the city and other areas within their retail trading zone.

Some newspapers publish a special tabloid section one or more times a week to accomplish the zoning option.

This tab section concentrates on neighborhood news, enabling papers to print school and club news, cover neighborhood sports and promote local events. Advertisers in these sections can target their copy to tie in directly with news of interest to these area readers.

Special Sections

Newspapers also have special sections several times a year.

These may include gardening, house, back-to-school, high school sports, travel, special festivals, and other sections.

Ads in these sections are often sold at special prices and enable advertisers to place ads alongside content that interests their customers.

Nearly all daily newspapers have at least some special sections – advertising rates are generally favorable and offer a good opportunity to target readers with interests in specialized products or services.

Subsidiary or "Niche" Publications

Many newspapers today publish subsidiary or "extra" publications targeted toward niche markets. These publications – which may look either like newspapers or magazines or can be in some other format – target special audiences.

These may be separated demographically, such as seniors or teens; by special interests, such as sports, auto, entertainment or gardening; or by some other category, such as real estate, brides, or jobs.

Some are geographically based and either supplement or replace geographic zoning.

In terms of circulation sales, newspapers are generally a paid reader medium, although some are free. Subsidiary publications are more likely to be free than are regular daily or weekly papers.

Preprints

Another type of advertising carried by newspapers is the preprint. These four-color slick ads are inserted into the newspaper as additional advertising.

The format and paper allows advertisers to use sharper color, to print the same ad pieces for a number of markets, and to be certain that these ad pieces are delivered to their target customers in all their markets on the same day. Preprints may be for local, regional or national advertisers. Sundays are a heavy day for preprints.

The rate structure for preprints differs from other ads;

preprint rates are discussed in a later chapter.

By keeping the cost of preprints at less than direct mail, newspapers are able to compete with this kind of delivery.

NEWSPAPER ADVANTAGES

Newspapers offer a good advertising opportunity for local advertisers because they can accommodate detailed copy, drawings, photographs, attention-getting headlines, innovative layout and design.

Lead time is minimized by deadlines that are a day or two (sometimes less) before publication time. Ad space in papers can be purchased for the full circulation run or for specific zones or zip code areas.

Because the product is paid for by the customer, it is possible to track consumers by where they live.

Paid circulation also indicates that the customer wants the paper and indicates a likelihood of use of the newspaper product, ensuring exposure to the ads.

Readership Studies and Measurements

Newspapers conduct readership studies to find out who their readers are, which sections of the papers are read most frequently, how readers use the paper for advertising information, how much time readers spend with the paper and the characteristics of non-readers.

A frequently asked question is: Did you read the paper yesterday? This is a very conservative measure that gives advertisers assurance that the numbers and preferences of respondents are indicative of actual reader behavior.

For More Information:

To help you find out more about newspapers, a more complete list of resources is at the back of this book.

WEEKLIES

Many smaller communities have a weekly newspaper.

They are similar to larger dailies that concentrate on a smaller geographic area.

Traditionally, they will feature more in–depth coverage of local events and activities and advertising will be predominantly from smaller local merchants.

"SHOPPERS" & OTHERS

There is another newspaper-like medium that is a growing force in many areas.

Originally, "Shoppers" were free newspapers which consisted largely of advertising, developed to provide additional low-cost opportunities for retailers. Since they have little in the way of an editorial staff and a fairly long shelf-life, they can be fairly profitable and can provide a stiff competitive challenge to traditional papers.

Another form of free newspaper has developed, with its roots in the alternative press of the '60s.

Today, these local newspapers often feature interesting editorial and graphics emphasizing local arts, particularly music and entertainment.

They are often distributed in local retail establishments, ranging from bars and record stores to local supermarkets.

They come out weekly or monthly, are usually free, and have circulations that range from a few thousand to over 100,000 for papers like Chicago's *Reader*.

They are generally targeted at a specific geographic and "lifestyle" demographic and offer another viable advertising opportunity for certain types of retailers.

On many large campuses, for example, there may be one or two "alternative" papers in addition to the on-campus student newspaper.

The growth of desktop publishing software has made these small special interest newspapers a new and vital force in the media world, both substituting for and reinforcing the traditional daily newspaper.

NEWSPAPER WORKSHEET

Now let's take a quick "snapshot" of the newspapers in your market, including the community weeklies and other types of newspapers.

You'll be using this information later as you develop your Local Market Profile.

You may want to input these questions onto your computer or set aside a few pages in your notebook so that you can add information as you go along.

How many newspapers are in your market?

How many are daily?

What is the circulation of the dailies?

What is their penetration?

(To calculate this number, you will have to know the circulation within the city zone area and the number of households in the city zone. You can get the circulation and household statistics from the "Editor and Publisher Yearbook" and other trade publications.)

Is zoned or part-run circulation available?

  If so, what areas are covered?

How often are the zoned editions published?

Are any subsidiary or niche publications available?

  If so, are they free or paid?

What kinds of content are in the niche publications?

Are there any weekly papers?

  How many have paid circulation?

  How many are free?

Are there any "shoppers" in the market?

  If so, what geographic areas do they cover?

QUESTIONS/ASSIGNMENTS

Here are some things to think about related to the paper(s) in your area:

1. Look into the main newspaper(s) in your market and into a weekly and determine who the advertisers are in each. What are the differences and similarities among advertisers in these two kinds of newspapers?

2. What geographic or demographic audiences does the weekly appear to serve?

3. If there is a "shopper" in your area, look at the advertising in it. What kind of markets (audiences and readers) does this publication appear to serve?

RADIO

Grabbing the audience on the go is radio's strength – people often listen to the radio when they're in the car. It's a medium that travels well.

Radio also provides background music and news highlights throughout the day in many homes and businesses. *Because the audience can listen to the radio while they are doing something else – typically driving or working – radio ads reach audiences at times and in places where other media cannot.*

The fact that radio does not have the complete attention of its audience can be a weakness as well.

Advertisers need to overcome that with frequency and with involving, attention-grabbing advertising.

Formats & Fragmentation

Listeners choose radio stations for the **format** – music and other programming – which appeals to them. While listeners may scan across stations looking for music that appeals, individual stations can also build loyalty among the audience through format and on-air personalities.

Some radio stations may buy standard or customized formats from syndicated agencies or consultants to enable them to compete for a specific audience segment within their local market.

Some stations may style themselves as country and western, as young adult, or as oldie stations. These formats are dictated by the desire to appeal to the particular age or demographic group the station considers its primary audience.

Every market has several radio stations, each one trying to appeal successfully to a certain kind of audience. The result is a special kind of demographic fragmentation.

So, while radio is a mass medium in one sense, it is also a very selective medium with well-defined demographic targets. Advertisers choose the radio "buys" based on their need to reach these specific and carefully defined audiences.

For example, one station may have the highest listenership among adults 18-34, another with teens, with women, or with the age 35-54 audience.

However, since there are so many stations in most markets, it is likely that there will be several audiences which appeal to the same age groups.

Competition for ad dollars among stations with "reach" into the same demographic audience profile can be very intense.

Advertisers buy time based on the viability of a station with the desired target audience – they use radio to select the market segment or niche that their store or business identifies as key.

Drive Time

Drive time – the time people spend going to and from work – is a valuable time for radio advertising. Audiences are high at these times as commuters listen while they are in city traffic or driving down the highway.

Roughly the time between 6:30 and 9:00 AM and between 4:30 and 7:00 PM, it is the most expensive radio ad time and it delivers the greatest audience.

Actual drive time boundaries vary with the size of the local market. The commuting hours are longer in larger cities and more compressed in small ones.

NICHE MARKETING – LOCAL & NATIONAL

While radio is largely a local medium, revenue for national and regional advertisers is beginning to grow as radio positions its programming for specific local audiences as a cost efficient way of hitting carefully defined niche audiences within a local target market area.

Radio is an ideal medium for niche marketing because it can deliver a defined demographic and geographic audience to an advertiser.

While no one station can reach teens, adults and seniors with equal effectiveness, specific stations within a market will have one of these audiences as their primary listeners.

This selective appeal is an important advantage, and stations can position their more narrow demographic focus in a very positive way in selling themselves to potential advertisers.

For example, the teen audience is growing in importance. This group has a high level of discretionary income, and teens are heavy radio users.

So if the target is teen-agers, chances are, radio should be part of the media plan.

FLEXIBILITY & FREQUENCY

Flexibility is a strong selling point for radio – and so is frequency, the number of times your audience will hear your commercial in a certain time period.

Adequate frequency is key for effective radio scheduling.

Since the radio audience is usually doing something else while the radio is on, some amount of repetition is often necessary for the message to "sink in."

And, since much radio time is non-drive time, many messages reach a smaller audience. Naturally, the price of non-drive time spots is less, but these smaller audiences also mean that more frequency is needed so that a large enough cumulative audience is exposed to the message.

Flexibility is also an advantage – with the ability to place many ads in a schedule at differing times of the day, to custom produce ads within a short time frame and to place ads on short notice, radio gives the advertiser an opportunity to respond quickly to changes in business and to competitive challenges.

Here are some examples of that flexibility:

Promotions

Radio is an excellent medium for promotions.

Announcements and reminder ads can draw an audience for a special event, and the radio format can get attention at times and in ways that other media cannot.

Remotes

Radio can go on-site as well. These promotional events, called "remotes," bring an announcer or DJ to a store or business to broadcast from that location.

The station provides refreshments and often games and small prizes, drawing a crowd to the store or mall for entertainment and a chance to see the radio personalities live.

The increased store traffic – often on a weekend – then results in increased sales and inquiries from potential buyers, not only that day but for days to follow.

The remote is often part of the incentive package offered with an advertising schedule and contract.

Precise Planning vs. "Spray and Pray"

As we noted, because there are so many radio stations, the audience is necessarily fragmented with many of the individual stations garnering only a small market share.

Some advertisers may feel they have to spread their advertising dollars over a number of stations in order to reach as much of the audience in the area as possible.

Station reps call that kind of placement a "spray and pray" technique that dilutes the frequency and makes the advertising ineffective. Used this way, radio can be very expensive for the buying audience reached.

Getting good results from radio advertising takes precise and careful planning.

The most effective radio advertising is usually a result of identifying a carefully designated target audience segment and placing a schedule on one or two stations in the market that have high listenership within that segment.

Radio ads placed with serious consideration of the desired target audience and an understanding of the appeal and specific audience reach of the available stations can be very cost-efficient.

RADIO IN A COMBINATION BUY

Radio is also an excellent supporting medium for those advertisers who may use print as a primary medium.

Used in this way, radio advertising can provide specific focus for a key demographic target even for those advertisers who can utilize print as a broad-reach medium.

Radio plus outdoor is occasionally referred to as "poorman's TV." One medium provides the visual, the other provides audio. Each has relatively low production costs (compared to TV).

Even their environments compliment each other – the perfect combination is when someone drives by your outdoor board while your commercial is playing.

There is some research to indicate that playing the audio track of your TV commercial on the radio offers some synergies. Assuming that a person has seen your TV commercial a few times, the TV commercial will be remembered just by replaying the audio track.

RADIO AUDIENCE MEASUREMENT

Radio use is measured by Arbitron, RADAR and others.

Radio use is reported by average audience over 15-minute segments throughout a 24-hour period.

The demographics of users are reported so that both advertisers and stations know their reach and impact within demographic categories (18-24; 25-34; 35-44; 45-54; 55-64 and 64 years plus). This is particularly important with the demographics of most radio stations.

Thus, a station that claims it provides advertisers with "Results with Adults" can use age and use figures to back up this claim.

For More Information:

You can find out more about radio in the Resources section at the end of this book.

RADIO WORKSHEET

Use this worksheet to develop a "snapshot" of the radio stations in your market. Be sure to indicate stations in nearby markets that may overlap.

You'll be using this information later as you develop your Local Market Profile.

You may want to input these questions onto your computer or set aside a few pages in your notebook, so that you can add information as you go along.

How many radio stations are available in your immediate market?

List as many as you feel are primary stations.

What are the formats for these stations?

What kind of demographic profile would be assigned to each station audience?

Which stations appear to reach the following most effectively: teens, seniors, adults 18-54, adults 25-54?

What types of on-air personalities do each of the primary stations have?

Which stations promote themselves most effectively?

List several types of local businesses and choose the best station for each.

THREE. Local Media.

TELEVISION

Television is the ideal medium for capturing the at-home audience. While many advertisers are national or regional in scope, network affiliates, independents and local cable offer many opportunities for local advertising placement.

TYPES OF TV

While there may be many stations in your market, they basically fall into three categories:
- **Network Affiliates**
- **Independents**
- **Cable**

Let's review them one by one.

Network Affiliates

Network affiliates run national advertising as part of their agreement with the networks, but there is local option time available at high viewership times as well.

The local news is a particularly high profile time for local advertising.

Independents

Many markets have independent stations.

Through the growth of "Fourth" and "Fifth" networks, such as Fox, many now deliver some degree of "network" programming, including NFL football.

The bulk of independent programming consists of syndicated shows and movies, some of which are quite popular.

Cable

Cable advertising provides a viable option for local advertisers. Audiences are more segmented, the costs are less, and advertisers can reach audiences with quite particular interests as well.

Many local advertisers are now using local cable and taking advantage of low-cost production offered by the providers.

For example, teen-agers have been hard to reach on TV in a cost-effective manner. Special cable channels, such as MTV, offer new opportunities for local advertisers.

As cable providers merge and consolidate, this will become an even more important area for both local and national media sales.

ADVANTAGES & DISADVANTAGES

Sight & Sound

Television provides advertisers with the message potential of sight and sound. This can be a tremendous advantage, but it can also be detrimental if poorly conceived and executed.

It's easy to say *"audio-visual integration"* or *"the words should match the pictures,"* but making a TV commercial that sells in a clear and entertaining fashion is always a challenge.

Cost & Competition

Television is also a challenge to many local advertisers because of high cost, production time and competition with national advertising. While television production in a few large cities may be equal to that produced for national ads, some local television ads do not compare favorably.

It's easy to understand. When a soft drink or automotive marketer can spend a million dollars and hundreds or even thousands of man-hours developing a message, it can be hard to compete with fewer resources overall and a production budget of a few thousand dollars.

Developing creative ideas and execution at the local level is a challenge for sales reps and advertisers alike.

Yet, while locally produced advertising may not have the budget of a national campaign, it is still possible to produce creative and effective advertising on the local level.

Longer Lead Time

Producing television usually takes time as well as money. Some local advertisers, particularly retailers, find this longer lead time to be an additional problem.

Resources for shooting and editing are usually much more limited (and much more expensive) than the production resources needed for radio and newspaper.

It is also true that most local television stations require a greater lead time than newspapers or radio.

Another concern – advertisers need to remember that viewers will compare their ads to the more expensively produced ads for national advertisers that run in the same commercial break.

Many local advertisers, such as car dealers, or local "co-ops" of fast food franchises, benefit from television ads (or "stock footage") provided by manufacturers or national ad resources. These ads only require a few seconds of local identification which can reduce costs substantially.

For these reasons, many advertisers find local television too expensive for their ad budgets.

Still, it is a powerful medium.

Types of Local Usage

Here are some of the reasons and some of the ways local advertisers can use TV effectively:

• Some advertisers use television selectively as a supporting medium.

• Some advertisers find ad placement on the local news provides both coverage and impact.

• Local television is effective in promoting recognition.

• If showing the product in use is critical, television should be considered.

• The large captive local audience can generate great reach in the marketplace.

• Institutional advertising on television allows a local store to get its name across to the viewing public without having to buy enough advertising to sell specific items. Many local stores and banks use television for this purpose around major holidays.

Clutter & "Zapping"

Local ads can suffer from the same viewer inattention as national ads – audiences who leave the room when the advertising comes on and audiences who zap commercials and graze among channels.

And, as we mentioned previously, locally produced television advertising often compares poorly with the national ads surrounding it.

For these reasons, smart tactical thinking, in addition to strategic thinking, is essential when a local advertiser decides to use television.

TELEVISION AUDIENCE MEASUREMENT

Television use is measured by the number and demographics of viewers watching quarter hour segments. Viewership is reported by time, viewer profile, and show.

[This is covered more completely in Chapter 6 – Terms You'll Use Every Day.]

Advertisers can match up the show itself with the viewers to make decisions about ad placement.

Television use is measured by Arbitron in quarterly ratings and by Nielson, which has recently incorporated the use of People Meters, measuring devices activated by viewers in the home. Local stations use rating points to sell their advertising time to advertisers.

The most popular times with local advertisers are generally the local news hours and local sports, both of which draw high viewership. These local programs are rated separately from the network and syndicated programming, allowing advertisers to know which local programs and personalities have the largest audiences.

TELEVISION WORKSHEET

Use this to take a quick "snapshot" of your local television "environment."

Remember, you'll be using this information later as you develop your Local Market Profile.

As we mentioned, you may want to input these questions onto your computer, or set aside a few pages in your notebook, so that you can add information as you go along.

Identify the television stations in your market that provide local news.

What other local programming do these stations produce?

What kind of local advertising runs during news hours and prime time on the stations in your market?

What kind of advertising runs on cable programming that originates in your market?

Pick two or three local advertisers who use television regularly. Check out the daily paper for their ads.

(Department stores, auto dealers and grocery stores are good categories here. You may find other types of specialty stores are also regular television advertisers.)

Does television appear to be a primary or supporting medium for these advertisers?

CITY MAGAZINES

This type of local magazine option offers an opportunity for certain kinds of local businesses to reach an upscale or geographically specific market.

They deliver a quality audience. Readers are generally in the upper economic levels with a higher-than-city-average of discretionary income.

The four-color reproduction in these magazines offers a good advertising option for specialty stores and restaurants.

Most local advertisers who include city magazines in their advertising programs use this as supplementary advertising.

For More Information:

Call the City Regional Magazine Association (listed in Resources) or call your local City Magazine and ask for a Sales Kit.

CITY MAGAZINE WORKSHEET

Add a quick "snapshot" of the City Magazine in your market, including any other upscale print vehicles that include four-color reproduction.

Does your city or region have a magazine?

Are there any other upscale print vehicles?

How many pages?

How many editorial?

How many advertising?

What types of advertisers use this magazine?

OUT-OF-HOME

Outdoor advertising billboards and posters provide large-scale messages for continuous exposure.

Other types of outdoor – kiosks, transit, benches, balloons, taxi tops, airports, stadiums, walls, and malls make up the larger category called "out-of-home."

Although the message is necessarily short, this kind of advertising can be effective in positioning a business in the audience mind and as reminder advertising.

Outdoor can provide such things as store or brand name awareness and location information (this type of board is often called a "directional").

Because the message has to be short, the combination of message and visual is crucial to success as is frequency of exposure. Simple messages can have a strong effect.

Some outdoor boards incorporate movement to draw further attention.

However, the speed at which the message is seen and the distractions inherent in traffic mean that the audience needs to have relatively long-term exposure to retain the message.

The driving audience is exposed to outdoor ads on a regular basis on well-traveled routes. This kind of high intensity can provide good supporting advertising for certain kinds of businesses.

This also allows for other tactical approaches.

For example, a directional – providing location information – can be very effective, essentially providing a store with an extension of their location.

Exposure vs. Recall

As with all advertising, exposure does not necessarily mean recall of the message.

Short, powerful messages are most likely to be effective.

Recent research also indicates that audience involvement can further increase the effectiveness of outdoor messages.

And, since outdoor can build up very heavy frequencies (it is not uncommon for your audience to pass the board once or twice a day), additional involvement – ranging from humor to the time and temperature – can provide additional effectiveness for your message.

Outdoor Audience Measurement

Outdoor is measured in terms of a "showing" or the number of people exposed to the advertisement over a given period of time.

This measurement indicates the level of exposure to an outdoor board in one day – a showing of 100 means that the number of people exposed to the advertisement in one day was equal to the number of people in the market.

This makes no distinction between reach and frequency.

For More Information:

To find out more about outdoor advertising, look in the Resources section – or call your local outdoor company.

YELLOW PAGES

The Yellow Pages – and similar directories – provide sales information that is always at hand.

While the basic directory listing provides only the name, address and phone number of businesses by category, many local advertisers use display ads in the directory for the following reasons:

- To attract attention
- To state the range of services provided
- To position the business as a category leader

Position within the listings, clever headlines and color make some ads stand out more than others.

Even position in the alphabet can have an effect – which you may see where someone has named their company AAAccurate – or something similar.

There are some restrictions and industry policies that work to prevent abuse in this area.

Listing vs. Display

Advertisers must balance the expense of the additional size and color in a display ad with:

- The size of the audience using the directory
- The ability of the ad to attract that key target audience
- Place of directory advertising in the available ad budget

This will vary for different advertisers – even those in the same category.

Location Issues

For some advertisers, a convenient location may be the primary reason customers shop there. In that case, a simple listing may be all that is needed to let potential customers know the store is nearby.

For advertisers in more distant locations, increased directory advertising may be necessary to compensate for the less desirable location.

For example, a key determinant of choosing a branch bank or drugstore may be convenience to work or home.

Then, as long as the service is satisfactory, customers are unlikely to look for other options.

Purchase Patterns

For less frequent and higher risk purchases – like building a fence, remodeling a kitchen, or having carpets cleaned – buyers will often choose among a number of local companies.

The company that provides the best information about itself may be the one that gets the first inquiry.

Annual Decisions

Directory advertising is a once a year decision and the influence on attracting buyers must be balanced with the limitations on spending in other media.

Virtually all businesses need some kind of listing. But, just as with all media choices, the place of each type of advertising in the overall media mix requires careful consideration.

The selection of categories and cross-listings with similar businesses is another choice that should be made with the entire year advertising plan in mind.

Many cities have several directories beyond the Yellow Pages – so advertisers must think of these options as well.

For most advertisers, directory advertising is a supplement to other local advertising.

Most local advertisers feel that basic information listings are essential, but that newspaper, radio and direct mail are needed to reach out to the audience with different messages throughout the year.

ADVANTAGES & DISADVANTAGES

Here are some additional considerations.

A Directional Medium

The Yellow Pages generally is not a medium that creates awareness of or demand for products or services.

People don't pick up the Yellow pages to look for a car. They do, however, pick up the Yellow Pages to look for a car dealer that carries a specific model after they have been influenced to make a purchase by advertising in other media.

Yellow Pages is a "directional" medium: its major strength is that it points willing consumers in a direction where their purchase can be made. Yellow Pages, then, can be said to be the final link in the buying cycle. After seeing ads in other media urging them to buy certain products, consumers turn to Yellow Pages to help them decide where to buy.

A Voluntary Medium

The Yellow Pages is "willingly consulted." Yellow Pages advertising does not intrude on editorial content.

When a consumer opens a Yellow Pages directory it is for the purpose of viewing advertisements and collecting infor-mation for a possible purchase – a significant difference from turning on the radio or TV or opening up a newspaper.

People voluntarily seek Yellow Pages information when they are ready to buy.

Wide Availability

Yellow Pages directories are just about everywhere.

They are distributed to every home and business with a phone and to many public phones, as well. Over 350 million Yellow Pages directories are distributed annually.

Long Life Span – Long Lead Time

Yellow Pages' main strength – long life span – can also be a problem. Directories are generally published once a year, therefore, a business's Yellow Pages ad cannot feature price, or other sales information that can change before the life of the directory is over.

Accuracy is even more important. A typo or phone number error in a newspaper ad is troubling, but minor.

In a Yellow Pages ad, it can be a disaster.

Sales representatives often call on advertisers six to eight months prior to directory distribution, due to production and printing requirements.

AUDIENCE MEASUREMENT

There are two measures of Yellow Pages' audience size: circulation and usage.

Circulation

Similar to other print media, Yellow Pages' audience size is measured in terms of circulation, which is either the number of households or individuals possessing a directory.

Circulation data is an important indicator of a directory's potential in a marketplace. After all, an ad cannot be seen if a directory is not in an individual's home.

Usage

Given the fact that many individuals have more than one directory in their home and use them differently, a method for distinguishing directory usage from directory possession was developed by National Yellow Pages Monitor (NYPM), a division of NFO Research.

Yellow Pages directory "ratings" are compiled by tabulating Yellow Pages usage data recorded in diaries over a one week period by a representative sample of consumers in a market area. Data collected from the weekly diaries are accumulated over a calendar year after which share ratings are calculated and reported.

These ratings are important because they allow advertisers to distinguish between two directories on more than the basis of gross circulation.

For More Information:

Check the Resources section.

YELLOW PAGES WORKSHEET

How many Yellow Pages directories are available in your market?

What cities, counties, and towns are included in the directories?

What are the demographics of the directories?

What is the distribution of the directories?

Do the directories offer value-added features, such as: color, coupons, and/or audiotext?

DIRECT MAIL

Direct mail is the fastest growing advertising medium and has gained share of advertising dollars steadily over the past ten years.

It provides an opportunity for local advertisers to reach the target audience in their homes with messages designed specifically for them.

It provides a self-contained sales message that can be targeted to specific demographics or buying history.

When direct mail incorporates couponing, or some other form of direct response, it also provides a built-in measurement device. Because it is measurable, direct mail, more than any other medium, is judged by specific results.

"DATABASE MARKETING"

"Database Marketing" is the name for the approach which is becoming increasingly popular with local advertisers who are now able to develop databases of current and potential customers.

Direct Mail is currently the major type of database marketing – but not the only one. The field also includes telemarketing and will probably include other forms of direct contact – such as computer e-mail.

Direct mail provides the retailer with a great deal of control. Messages can be customized for certain types of customers, and the customer's name can even be integrated into the printed piece.

Direct mail is relatively easy to measure. It is possible to provide the advertiser with information about what kinds of ad messages and approaches work in different situations.

For example, advertisers can try different types of messages and test which draws the most store traffic or sales.

Database formation is relatively easy for any advertiser who has a computer. Lists can be purchased or developed from a customer base of checks, charges and mail response. Some local retailers share database information.

Lists can be segmented by neighborhood, by buying history, by location or other categories. Commercial lists are also useful for some kinds of local businesses.

For example, suppose a local car dealer decides to target all owners of the type of cars he sells and particularly wants to reach owners of cars three or four years old – people who may be ready to trade in their older cars. The dealer can buy a list of all such owners in his market area from the state Division of Motor Vehicles.

COSTS & PROBLEMS

One problem with database use is the continual need to update. Local advertisers who develop their own lists may find that many names are no longer useful, particularly in areas where there is high mobility.

Another issue is cost. Even with slightly reduced postal rates, your message, including postage, printing, envelopes and tasks such as folding, stuffing and sorting, can result in a piece that costs 25-50¢ a customer – or more.

On a per impression basis, this is far more expensive than other forms of advertising. Of course, you can do much more with that single impression.

Other cost-reduction options, such as group mailing with other marketers, accomplish the reduction of costs, but they also reduce the impact. Card decks, for example, have a notoriously low response rate.

The customization capability of direct mail makes it attractive to local advertisers. Other local media find it to be a challenge to their own advertising sales success.

Computer-based technology is evolving the direct mail tools available to the small advertiser.

From mailings to your customer base, group mailing to nearby zip codes or mailing to special lists, every marketer should examine some sort of direct marketing program.

Many direct mail providers feature a sales force where the sales representative plays a key role formulating the program.

Other programs, such as Val-Pak, feature a local franchise arrangement where each franchisee will focus on retailers in a specific area.

"NEW MEDIA"

New media development is rapid in today's technologically advanced world.

A convergence of technological capability provides new means of reaching audiences with information of all types.

Now messages can be targeted more exactly and transmitted almost instantly to all parts of the world.

Much of this new technologically driven media offers opportunities for advertising as well. Here are some of the most important new areas – in alphabetical order:

AUDIOTEXT

Audiotext uses a combination of phone and computer capability to provide users with instant on-line connections to advertisers and information.

Daily newspapers are rapidly developing audiotext capability that allows readers to call in for additional information – sports scores, stock market prices, updates on developing stories – and allows advertisers to provide a voice message as an additional service to their other advertising.

For example, with audiotext, an employer can list a phone number in a classified ad. When interested applicants call the number, they may be asked a series of screening questions designed to sort out eligible applicants. Employers can then review the taped interviews and call back selected applicants.

A similar technique can be used for other kinds of sales, including real estate. Advertisers may receive a certain number of free call-ins and reviews for the price of the ad.

Audiotext capability may be offered at a special rate with regular advertising or it may be sold separately depending upon the policies of the provider.

Advertisers can provide "800" numbers (which are free of charge) or "900" numbers (which have a per-minute charge). These calls provide respondents with additional information.

Many papers are initiating voice personal services – allowing readers to respond to personal ads in the paper. Responses are recorded for the person placing the ad to review. Again, these calls may be free or there may be a charge.

ALTERNATE DELIVERY SYSTEMS

These systems provide home delivery of advertising, magazines and other information as a substitute to using the mail.

Some newspapers provide alternate delivery utilizing their regular carrier service; there are also separate companies that provide this kind of delivery.

The charge to advertisers is calculated by the type of pieces and by the length of the route. This kind of service provides advertisers with control over both content and delivery time.

IN-STORE COUPONING AND TRACKING

The introduction of scanners for bar codes now allows tracking of purchases as well as inventory control.

Many stores have also added coupon generating capability at the cash register. With this, scanning of one product may produce a coupon for a discount at the time, a special offer for a next visit or a coupon for a competitive brand.

Some stores have developed a database of regular customers who receive a "Preferred Customer Card." When the card is scanned, all purchases are recorded in the database, giving the store a complete shopping profile of that customer – who is then sent special offers and information in the mail and provided with coupons and recipes from a dispenser at the check out counter.

VisionValue is one of the leaders in this area, with initial funding from Procter & Gamble and RR Donnelly.

Kiosks and "Interactive"

More stores and malls will have kiosks with interactive computer programs for locating items within the store and distributing material like coupons, product information and recipes.

ON-LINE AND CD-ROM

Media and messages can now be delivered via modem through a variety of different on-line services.

Most of these interactive systems are programmed to carry advertising as well as information and often offer the opportunity of buying directly through the program – or at least receiving more information.

You can literally have your own custom newspaper, magazine or information delivered by modem to your computer.

In addition, several media companies are developing

publications that will be delivered via CD-ROM and feature music, moving pictures and interactive features.

Although some of these systems are in the fledgling stage at present, they do offer the potential for advertising messages as a means of reaching customers.

Catalogs are already being offered in a CD-ROM format, where the computer can even transmit your order over the phone lines.

As we get up to speed on "The Information Highway," there will be more and more activity in this area.

NEWSLETTERS FOR NICHES

Another result of the computer has been the increased ease of creating and producing quality newsletters.

Many marketers use newsletters to reach their niche markets. While these are similar in some respects to direct mail and database marketing, they have an additional function.

The integration of information and selling messages directed at an identified and segmented target market make these newsletters – which may be delivered by traditional methods or through interactive computer – a key medium for not only selling very specialized products and services, but for building a relationship with the target group.

"RELATIONSHIP MARKETING"

For years, advertising's job ended when the sale was made – and advertising, quite properly, focused on recruiting new customers.

Today, advertisers and marketers also need to be more concerned with maintaining and building a relationship with current customers.

In addition to starting the initial dialogue with a new customer, marketing programs are working to develop a deeper dialogue and relationship with their current customers.

Each of the media forms we've discussed can play this relationship-building role as well – strengthening the relationships between marketers and their customers.

It's one more way to "Make The Sale."

4. THE LOCAL MEDIA MIX.

*"Advertising nourishes
the consuming power of men.
It creates wants for a better standard of living.
It sets up before a man the goal
of a better home, better clothing,
better food for himself and his family.
It spurs individual exertion
and greater production.
It brings together in fertile union those things
which otherwise would never have met."*

Winston Churchill

FOUR. The Local Media Mix.

Your market – every market – contains a dynamic combination of media choices.
They compete with each other.
They reinforce each other.
They can work individually or in combination.
Now that we've covered each medium in detail, let's see how they all work together.

AN OVERVIEW

Let's take a quick "snapshot" of the overall media mix in a local market.

Newspaper and radio remain top local media choices.

Direct mail is strong and increasing in share every year.

Television – local network, cable and independent – provides a growing array of options.

Other traditional forms, such as outdoor, transit and specialty advertising may all be used by local merchants depending upon budget and strategy.

Local listings – Yellow Pages and other directories – are a necessity for every business, and today there are new electronic options for the listings as well.

New technology adds opportunities for retailers and service businesses on an almost daily basis.

With electronic options, like on-line computer services, a phone call can put would-be customers in touch with stores and businesses in virtually every category.

Increasing choice (and expense) makes it harder for retailers to choose where to place messages.

Matching media with markets

Some businesses need to focus their messages and media on narrow target markets, while other businesses want to reach as broad a market as possible.

The right media match will make it easier and more efficient for retailers to get in touch with would-be customers.

To do your job, you need to understand the market overall, and then understand the best ways to match this wide range of media options with specific marketer needs.

Sometimes you will help marketers select media choices.

And sometimes you will target the marketers who will benefit most from the specific media vehicle you represent.

This is a decision process that demands good information on the media options in your market.

IMPORTANT DECISIONS

Here are some key factors in making those media choices.

Broad or Narrow Audiences

Local media can reach broad or narrow audiences. Depending on client needs and strategy, one medium or a combination may be used.

A single client may vary the media mix throughout the year according to differing goals.

Some Examples

For example, a local restaurant in a resort town, where summer tourists add to both the population and business, may use the Thursday or Friday newspaper on a regular year-round basis. They may also run radio and television ads throughout the year as reminders for weekends, holidays, or special occasions.

During the busiest time of the year, additional radio and television may be used. Ads may also be placed in a local magazine highlighting weekly events during the busy season.

A toy store may rely on radio, some newspaper and direct mail with special offers, coupons and special birthday offers to a database of customers on a regular basis. But during the Christmas season, an additional newspaper schedule and local television may be added.

Geographic Considerations

Geographic considerations are also important.

Here are some examples of the questions you need to ask.

Is a large, broad-audience medium needed for the job?

Or can a small newspaper or other local publication that circulates in one area of the city or county do the job as well?

Would a concentration of outdoor along a well-traveled route or within one neighborhood area be effective?

How close is the audience to the business?

A small restaurant may draw from an entire city – but the surrounding neighborhood may be the prime target and return the most business for advertising dollars spent.

If that is the case, a truly local medium, like a zoned newspaper section, a neighborhood paper, direct mail within a local zip code (or, more targeted yet, to a specific customer database) may be both less expensive and more effective.

What the savvy retailer must think of is cost per actual customer or cost per sale.

While a larger circulation medium may offer less cost per person or cost per thousand, much of the advertising dollar may be spent to reach people outside the primary audience.

For this reason, many advertisers consider this kind of buy to be a waste of their ad dollars.

New Technologies – New Options

As technology adds options for even the smallest businesses, new media opportunities will evolve.

It is important for both retailer and sales rep to be aware of all the opportunities available and their potential effectiveness in meeting the specific goals of the business.

Understanding all available media options is also a part of knowing how to develop the most advantageous media mix.

SAME LOCATION – DIFFERENT MARKETS

An Example

Let's consider two local retailers right next to each other in the same small shopping strip.

DeLuxe Cleaners is a dry cleaner owned by Fred Brown.

Betters' Better Gourmet is owned by Sally and Bill Betters and is a gourmet take-out food store/deli primarily featuring pastas and sauces that come ready to heat or frozen. The deli also offers salad greens and a selection of wines, sparkling waters, and fruit juice.

All food is freshly made on the premises using only the finest quality. (Of course, the food is somewhat more expensive than pasta from the frozen food or deli section of a local grocery chain.)

They also offer special orders for large parties on a pick-up-and-go basis with a two-day advance order policy.

The two businesses share these things in common:
- **Same location**
- **Sufficient on-site parking**
- **Shopping center on a major commuting street**
- **New buildings with plenty of light and space**
- **Locally owned and managed**
- **Neighborhood identity**
- **New residential areas nearby**
- **Repeat business – ability to build loyalty**
- **Personalized, friendly service**
- **Lack of competition in immediate area**
- **A history of successful operations**

A media sales rep might hope to sell his medium to the entire shopping strip based upon geographic location, small business size, and local ownership factors. .

But the needs and goals of these businesses are very different. Let's think about them.

Business #1 – DeLuxe Cleaners

Customers come to Fred's because of convenience and quality of service. Although Fred's has only been in business seven months, it has already earned a reputation for good workmanship, pleasant service, and on-time work.

Many patrons drop off clothes on the way to work, so Fred opens the store at 7AM and business is steady until 8:30 or 9AM. Customers also come in on their way home, so he stays open until 7PM.

Fred knows many of his customers by name and most of them live within two miles of the business. He estimates 10 percent of the customers live beyond his primary neighborhood area and use him because he is on their way to work.

Typically, these customers bring in bigger loads of shirts and come by once a week at most, on the way to or from work.

Fred thinks of DeLuxe as a largely neighborhood business. He knows of two other dry cleaners within three miles, one of them on the same major thoroughfare.

Business #2 – Betters' Better Gourmet

Now let's consider Bill and Sally's business.

Some of Fred's customers also shop at Bill and Sally's gourmet food shop. It's not such a routine stop as Fred's, but Bill and Sally stay open until 7PM too, hoping to get some hungry customers who are picking up cleaning at Fred's.

In fact, Bill and Sally offer a dinner special – pasta and sauce of the day – on week nights. Their big selling items are frozen pastas and special orders for parties.

Their competition is diverse. While they don't have any real competition within a five to seven mile radius (except grocery stores), they rightly feel any take-out food is competition, and they feel the need to draw from a wide geographic area.

Bill and Sally have identified two primary audiences:
- local people for weeknight take-out and party food
- those who will drive over on Saturdays for weekend and "freezer food." They live further away.

Both audiences are important to this specialized business.

Different Audiences demand different Media Plans

The same local advertising plan and media for both? Perhaps both Fred and Bill and Sally could use the same neighborhood medium. And certainly both benefit from word-of-mouth from happy customers.

But the gourmet food business needs a geographically broader base medium as well and for two reasons:

One, this non-routine business probably cannot survive – and is unlikely to thrive – with a strictly local clientele unless they are located in a major business center.

Two, Bill and Sally are missing potential customers if they fail to advertise more broadly. There are lots of people in other parts of town who might like to sample the gourmet pasta. Since much of it is sold frozen, a monthly trip to stock up is a definite possibility. And since supplying special orders for parties is another goal of this business, the more people who know about this service, the better.

Possible Plans...

One possible plan for Fred might include a local neighborhood paper (if available), direct mail (zip code and customer database), and (perhaps) local radio.

Sally and Bill can use some of the same, but their newspaper dollars might be better spent in a larger daily, particularly in the Wednesday food section and weekend editions.

They might also want to consider the local weekend entertainment section and a few newer "free" papers with an arts and entertainment focus.

Both businesses would want to have some kind of promotion targeted to newcomers to the area. They might do this through a Welcome Wagon promotion, through local realtors or by direct mail to the newer areas.

LOCAL MAP EXERCISE

One way to begin to think about how local retail markets are organized and the needs of different kinds of businesses is to choose one area of your own city and map out the kinds of businesses in that area.

Get a good-sized map and find a wall where you can hang it up for a while as you get a feel for the area.

• Use colored pencils, pins, or dots.

• Have at least five retailer categories: clothing stores, supermarkets, family restaurants, fast food restaurants, etc.

Write some category candidates for your map here:
1.
2.
3.
4.
5.
6.
7.
8.
9.
10.

Make a sheet that indicates the category code with the names of the retailers in the area in each category.

Note how many are in each category type (dry cleaners, grocery, shoe store, video store, etc.) and how close they are to one another. Which stores are most competitive with one another by both category and geography?

With your colored pencil, also note major routes nearby that would make it convenient for shoppers to reach these businesses on the way to and from work.

Think about the most effective media for each of these businesses. How often do you think they need to advertise?

Do they need media that would reach the whole city or are they better served by a neighborhood medium?

Thinking about the individual businesses as needing to position themselves competitively and reach their target customers in the most cost efficient and effective way possible will make you better able to think about all the media choices they must make.

Getting a "bird's eye view" gives you a perspective you don't always get at the ground level.

DIFFERENT MARKET CHARACTERISTICS

Now, let's try to look at an entire market.

First, we'll cover three examples and then you need to develop a profile of your own market and the Media Mix.

There are similarities and differences in every local market. Let's look at three examples:
- **Market A – a large city**
- **Market B – a small city with a major university**
- **Market C – a tourist area**

FOUR. The Local Media Mix.

MARKET A

Market A is a large city with many suburbs in the counties surrounding it.

Media Summary:

There is a major metropolitan daily in the main city.

Several smaller dailies serve the suburbs and, in addition, the metro daily publishes zoned tabloid editions targeted toward each of the suburban markets and inserts them into the larger papers delivered to these suburbs.

In addition, there are several weekly papers serving smaller areas and a monthly city magazine.

On the broadcast side, there are several local television stations, including network affiliates and independent stations. Two cable companies split this market.

There are over 40 radio stations, and every format imaginable is represented from all-news to religious.

Other media forms are also in great abundance:

• Two major outdoor companies and a company that sells signs on the sides of busses. A bus stop poster franchise has recently been awarded by the city.

• Numerous direct mail services are available, including Val-Pack. Mailers and inserts are also done by some of the weekly newspapers.

• There are two competing phone directories.

Major Challenges and Unique Opportunities

Clearly, Market A offers options for nearly any kind of local and regional advertising package. The larger advertisers use a mix of mass reach media – newspapers and TV – and supplement with direct mail, radio and outdoor.

Since special events, such as sports and concerts, bring a number of people into the area on a regular basis, hotel magazines are also popular with some retailers.

Specific neighborhoods may be targeted with any of the smaller media. Several larger advertisers – such as department stores at the large regional malls – regularly place full-page ads in the suburban dailies as Market A has a large retail trading zone that draws from a 50 to 70 mile range for regular shopping and from an even broader range for seasonal shopping.

Smaller advertisers find the metro paper expensive. Many feel the geographic reach is much more than they need.

Some place small ads on a weekly basis for fear of losing some potential customers. Others rely on the zoned neighborhood editions to concentrate on their own local area exclusively. Still others do not use the print media at all, but rely on a combination of radio and direct mail.

Many of these smaller advertisers have figured out their own markets and found media combinations to serve them in the most effective way they can afford.

Although every type and size of business has differing media needs, most of the smaller, truly neighborhood businesses find a combination of zoned editions, radio, occasional direct mail and special promotions works well.

Cable TV is popular with some businesses, due to the relatively low cost, but many feel the reach is too great, since their cable systems reach far beyond the local trading area.

Some smaller businesses have an appeal beyond their own locality. They tend to rely on the metro paper and TV in a way similar to larger advertisers, although budgets are smaller.

MARKET B

Market B is a small city with a major state university.

Although the university is a dominant presence, the town also serves as a suburb for a larger metro area nearby.

Retailers and businesses in Market B distinguish between the college student market and the regular town market and tend to use different media to reach each contingent.

Media Summary:

For the college market, the college newspaper, three popular radio stations, flyers, posters and word-of-mouth are the usual media choices.

Reaching the regular town market is more difficult. Print options are a small five-day-a-week local paper, a large daily from the nearby metro area and a shopper.

Local cable is available, as is network affiliate television from the metro area. There are fourteen radio stations.

Long-term local residents tend to use a lot of the media from the metro area, but many smaller businesses feel the rates are too high and the reach much more than needed for the kind of traffic they could generate.

The metro daily puts out a local insert three times a week which is popular with advertisers.

Major Challenges and Unique Opportunities

The general feeling is that it is harder to make media choices in this market than it would be in a city of similar size but without so much media coming in from the outside.

Local merchants feel the town is neither a real stand-alone city nor a real suburb. The usual media mix is the local paper, local inserts in the metro daily, cable, and radio.

For the college market, coupons in the college paper are quite effective for some local restaurants, but some managers feel they only bring in customers during the coupon discount time.

MARKET C

Market C is a tourist area with several small towns strung along a beach. Year-round population is around 30,000 and much greater during the heavy tourist season.

The nearest shopping mall is 20 miles away, although there is an outlet strip.

Market C is filled with small stores of all kinds to serve both year-round and tourist shoppers. There are numerous restaurants, hotels and condos throughout the area.

Media Summary:

Market C has one small daily newspaper, one semi-weekly and 14 radio stations. While cable is available throughout the area, both it and all network affiliate television comes from a larger city 50 miles away.

A special weekly magazine is published during tourist season. An annual directory and tourist attraction magazine is published every year.

Major Challenges and Unique Opportunities

Businesses in Market C rely heavily on radio.

For entertainment businesses, a special Friday section of the daily paper is important, as well.

There's not as much direct mail in Market C as in non-tourist markets of the same size since even regular year-round residents move in and out more often.

Virtually all businesses are listed in the directory, and many participate in a hotel package which offers listings and coupons. Outdoor is popular with restaurants and hotels, although there is a move to ban outdoor boards from the more scenic areas.

Market C businesses also advertise in the markets where tourists come from. Newspaper ads in Sunday travel editions in cities within driving range are judged quite effective.

THE MEDIA MIX EVOLUTION

The previous examples are three very different markets with many possible choices and combinations in each.

Notice how media forms have developed to meet the needs of each market. Sometimes they are the result of large media companies modifying their products to meet local needs and sometimes they are the result of an entrepreneur seeing an unfilled niche in the marketplace.

This evolution is going on all the time.

It is simultaneously primitive and sophisticated – local "shoppers" make old-fashioned sales calls at the same time they use the latest computer technology for their paper.

This evolution simultaneously features success and failure. New media forms emerge, old ones go their way.

This is the way media evolves to meet the needs of business. As you look at your market, be sure to look for the evolutionary trends taking place.

MEDIA MIX WORKSHEET

Develop a Market Profile that includes the following:

Market Summary:

Metro, suburban, small city or rural

Regional or local shopping areas

Major department stores and malls or smaller, neighborhood shopping areas, or both

Major employment: Industry, professional, small business, tourism, etc.

Media Summary:

Types of available local media

Number of different types of media available

Major Challenges and Opportunities:

Major challenges to effective advertising

Unique opportunities and advantages

√ LOCAL MEDIA CHECKLIST

This Checklist provides a format for comparing relevant data from competing media in your market to determine opportunities for competitive advantage and disadvantage.

	Broadcast Television	Cable TV	Daily Newspapers	Radio	Direct Mail	Other
Cost of Advertising						
Cost Effectiveness						
Control of Timing or Placement						
Relationship with Sales Rep						
Quality/Reliability of Service						
Ease of Preparing Advertising						
Effectively Reaches Target Audience(s)						
Effectively Counters Competitors' Ads						
Lead time						
Other						

III. GETTING STARTED.

"You gotta know the territory."

The Music Man

Charlotte, NC. Photograph Curt Peters. Courtesy Charlotte Chamber of Commerce.

*Y*ou have to know your market.
You have to know the people in the market.
You have to know how things work in your market.
After all, how can you sell unless you do?

Homework and Fieldwork

A strong overall knowledge of your local market is the foundation of successful media sales – it helps you to become a knowledgeable marketing partner. And it helps you know where to look for new opportunities.

If you change jobs, as often happens, this knowledge will become the foundation for greater success in your market. Whatever medium you work for, your knowledge of the local market will be key.

If you change markets, as also often happens, knowing how to develop local market knowledge from scratch will become the foundation for greater success in your new market.

5. LOCAL MARKET RESEARCH.

Researching your market is both a methodology and a way of thinking. And they work together.

In this section, we'll first cover those two dramatically different mind sets you need for local media sales – a combination of state-of-the-art and "street smart."

Local Market Profile

Then, we'll show you a format for developing a fairly complete Local Market Profile. We'll give you sections where you need to fill in a few blank spaces – filling in those blank spaces for your own market will take a lot of time and effort.

Research Tools

Next, we'll cover some Research Tools you can use to fill in the blanks in your Local Market Profile.

Implementation

Finally, we'll show you local market research in action – we'll show you a few examples of how you can pull together state-of-the-art information and "street smart" judgment into a proposal that will result in more business for your client and a media contract for you.

GETTING TO KNOW YOUR MARKET

Two Kinds of Thinking

To really get to know your market, you have to be state-of-the-art and "street smart."

Sometimes you can use sophisticated marketing information to help an unsophisticated client make important marketing decisions.

And sometimes you have to go with your instincts.

Spotting a trend or opportunity and being the first to capitalize on it often means getting there before some market survey makes it obvious to everyone.

Sometimes you can use impressive amounts of data to show the characteristics of your audience. And sometimes you need impressive amounts of insight and empathy. Sometimes understanding what's important to a client and that client's customers is as important as a demographic profile.

Successful selling also means that you need to know how your clients think. You have to match market information with the client's view of the world – sometimes confirming and sometimes challenging that view.

You have to know what's important to them as well as what's important to their customers.

Market Knowledge = Added Value

To function as a marketing partner, you must know your market in all its dimensions. For, in addition to delivering your medium's audience, you are delivering market knowledge and market opportunity.

That's the added value that today's successful Media Person brings to every transaction. That's the extra dimension of effectiveness added to every successful program.

It pays off in a better match of marketers to a media's audience and a better developed message for that audience.

And it pays off in a faster more effective response to opportunities in the local marketplace.

Existing Knowledge + New Information = Opportunity:

What would you tell someone if you were pitching them to locate a new business in your market?

- Is the market growing?
- What kind of businesses are already there?
- Are some businesses moving out?
- Are new shopping centers coming in?
- Who competes and where? What's going on?

Whichever you choose to emphasize, all of these factors depend on local market knowledge.

When a new question arises, you develop answers (or hypotheses) by integrating new information with an existing (and expanding) knowledge base.

That's why it's worth saying again – to sell successfully, you have to know your local market.

So, let's get started.

AN OVERALL APPROACH

First, you have to know what to look for.

Differences and Commonalities

Every market is different.

Each city and town has strong points – and they are sometimes quite unique.

A comparison of seasonal sales curves would show that Destin, Florida, a Gulf of Mexico beach and fishing community is quite different from Nantucket, Massachusetts, an Atlantic Ocean beach community.

Demographic analysis would show that Tucson, Arizona is quite different from Fort Wayne, Indiana.

Yet, they all have some things in common. Destin and Nantucket have very similar types of tourist-based industries and both the high-tech market of Tucson and the "Rust Belt" city of Fort Wayne have a very diverse and dynamic industrial base with some surprising similarities.

More Diversity – More Similarity

Nationally (and internationally), every market is becoming more diverse and, at the same time, every market is becoming more similar.

What does this mean?

Once, small markets were fairly homogenous – even though there were income differences, people were very much like each other, went to similar churches, held similar beliefs, had similar (and narrower) purchasing habits and they even had fairly similar media habits. After all, there were fewer choices.

Today, virtually every market is more diverse – within each market are people with a broader range of interests, consumption patterns, and lifestyles.

Across all of those markets, there are more and more "niche" markets that have a lot in common with each other.

Understanding this complex set of relationships and how they apply to your local market is an important part of a media sales person's intellectual capital.

State-of-the-Art & "Street Smart"

As we said before, you need both methodology and instinct.

You will have a wide range of marketing research tools at your disposal. In the world of local media, sometimes you can base your decisions on state-of-the-art research and sometimes you have to operate on "street smarts."

It's more than intellect. The best salespeople are the ones who can sense when something is going on – and come up with 10 ways to make that something work to their advantage. It's almost instinctive.

It's understanding how a new shopping mall on one side of town may have an impact on businesses all over town.

And it means knowing about a change in your market as soon as possible – before it shows up in a research report.

That's why getting to know – and understand – your own local market is one of the most productive things you can do for yourself. To accomplish this, you need to work on two areas:

• Learning as much as you can about your market – through all kinds of sources and research resources.

• Developing contacts – meeting the people who are in touch with what's going on in your market.

"Learning" Your Market

Developing a feel for your local market is both high-tech and "high-touch."

Your information can come from such diverse sources as: Chamber of Commerce reports, secondary and primary data sources, local publications, and industry studies.

It also comes from making friends with your dry cleaner, a few real estate agents, and becoming a regular reader of all the local business news you can get your hands on.

The good part is you get to know everyone and develop resources that become more valuable over time.

The bad part… you're never really off the job.

James Webb Young deals with this in his wonderful book, *A Technique for Producing Ideas.* He talks about the need for two kinds of reading:

1. General Reading – to develop a broader background.

2. Specific Reading – to become more expert on the subject at hand.

Your task will be very similar in "learning" your market.

You will be developing general background on the market and then doing specific research on a client industry.

Market Background & Market Changes

Everything you can learn about your local market gives you some of the background you need.

With this background, you will then be able to figure out what every change means to the market and to you.

Sometimes these are big changes – a major league team or new store coming in, a business closing, a mall being planned. Sometimes the changes are more subtle – a transfer of an executive, a conference coming to town, a restaurant chain taking an option on a piece of property.

You have to look for clues and put it all in context.

A Few Rules to Remember

There are several rules to remember when you're getting started in the media sales business:

Rule #1: Things never stay the same.

Stores move, owners sell, new competition comes in, new shopping centers are built.

Rule #2: Keep your sensors on.

You have to stay tuned in – morning, noon and night.

You have to be able to make quick and sound assessments. Good salespeople pick up leads and tips wherever they are.

Rule #3: You have to build – and nurture – your network.

You'll be amazed at all the people you get to know.

But with relationships come responsibility. Sometimes it means being a good friend – and sometimes being a good business acquaintance – steering business someone's way – or letting others know about opportunities.

There's an old saying, "What goes around comes around." If you want people to help you with good information, you should look for opportunities to help others.

Rule #4: You can make change work for you.

There are opportunities everywhere.

Think creatively. If a store is closing, it means opportunities for its competitors. They'll need a new plan. If a store is moving in or expanding, there's a two-fold challenge – to get the ad dollars <u>and</u> to keep serving your old clients at the same time

LOCAL MARKET PROFILE.

Now let's examine some of the techniques we need to start building our knowledge base.

First, start a Notebook.

As you read through this list, you might want to start putting together a notebook on your local market.

It should not only have blank pages for writing notes, but also pockets, for stuffing in articles and reports.

Second, start filling out this Local Market Profile.

With each category of information, write down the question and category and, either write down the answer, or leave a blank. (We'll show you how to go about filling in those blanks later in this chapter.) You might also want to guess, so you can see how accurate your instincts are.

You'll also see that, in many areas, we've already covered the preliminaries in previous chapters – you already have some important pieces to the puzzle.

The media information you pulled together in Chapters Three and Four will be important here.

This profile will help you put it all in one place.

Before you think about innovative ways to sell your medium to a retailer, you need to know the kind of people who could be that retailer's customers.

• What kind of people live in your town or city?
• Where do they live and work?
• How much do they make? What do they spend it on?
• What are their media habits?

Smart marketing depends on digging up the facts of the marketplace. And to do that, you need the right tools.

Coming Up – Research Tools

After this questionnaire format, you'll find the RESEARCH TOOLS section. Review the questionnaire first, to see what you need. Then read the next section, to help you track down the tools you need to do it

When you're done with this profile, you'll have the answers to these questions – and a lot more.

MARKET PROFILE QUESTIONNAIRE

NOTE: "Your market" may have more than one definition.

Your city might be part of a larger "ADI." Select your definition of your local market and, where appropriate, also indicate the larger ADI number.

Population

How many people live in your market?

How many households?

What is the median household size?

How many people live outside the immediate area, but come to shop? (Hint: The Chamber of Commerce often provides this type of information)

What is the median age of the population?

How many people have moved into the area in the last year? In the last five years?

How many people have moved out of the area?

> Why?

How many people have stayed in the area, but moved into a different house within the last five years?

What percentage own their own houses or condos?

> What percentage rent?

Employment

Who are the largest employers?

What kinds of business are they?

What is the level of unemployment in your area?

Geography & Traffic Patterns

Where do the people who work live?

> In the city itself?

> In a suburb or rural area outside of town?

What kind of public transportation is available?

How many people commute into the city?

> Where do they live?

How do people who commute get into the city? What percent drive? What percent use mass transit?

NOTE: People who commute daily have interest in both the place where they live and in the city itself. They are likely to be regular users of the local media and thus get a lot of their shopping information from them.

They may shop or bank in the city during lunch hours or after work. Those who commute may have their cars repaired or serviced during the work day. (If they don't, perhaps they could be encouraged to do so!)

Geography & Retail Trading Zone (RTZ)

What is your RTZ?

NOTE: Newspapers call this area a Retail Trading Zone (RTZ). Newspaper circulation is described as the city trading zone (CTZ), which is within city boundaries, plus the larger area outside where people use the city as a shopping center (RTZ).

Education

How many people (or what percent) in your market area are high school graduates?

How many are college graduates?

How many have graduate degrees?

How do local elementary and secondary schools rank in your state? How does your state rank nationally?

What percent of high school graduates go to college?

What colleges or universities are in your community?

NOTE: People with more education tend to have higher incomes and may have different tastes in stores, restaurants and leisure activities.

Income

What's the median household income in your city?

What's the per capita income?

NOTE: Income levels as reported by the U.S. Census are from under $15,000 to over $500,000 with $5000 category breakdowns under the $50,000 level and increasingly wider categories as the level goes up.

Businesses and Local Tax Base

What is the tax base of the area?

What kind of businesses does the tax base come from?

What percent of property in your area is tax exempt?

Retail Sales

What percentage of income in your area is spent on: Automotive, Apparel, Food, Furniture, General Merchandise, Lumber and Building Materials, Fuel, and other categories?

The Department of Revenue in each state publishes a list of retail expenditures by category for every county. You can use this to spot differences in spending patterns for your area.

Area Media

Pull out your worksheets from Chapters Three and Four.

What is readership, listenership or viewership of:
    Newspapers (including weeklies and dailies)

    Radio

    Television

    Specialized publications

    Other

How are ad dollars spent by media form?
    Newspapers (including weeklies and dailies)

    Radio

    Television

    Specialized publications

    Other

How is money spent by retail category? (Automotive, Apparel, Food, Furniture, etc.)

Special Local Information

What would be of specific interest to retailers and other businesses in your own market?

Are there special local events or circumstances that would take some of the advertising/promotion dollars in your market?

NOTE: Look at spending in sports programs, in athletic programs, in other kinds of media.

RESEARCH TOOLS.

You need research to get to know your market.
These are the tools that will help you "fill in the blanks."

Knowledge is Power

The more you know, the higher your credibility with your clients and the better you'll be at your job.

To build that knowledge, you need the right tools.

Primary and Secondary Research

First, you will need to get information from **Secondary Research** – material that is already available. There is a lot of it – we'll show you where to look and what to look for.

Then, you may need to do **Primary Research** – where you generate the information yourself.

You will be doing some of this on an informal basis with your store visits and interviews, but we're going to show you more comprehensive techniques, as well.

Secondary Research tends to be inexpensive – it's often free for the asking. Primary Research can be expensive – even when you do it yourself, it may take a lot of time to do it right.

Secondary Research is usually done first.

SECONDARY RESEARCH SOURCES

Here are some of the main sources of Secondary Research. Within these sources, you will find much of the information you need for your Local Market Profile.

Chamber of Commerce Reports

Cities and towns of all sizes have their own reports. They are both informational and promotional, ranging from flyers to complete packages – even books. Some are updated yearly.

Chamber reports give a good overview and are likely to include some area history, list major employers, industries, churches and schools, provide a demographic overview of the population, give phone numbers for local service agencies, and show a map with areas of major interest highlighted.

Survey of Buying Power

This book, published and regularly updated by *Sales and Marketing Management*, gives a breakdown of both population and retail spending in all counties in the U.S.

It lists major industries and payroll information as well.

The breakdowns are for all states and counties and for

major cities as well.

Donnelly Demographics

Donnelly provides census data in a number of demographic categories and also contains some trend estimates of its own.

U. S. Census data

The Census is updated every ten years.

It provides population, income, growth, employment, education and other demographic data which can be extremely useful in both understanding your own market area and comparing it to others.

Larger newspapers and broadcast stations may have census data in either printed form or on-line. If that is not available, a state library or research institute will have it. There are also many sources that print certain facts from the census data – such as Donnelly (mentioned above).

U. S. Government studies and booklets

The Government Printing Office publishes information and study summaries in a wide variety of categories.

This is one inexpensive (sometimes free!) source for both basic and detailed information about industries which may be important to your clients – and therefore to you.

U.S. Statistical Abstracts

This book, published yearly by the U.S. Government, gives vital statistics for the country by state and specific categories such as health, sales, population, government structure, growth charts for gross product, manufacturing, and mining.

It is a valuable source for understanding trends.

Regional studies

There is a wealth of information available from state government sources.

In addition, many state universities have urban study centers which produce specific regional reports. Particularly valuable are reports in such areas as growth and planning.

Industry publications

Every business has its own set of trade publications, and you should be familiar with those of interest to your clients.

These are the publications your clients read on a regular basis. They range from automotive publications to hardware, home-builders to food and sports – every area you can imagine.

You should at least be familiar with these kinds of publications and keep up with the major trends. This shows the client that you have a sincere interest in his business.

Specialized reports

Just as with trade publications, your clients receive reports and newsletters.

Many businesses have associations of their own which publish newsletters and other publications of interest to those in that business. Again, you should be at least familiar with the major sources.

"Instant Backgrounders"

The Radio Advertising Bureau, and other media sales groups, often prepare category profiles that can be very useful.

They will provide you with summaries of the specific product category and other helpful marketing information.

Local newspapers and magazines

The local news and business sections of local publications are full of news you can use in the sales business.

Every change in the market – from promotions to store additions to road plans – can mean opportunity for you. Reading regularly also means you can discuss local events of importance with your clients.

Many papers have a special Business section (sometimes it's in tabloid format) and all have listings or transfers and promotions of people in the various businesses in town.

Awards, speeches, committee actions and other activities often appear in the Business section. If these mention the name of a possible contact, that's even better.

To get the most use out of the media news, start making a file of news and people who will be important in your territory.

For example, if you work on a bank account, you want to keep names of bankers in the news, clippings about special services and announcements.

And you want to keep information not only about your clients, but also about their competition.

Remember, ads in media other than your own are also a source of information.

There's more about this in the "Keeping Records" section.

National newspapers and magazines

The important ones for you are the industry and trade magazines mentioned previously as well as *Business Week, The Wall Street Journal, Time* and *Newsweek*, and major newspapers such as *The New York Times* and *USA Today*.

What you want to look for here are the charts, graphs and information pieces that give you some details about trends that affect your clients and business in general.

American Demographics is published monthly and can be a valuable source for tracking changes in customer habits, including leisure and shopping trends, and growth and change in certain demographic categories.

Advertising journals and papers

Many people might think these national advertising trade publications are not much use for local media sales.

But *Advertising Age* is important, particularly if you work with big clients or have a regional territory. They also feature regular articles and special sections covering various industry groups, which can be helpful.

There's also *AdWeek*, which also features good regional coverage of the advertising business, *Media and Marketing, Editor and Publisher, Radio Ink, Presstime* and the *Journal of Broadcasting*.

You'll want to look into these on a fairly regular basis to keep up with trends in your own industry.

Radio Ink, for example, covers the activities of radio stations with emphasis on local sales and promotion.

If you want to know about other media to compare to your own, there's *Editor and Publisher Yearbook, Broadcasting/Cablecasting Yearbook, Standard Rate and Data Service* and other similar publications.

These include basic information about markets and about rate charges and services provided.

Finally, if a client mentions some source as particularly useful for him or quotes from a source, ask about that information source. Asking will make you seem interested (not uninformed), particularly if the source is one only those truly inside that business would be likely to know about.

CD-ROM Databases

Some of the newest sources of information are the many databases available on-line and to CD-ROM users.

With these sources, you can locate almost any kind of published or catalogued information, read it on the screen and print pages right in your office.

The only limitations are access and expense.

ABI/Inform provides database information from business journals in all areas.

This is a valuable source for information about businesses, market trends, new products, financial news and economic indicators about business.

You can also retrieve information from trade magazines in many retail and small business categories.

Other databases provide governmental information – publications from the Government Printing Office, U.S. Census data, bibliographic information and many others. A visit to your own library will tell you what is available locally.

If you are working in sales, your own business is likely to have access to a variety of pertinent database programs.

Here's a quick example of using secondary data to build a sales program.

AN EXAMPLE:

Here's an example of how you might use specialized information to develop new business with a client.

Suppose you've just read about a new regulation concerning lawn mower safety and the publication says that a safety feature will be required in 18 months.

One of your clients is a hardware store that sells lawn equipment. You visit that client soon after this information comes out.

You are now in a position to ask him about what he has heard from the manufacturers who supply him about their timetable for getting this new feature on the market.

He volunteers that he'll have a piece to retrofit mowers bought within the last two years – and that he'll have it well before the mowing season begins.

Now you have accomplished two things:

1) Your client thinks you are not only interested in his business and his customers, but that you're really up on regulations that affect him, and

2) You have the basis for a pre-season ad campaign to tell past and potential customers that this special equipment is available, and positions your client as concerned about safety. (A family-friendly store.)

And your new ads (with extra space or time purchased) are just the way to get that across.

You've made the sale by functioning as a marketing partner – and it's all based on knowing the market.

Look for sales opportunities in secondary data

Trends and growth patterns can provide valuable clues for local use. There are a variety of primary and secondary sources to supplement your own day-to-day observations.

As an aspiring salesperson, you may get the impression that you'll spend most of your time reading rather than selling. That's not true.

But it is true that, as an aspiring salesperson, one of the best investments you can make in your own career is building up that knowledge base.

And, at the beginning of your career, the better you build your market knowledge, the sooner you'll become more than an aspiring salesperson.

You'll become a valued marketing partner.

PRIMARY RESEARCH SOURCES

Though you will always be using your own "primary research" of store visits and interviews, there are two basic areas for more formal primary research that can be used for local selling:

1. Store or Customer Research
2. Media Research

Sometimes these are separate studies, but many times a local medium will find out information about both areas in the same study, which may be a survey, or a focus group, or some other method – such as a mall intercept study.

Stores use scanner data and databases of customers to find out detailed information.

The media also use databases of their users as well as of their advertisers.

Newspapers and broadcast stations may do research about the market and their users on a regular basis.

Primary research is expensive, but it can provide very specific information about the media product, user and non-user perceptions and use patterns and importance of the media product for providing advertising information.

Information about the importance of the media product and its advertising messages to users can be very valuable.

Primary research can enable a newspaper, radio or TV station to compile a profile of readers, listeners, or viewers – this can help sell advertisers on the value of the medium as an advertising vehicle.

Here are some of the things that primary research can help you learn:

1. Store or Customer Research

Awareness level of different stores
Shopping habits
Attributes customers find important
How much customers spend on each store visit
How customers feel about/use the competition
Store traffic and patterns of use
How customers use local ads
Where customers get shopping information
Problems: location, prices, image or parking
Major goods bought by customers in past year
Plans to buy major goods
Where customers/prospects work
Where customers/prospects shop
Which stores customers/prospects pass on the way home from work
Which stores have the best values for certain products
Which stores have the best customer service
Restaurant use
Bank and other service use

2. Media Research

Media use habits
What attributes customers find useful/important
How much/how often read, viewed or listened to
Time of day read, listen or view
Which medium provides best news
Media features: personalities, subject matter, articles
Use of different sections in local newspapers
Reliance upon local media by differing demographics
How customers read or use ads
Coupon clipping/availability
Level of coupon clipping and use

TYPES OF PRIMARY RESEARCH

These are the most usual types of local primary research:

Surveys

Surveys are a means of obtaining specific information – such as shopping habits, attitudes about specific stores, media use, use of competitors, frequency of visiting certain shopping areas or stores, average dollars spent per visit, and demographic data for users as well as non-users.

A survey is a tool that can be tailored for specific needs and, with good questions and respondents who are representative of the group you want to know about, a survey can yield very useful answers to help both media and retailers plan advertising plans and ads for businesses.

Media such as newspapers or radio stations often do readership or listenership surveys for their own products.

The purpose of these surveys is to get a profile of the reader or audience including how often they read or listen to the medium (and to competitors) and how much time they spend reading or listening every day.

Some surveys, such as those about shopping habits, include store preference, frequency, location, dollars spent, use of local advertising in making shopping decisions and other shopping information.

Demographic data is gathered as well: age, income, housing, employment, number of children at home, length of time lived in the area and other similar facts.

With this kind of information, the medium can talk to advertisers about specific buying habits of readers or listeners and use the survey facts to show that buying advertising in their medium is a good investment.

Questions should generally move from the general to the specific. In order to generate the most honest answers, the respondent should not know who the survey is for.

EXAMPLE: JONATHAN'S PIZZA

Jonathan's is a one-location pizza store located in the main shopping district of a medium-size town.

The distinctive selling point for Jonathan's is the wide variety of fresh toppings available: daily selections might include shrimp, fresh vegetables, green and black olives, garlic, two kinds of onions and pineapple in addition to the usual kinds of pizza toppings. Pizzas are made from scratch on location.

Jonathan's competition is all the usual franchise pizza stores who have both eat-in and delivery. Jonathan's does not have delivery because it is

a.) too difficult to park cars in their location and

b.) it is a small store and they can only make enough pizzas to be consumed on location.

FIVE. Local Market Research.

Here's a possible phone questionnaire for some store research – a survey for Jonathan's Pizza.

JONATHAN'S PIZZA SURVEY

1) How often do you eat fast food?
- ☐ More than once a week
- ☐ Once a week
- ☐ Less than once a week
- ☐ Never eat fast food

2) I'm going to read you a list of fast food items. For each, please tell me if you eat this food often, occasionally or never:

Hamburgers	☐ Often	☐ Occasionally	☐ Never
Chicken	☐ Often	☐ Occasionally	☐ Never
Chinese	☐ Often	☐ Occasionally	☐ Never
Mexican	☐ Often	☐ Occasionally	☐ Never
Pizza	☐ Often	☐ Occasionally	☐ Never

3) When you go to a restaurant for a fast food meal or snack, how important to you is each of the following?

Atmosphere
☐ Very Important ☐ Important ☐ Not important

Speed of service
☐ Very Important ☐ Important ☐ Not important

Dollar value
☐ Very Important ☐ Important ☐ Not important

Food quality
☐ Very Important ☐ Important ☐ Not important

Additional Questions

The next questions might ask about locations visited and then move on to specific questions about different pizza stores in the area or about coupons.

If the survey is for Jonathan's specifically, more detailed questions about that particular store would follow.

If the survey is about shopping in general, such specific questions would not be included.

Some surveys ask about future buying plans for large items such as houses or condos, autos and furniture.

Using surveys for sales success

A newspaper or radio/television station could use information from this kind of survey to talk about the kind of people who are in their audience and their buying habits.

By showing an advertiser just how people use their medium to make shopping choices and the demographic profile (income, education, age) of the buyer, the value of the medium in reaching the customer is clearly demonstrated.

Example 1. (General Survey):

"Did you know that people who read our paper go out for pizza 2-3 times a month and spend $20 each time?

According to our most recent market survey, single people are likely to go for pizza with friends at night after work and readers with kids say pizza is their number two choice for fast food.

How about advertising an early special for three or more sharing an extra-large pizza with salads?

Example 2. (Survey questions specifically for Jonathan's):

"Our readers spend a lot of money on fast food – and 70% say they eat pizza out in a restaurant at least twice a month. But our market survey showed that most don't know about your fresh toppings.

Here's a campaign that might work with that."

Example 3. (General Market Survey):

"Over a fourth of the readers we talked to said they were planning to buy new furniture within the next year.

With an average income of over $26,000, they'd be great prospects for your store.

We reach 60 percent of that buying market everyday – 73 percent on Sunday.

A Sunday ad campaign would reach a lot of those potential furniture buyers."

Example 4. (Radio):

"More than half of adults 18-44 listen to us at least three times a week. And our listeners go out to eat an average of two times during the work week.

Ads for your restaurant placed during evening drive time would get them when they're hungry.

Here are some ad ideas to help bring them in here."

MORE PRIMARY RESEARCH TOOLS

Focus groups

Sometimes a newspaper or broadcast station will bring in a series of small groups (8-12 users – or non-users – of the media product) to ask their opinions about the kind of job the medium is doing.

The group might talk about what features they'd like to see, what they like or don't like, how they use the media product, how they use the ads and other information.

Although focus groups are small, the participants may bring up points that might not be included in a survey. Because of the face-to-face discussion, the moderator can follow up on points and explain difficult areas.

It is also possible to let participants see the newspaper, listen to tapes or watch programs.

While this kind of group is often used to get information and understand issues before writing survey questions, it can also be used just to find out more about the product use.

Asking about advertising use can also be a part of it.

Focus groups can even be used to find out more about advertisers and their perceptions of the medium itself.

Focus groups produce qualitative data in a setting that encourages many different ideas to emerge.

Though the results are open to subjective interpretation, they are easier and less expensive to implement than more formal studies.

Mall intercept data

Another method of finding out information about consumers is a mall intercept study. Although this kind of study is not statistically significant, it does give a retailer or a medium some kinds of information about people who are actually in the mall or other shopping location.

Typical questions concern frequency of shopping, favorite stores, reasons for choosing the particular shopping area and opinions about differing kinds of products. Sometimes people are taken to a research area and asked to test products or fill out questionnaires.

Although this kind of study does not give you information from the broad range of customers in your retail trading area, it can give you some very specific information about people who are actually shopping or browsing on a given day.

One-on-One Interviews

Finally, just talking to consumers can be helpful. If you can find a few "Heavy Users" of a store or product category – those with a lot of real world consumer knowledge – you can find out a lot very quickly.

They can be a rich source of information – and you can do

it on your own. One-on-one interviews can be a good way to do some primary research for almost any client.

"Di-ads" and "Tri-ads" are similar to one-on-ones, only they use two or three respondents instead of one.

Computer Mapping

This sophisticated technique takes past growth patterns, census data, area trends, and an overview of the local area and makes projections for growth and changes within the local area for a period of time to come.

Regional and urban planning institutes are a valuable source for information of this type.

TRACKING THE COMPETITION

The importance of competitive information

One important research tool for developing sales opportunities and your own marketing skills is an ongoing competitive analysis of other media – you need to track advertising in other media from your actual or prospective client list.

Looking and listening can do a lot.

Tracking other advertising keeps you up-to-date on the other media outlets your clients are using.

It alerts you to prospective clients who are not in your medium. It may also inspire new ideas and opportunities.

Keep a Log Book or Clip File

One effective technique is to start keeping a log book (for radio or TV) on frequency and type of ads used other places – and, for print, a "Clip File." This can give you a good idea of the audience, advertising objectives and creative appeals those clients think works for them.

Not only do you know more about the competition, you now have valuable information to use on your own sales calls to these clients you'd like to have on your own list.

Look at ads from other markets

Ads from other markets can help, too.

Not only will there be new creative ideas to bring to your clients, but there may be whole new categories of businesses who advertise. Perhaps these kinds of businesses are just moving into your local community.

Your "Clip File" will grow. Soon, you'll be filing the tear sheets by category – by industry (fashion, etc.), by technique (coupons, etc.), or both.

SPOTTING SALES OPPORTUNITIES

Secondary data can be an ongoing source of sales opportunities. Here are some places to look:

1) Business pages of newspapers run stories about new businesses and expansions in the area.

2) Local stories about new schools or planned new subdivisions tell you to look in those areas for increased growth and new retail outlets.

3) Requests for or changes in zoning often signal growth or commercial development in an area.

4) Census data, or *Chamber of Commerce* publications from areas similar to yours, can enable you to make comparisons between your own area and others.

5) *The Survey of Buying Power* gives easily used data that compares your area to others in your state or region. Using data like this can generate trend lines to follow.

6) The *Radio Advertising Bureau* provides instant background on store categories in your area.

7) Other media organizations, including the *Newspaper Association of America (NAA)* provide similar data.

RESEARCH AT WORK.

Now let's use some real life examples that can help you use research to sell. We also need to talk about some real life habits that can help you expand your knowledge and discover new opportunities.

As we said at the beginning of this chapter, it's often a combination of using sophisticated data and "street smarts."

Here are some examples of how they can work together.

CHECKING IT OUT

Sales ideas from a ride around town

As you become a media person, you'll discover that even when you're just driving, your antennae will be extended – looking for new opportunities.

Each time you're out on the street, it's a chance to develop your "street smarts."

Here are some things you should do.

Look for new businesses

• Check out existing shopping areas and malls for movement. If you know that some stores are moving or expanding, find out who is moving into their old space.

• New shopping areas are fertile ground for an alert salesperson. Stop by and talk to anyone you can find – even if building is still in progress. Construction workers and others on the site may be able to tell you who is coming in and the estimated date of completion.

• A new residential building in an established area is also of interest. Find out who's in charge. If it's an apartment or condo, there may be advertising opportunities right there. If not, keep looking for nearby businesses to change or new ones to move in to serve the expanded residential base.

• New office buildings may want to advertise for leases. Stop by and check out the completion date, projected types of tenants and percentage already rented. Not only might you get ads for the building itself, you may be able to get ads from the new occupants.

Look for business growth

When a business is growing, your antennae should start to tingle. Is a store that is on your list – or should be – expanding? It may be adding new features, new departments, or just accommodating increased business.

Either way, it may be an opportunity for more advertising.

Look for competition

When businesses compete, they all look for new ways to reach new customers.

The reaction to new businesses by existing businesses also spells opportunity. Soon, you'll be able to feel the rumble of businesses gearing up to compete.

With smart marketing, you can provide a competitive advantage to businesses that want to compete.

Look for opportunity

Whether it's new businesses, growing businesses or competing businesses, each offers opportunity.

And, with each of these leads, you can dip into your research resources to find out more.

All it takes is starting your car.

And getting started.

LOOKING FOR CLUES

Now let's try looking at information like a detective.

Unraveling data for problem-solving clues

You have to do more than collect data – you have to convert it into usable information and actionable insights. Often, this means looking for "clues."

The sequence Lisa Fortini-Campbell describes in her book, *"Hitting The Sweet Spot,"* is…

Data>Information>Insight>Inspiration

Lisa talks about becoming a "Consumer Detective." In the same way, you want to become a "Sales Detective."

You want to "unravel" all the data and then tie important pieces together into information that helps you understand the business.

And remember, you want early insights.

After a market has been developed, the potential is clear to everyone. You want to find the winners early on.

Finding a situation as it's just developing is the kind of opportunity-laden situation that can result not only in sales, but in being part of helping an exciting new business grow.

Discovering Insights

Generally, two pieces of information will tie together to create an insight. As James Webb Young reminds us, *"an idea is a new combination of two previously existing elements."* In this case, that idea, that new combination, is your insight.

Using that insight, you can build a sales presentation that inspires new sales.

Here, we will take you through two cases to show you where insights can be generated by the sales rep doing some detective work. The result can be a successful sales presentation and advertising program.

Then, we'll give you an example to see if you can unravel the data and tie it together.

MINI-CASE #1

Franklin's Clothing Store –
Using secondary data to help a client

Franklin's is a traditional men's clothing store offering clothing in the mid-price range. It was started just after World War II by old Mr. Franklin. His two sons now own and manage the original store and two branch stores.

Franklin's ads (which are infrequent and conservative) have always stressed the fact that the store caters to men of all ages – "all generations" as old Mr. Franklin said.

The mission of the store has been to convert customer's sons in their teen years to loyal Franklin customers.

Records of all charge purchases, size changes, preferences as to style and color are kept for all charge customers. Customers are encouraged to open a charge account – in fact, charge customer's sons are awarded their own account at the time they go to college.

Franklin's has always been a family-oriented business and customers in the past have tended to remain loyal. Customers who move out of town often call Franklin's to order and often stop in when they are back in town.

Franklin's ad policy has been, and still is, very conservative. The store has prided itself on word-of-mouth and maintained a very minimal ad schedule in the local media.

Sales reps are always greeted cordially, but soon find that the Franklin's management team has their own inflexible ideas about advertising based on what has been done before.

Franklin's has not changed over the years, but the town has. The store is doing well enough, but is missing many opportunities – leaving itself open to another, more savvy retailer to come in.

What are your clues?

First, Franklin's is a typical case of a well-established retailer in a market that has changed.

Your clues are that the market has changed and Franklin's is maintaining a policy that resists change.

Your next task is to find market information that helps Franklin's management sell themselves on the need for change.

Use secondary data showing population, age and growth trends over the years – help Franklin's see the opportunities that can come from expanding their target market to new audiences.

Show them the potential new business out there.

Although you'll have to be tactful, suggesting additional audiences and media may help Franklin's to see that they must update and expand their approach to keep their market share and protect themselves.

Play to both generations of Franklin's management by giving them useful information about "all generations" of new business in their market.

MINI-CASE #2

GreenStuff Nursery –
A Media Survey finds a problem

GreenStuff Nursery (GS) is a three-year old business run by a husband and wife team (Arlene and Ed) who are both botanists.

A combination nursery and yard store, GS is a year-round business with three distinct seasonal selling peaks: spring for vegetable and flower gardens, fall for trees and yard clean-up, and Christmas for decorations.

The remainder of the year, customers will buy house plants and herbs. Plants and trees are of the highest quality and are guaranteed. Prices are somewhat higher than the grocery store and chain garden centers to reflect the quality.

The advertising plan has been to use local newspaper and radio at a reminder level much of the year, with additional ads at peak times.

Last year, the nursery placed a quarter page in a gardening tabloid run in the local paper using a coupon for 10 percent off any purchase of $25 or more or a discount on tree planting.

These special offers brought some additional business. But, despite what GS feels is a good ad schedule, their business isn't growing and customers brought in with special discount offers don't seem to come back on a regular basis.

There's strong competition from the chain store garden centers in both price and convenience.

Although the ads seem to attract some new customers – particularly at peak seasonal times – the average spending level is disappointing, with most shoppers spending less than $15 per visit. A typical purchase would be a couple of herbs that the local groceries didn't carry, a tomato variety that was scarce or a house plant for a gift.

Ed complained to his local ad reps, *"Our ads aren't doing us any good – or at least there is no gain we can measure over any kind of time. Ads should be an investment – but ours don't bring any long-term return.*

People seem to think of us as a supplementary place, but not as the place to buy plants for the whole yard on any kind of regular basis."

The paper included GreenStuff as one of the nurseries in the next general survey. Responses showed that GS was regarded as a place to buy specialty items, but not as a general plant source – confirming what Ed and Arlene had thought.

But another important clue emerged. The survey showed that 73 percent of customers for all nurseries were afraid the plants they purchased would die or not produce well – so they hesitated to spend top dollar for vegetable plants or for small trees they could get at low prices.

Here was a clue that helped GreenStuff develop a more persuasive message.

Working with their ad reps for both newspaper and radio, Ed and Arlene developed a new ad campaign to stress that the owners were botanists who grew their own plants from seed and would give professional advice about planting conditions and requirements for all sales – big and small.

The ads also contained tips for different kinds of plants, positioning GreenStuff as a reliable and knowledgeable source.

By inference, the ads showed the value in buying from local experts as opposed to mass-produced flats of vegetables and other plants found at chain stores. Sales grew and Ed and Arlene could track repeat customers. After talking to their rep, they instituted a weekly hot-line so customers could get some help in making decisions.

They also started a series of classes in small garden planning and gave discounts to customers – who bought the plants for their garden designs exclusively from GS.

In this case, survey results and owner insights were the critical combination that led to developing a more effective message and a stronger long-term position in the market.

Digging for Information

Whether it's a garden shop, a pizza place or someone who's never advertised before, you should be looking for information that is "advertisable."

"Find the problem the advertising must solve." You're a detective, a "problem-finder." You're looking for the insight that will be the key to unlocking those problems.

That's the key to being a successful marketing partner.

Now it's your turn to take a look at the information and unravel the clues.

ASSIGNMENT:

Sweeney's Ice Cream

Sweeney's is a modern ice cream store that works very hard to be like an old-fashioned ice cream parlor.

Their specialty ice creams are made in-house and Sweeney's has expanded to a sandwich menu as well.

Business is pretty good. Sweeney's attracts working people for lunch and families for dinner on weeknights and weekends.

Late nights are popular with the teen crowd.

Although locally-owned, Sweeney's has begun to expand and they recently opened another store in a nearby city.

The advertising campaign is consistent with that of the first store, but the ads in the new location do not seem to be working as well as projected. Lunch business is fine, but traffic really slacks off around 5PM.

Sweeney's manager finds it hard to believe that the ad campaign is not working. You're pretty sure the problem is not with the ads, but with the media placement.

You represent both the newspaper and one radio station in the new market. You point out that this town is different from the first location. The manager's reaction to this idea is that he'll give your medium a chance if you can give him any evidence to prove it might do a better job.

1. Make a list of the possible problems. How will you narrow this list down? How will you search for clues?

2. Outline your plan for showing this manager why different media and a new approach may be needed for this market even though it is not far away from the first location.

3. What sources will you use for this research?

RESEARCH = THE RIGHT START

Whatever the problem, whatever the solution, it starts with the right information to help you develop the right focus and the right direction.

That means knowing how to do the right research.

That means:
- The right mind-set – state-of-the-art and "street smart"
- The right research tools:
    - Secondary Research
    - Primary Research
- Looking for clues and opportunities
- Identifying the marketing problem
- Putting them all together into a program that solves that problem and builds long-term growth

It's a big job.

The right research will help you get started.

6. TERMS YOU'LL USE EVERY DAY.

*"Words are the dress of thoughts,
which should no more be represented
in rags, tatters and dirt
than your person should."*

Lord Chesterfield

Every profession has its own specialized vocabulary. *When you're selling – or buying – media, you need to know the terminology and be able to use it.*
Here are some terms you'll need to know on the job.

Not Alphabetical

We've sorted them by media form, with general terms coming first followed by terms more specific to newspapers, broadcast (radio and television), outdoor, direct and Yellow Pages.

Rather than list the words alphabetically, we've tried to put the more important words first – a sequence that makes it easier to understand the category.

GENERAL MEDIA TERMS

Advertising

A means of telling prospective buyers about your business or service or about specific offers or goods you have for sale through placement of a written or spoken message in a medium. As legendary copywriter Claude Hopkins said, *"Advertising is multiplied salesmanship."*

Marketing

Marketing covers all aspects of the sale or exchange of goods and services from promotion through distribution. Advertising is one aspect of marketing.

Marketing may be "customer-focused" or "product-focused."

Promotion

A specific event or offer designed to call attention to a product or service in a way that often gives the prospective buyer something extra for the money. For example, a two-for-one coupon or a radio remote with live music and giveaways at a client's business location are promotions.

Objective

A goal. A mission to be accomplished. Advertising campaigns should have specific objectives in terms of new clients reached, sales or market share gained, increased loyalty of present users and other similar accomplishments.

Strategy

How you accomplish that goal. Remember, there are many kinds of strategies in business – there are marketing strategies, creative strategies and media strategies. When someone wants to talk about "the strategy," make sure you know which one is being talked about.

Another thing to remember — a strategy is often an hypothesis or a "best guess" as to how to accomplish a certain objective. There may be other alternatives as well.

Target Audience

This term has many synonyms. "Target Consumer," "Customer," "Target," and "Prospect" are some of them.

Basically, it is a description of the audience you want to reach with your ad campaign, promotion or other marketing effort.

Reach

Refers to the number of people who have been exposed to your message. Using reach, you count each person one time.

You might also use the term, "effective reach," which measures how many people in your target audience have been reached by a message.

Frequency

Frequency counts how many times each person has been reached. You could say that reach is talking about the first time a person has been exposed to your message while frequency is adding up all the times that person was reached.

Contract

This is the agreement dealing with how many times the message will be placed, how often, for which days or times, size of the ad (space or time), cost of each ad and the total cost of all advertising covered under the contract. It specifies what the client will get, the cost, and terms of payment.

Commission

There are two types of commission common to our industry.

The Sales Commission goes to the Media Representative who handles the business.

An Agency Commission may also be paid, or deducted before payment, either by the agency of record, an advertising agency, or by a client through some sort of "house" agency.

Agent

This may be the person who represents the medium or it may be the person who represents the client in a transaction.

Vendor

A supplier.

Representative

As used in the media sales business, it refers to the person who works for the medium and acts as the account person in selling space or time and arranging advertising placement.

Book

This word has a number of definitions in our industry:

1. A sales representative brings a presentation book to the client. This book explains market facts, facts about the medium, rate schedules, placement, and contract terms.

Used during a sales presentation, this book will also contain specific information gathered for the particular client as well as some speculative ads made up just for that client.

2. A sales representative's "book" may be his list of clients.

3. In radio, it may refer to Arbitron ratings.

4. For creative people, it may refer to their portfolio.

Cold Call

This describes a visit without prior contact by a sales representative to a prospective client. It is termed a "cold call" because the sales rep knows nothing about the business at the time, nor has there been any contact. However, one should never go in without knowing something.

A "cold call" is a getting acquainted and fact-finding sales call rather than one where the goal is to actually make a sale.

House ads

These ads are for the newspaper, station, or other medium and are run in that medium as a promotional device.

They usually run when there is space or time to fill.

Niche marketing

This refers to marketing that focuses on specific groups (demographic or geographic) or a narrow market segment.

Media mix

Sum of media used for advertisements. One of the jobs of the sales rep is to understand the optimum media mix for each client and position his medium as primary within that mix wherever appropriate.

Position

This is an important term with a number of definitions.

1. Position can be a verb meaning either to "position" a product or service within the mind of the consumer (as defined by Trout & Ries).

2. Position can also be a verb describing the process of determining the "relative position" of a product or service within the category.

3. Position can be a noun referring to the position of the ad within a publication or the placement of the ad within a broadcast period relative to the program or time slot.

NEWSPAPER TERMS

Column inch

A newspaper measurement and the usual way newspaper is priced and sold. A column inch is one inch in depth by one column wide – no matter how wide the column.

Usual newspaper column width is $2 \frac{1}{16}$ inches.

Broadsheet & Tabloid Sizes

Broadsheet is the usual format. Page measurements may vary slightly, but are usually about $22 \frac{1}{2}$ to $23 \frac{1}{2}$ inches in length and $13 \frac{1}{2}$ in width.

Tabloid papers are approximately 13 $\frac{1}{2}$ inches in length and 11$\frac{1}{2}$ to 12 inches in width.

Standard Advertising Unit (SAU)

Originally developed as a way to make newspaper advertising units uniform for national and regional advertisers.

The SAU provides standard sizes honored by all newspapers offering the SAU option.

Each different size has a number; ads of a certain number will look the same in any newspaper, making it possible for an agency to develop one ad in one size to send to all papers.

Standard page

The SAU page is six columns wide with 21 ad inches per column for a total of 126 column inches per page. Some papers add $\frac{1}{2}$ inch per column for a total of 129 inches for a full page, but also honor the SAU sizes on that page.

Total market coverage (TMC)

This term refers to a newspaper's practice of printing a special, smaller section, once or twice a week, with highlights from the editorial (mainly feature) sections of recent papers and ads. The TMC sections are delivered free of charge to all people within the paper's target area who do not subscribe to the paper.

If advertisers sign a contract for TMC coverage, their ads appear in the regular paper and also in the TMC section.

This provides complete coverage of the area and assures an advertiser that the ads have reached everyone in the market, whether or not they are newspaper subscribers. The cost for using TMC coverage is the cost of a regular inch plus a small additional charge.

Bulk or volume discounts

Advertisers who sign a contract for a given number of inches to be placed during a one-year period are eligible for a discount based upon the number of inches to be used. The larger the number of inches in the contract, the greater the discount.

For example, if the open rate at a newspaper is $71, an advertiser agreeing to run 50 inches a year might be eligible for a price of $62 an inch. For 800 inches, the cost per inch might be $56. This type of contract means that the advertiser can use the ad inches at any time during the year.

For this reason, a bulk or volume discount is ideal for an advertiser with a seasonal business.

Frequency contract

This type of contract refers to an agreement by the advertiser to use some number of inches every week* for a period of time ranging from 13 weeks to a year. The discount is based on the number of inches to be used, with increasing discounts for greater numbers of inches.

For example, an advertiser agreeing to four inches every Thursday (weekday rate) might pay $47 an inch while an advertiser agreeing to 32 inches might pay $43 an inch.

Because it guarantees a consistent amount of advertising and cash to the newspaper every week, a frequency contract generally offers the lowest prices for an advertiser.

*[Some papers allow an advertiser to miss one week of every quarter and still receive a frequency discount. Thus, a contract might read that the advertiser must place ads in 12 of 13 weeks, 24 of 26 weeks, 36 of 39 weeks or 48 of 52 weeks.]

Circulation

The number of newspapers that are sold each day, either by subscription, or by single copy sales, or both.

Penetration

The number of newspapers sold within a defined market area as a percentage of all available households.

Thus, if a community had 31,554 households in the city zone and sold 26,239 papers on weekdays by carrier delivery, single copy sales and mail subscriptions within that city zone, the penetration rate would be 83 percent. This would be a very high rate of penetration in today's markets.

Duplication

Used in newspaper markets where there is competition, duplication refers to readers of more than one paper. The advertiser then, is getting duplication or frequency with these dual readers by using both papers. For the readers of only one of these papers, the advertiser is getting reach.

Preprints

These are sections that are printed separately from the regular paper and inserted into it before it is delivered. They may be printed at the paper, but it is more likely that they will be printed elsewhere and delivered ready to insert.

By using preprints, the advertiser has complete control over the ad format and, often, better color reproduction. The same ad preprint may be inserted in a number of newspapers in a region on the same day by national or regional advertisers.

Newspapers charge a fixed amount per thousand inserts with the price based on the size of the preprint and the number of preprints the advertiser will run through the contract period.

Inserts

Same as preprints. Some papers call single sheets "inserts" and tabloid or multiple-page inserts "preprints."

All are inserted separately from the regular press run.

Zoned editions

Targeted for special areas of the city or market area, these sections carry news and advertising for that section.

Zoned editions may carry local school information, special neighborhood coverage, sports scores and local advertising. These editions give a small advertiser with local customers a chance to advertise directly to the geographic area nearby at a much reduced rate.

RTZ stands for Retail Trading Zone.

CTZ stands for City Trading Zone.

Run-of-press (R.O.P.)

This term refers to advertising that is placed in the paper's regular page as opposed to preprints.

Display advertising

This refers to the ads you see throughout the paper.

Most retail ads are display ads.

Plates

Ads and news copy are typeset and then a negative is shot which is then burned onto an aluminum or plastic "plate" which is then ready to be placed on the press.

Camera-Ready

This refers to an ad that comes into the paper already typeset and ready to shoot for a plate.

Classified advertising

Ads that are placed by category and are generally line ads without headlines or graphics.

Classified ads may be placed by individuals or businesses.

Classified display

Some ads in the classified section look like display ads because they have headlines and photos or drawings. These ads, often placed by car dealers, are "classified display."

Subsidiary publications

These may be magazines or other newspapers published by the main paper, but focusing on either a special topic (jobs, real estate, auto, entertainment, senior citizens, brides) or a special geographic area.

Subsidiary publications may be distributed though the main paper (inserted), but they are likely to be distributed separately either by home delivery or on racks.

The publications may or may not be free.

Special sections

These special topic sections are delivered with the paper. Most newspapers have many special sections a year.

Topics may include local parks, gardening, high school football, a special festival or any other topic that lends itself to occasional heavy coverage and provides an opportunity for special editorial and advertising information.

Advertisers in businesses that relate to that topic area are assured that readers are likely to be potential customers.

Pick-up rate

This is an add-on rate given to those regular advertisers who "pick up" or add another product such as a zoned or subsidiary paper. The cost for the ad in the second product is much less than it would be if bought alone.

Short rate

For bulk or volume advertisers who do not meet the terms of the contract, the bill is adjusted to the level actually placed.

For frequency advertisers, there may be a penalty or the contract may be back-billed at the open or other adjusted rate. If an advertiser comes up short on the contract commitment and is billed, he is said to have been back-billed.

Gross billings

When agency commissions must come out of the total price, the costs quoted are gross prices and are adjusted for the amount paid (usually 15%) to the agency.

Net billings

This is a non-commissionable rate. No money is rebated to an agency on this kind of charge.

Cost-per-thousand

The cost to reach one thousand readers, listeners or viewers.

To find the cost per thousand (CPM), divide the cost of the ad by the number of readers, listeners or viewers and multiply by 1000. Or, divide the cost by the number in thousands.

Example: Cost of ad is $48,000 and circulation is 280,000. Divide 48,000 by 280 for the CPM. [$171.42]

Audit Bureau of Circulation (ABC)

This is a service that measures newspaper circulation for audit purposes. Most newspapers are members.

Measurements are certified by the ABC in March and September of each year. At-home delivery, single copy and mail subscriptions are verified. Advertisers rely on these figures to know how many households their ads are reaching.

Co-op Advertising

Manufacturers may agree to share the cost of an ad with a retailer who features their products.

This sharing is called co-op advertising.

The practical result of this is that the retailer's ad dollar is stretched and that the manufacturer gets an ad featuring his own product exclusively.

There may be special rates for co-op, and there are always conditions to be met in the ad copy and placement.

The usual conditions are:

1. The product or service must be featured in the ad and must be the only one of its kind featured

2. No competitive advertising must appear on the same page or on a facing page

3. A copy of the page where the ad appeared must be sent to the manufacturer with a copy of the paid bill.

After the specified conditions are met, the manufacturer will send the promised percentage to the advertiser.

Make-goods

This term refers to a reprinting and rerunning of an ad that has had an error in copy or is wrong in some other way. Rather than refund the price of the ad, the medium will run another ad free to make up for the error. If the timing of the ad was critical, some other concession may be negotiated.

Screen or Line-Screen

This refers to the "dots" that make up a reproduced photo in an ad. The finer the dot "screen," the smaller the dot. Different papers, presses and printing processes handle different line screens. **This is a key piece of information in the preparation of an ad that has a photo in it and may vary from publication to publication.**

BROADCAST TERMS

Daypart

Broadcast is divided into dayparts based upon the amount of use. Rates are set proportionately to audience levels.

For example, radio has its highest rates during the day, while television's highest rates are at night.

Spot

There are actally two usages of this word.

1. It may mean a broadcast commercial. Either a radio or television ad may be referred to as a "spot."

2. It is also a type of media buy or schedule for individual 15 to 60-second ads placed throughout the contract term.

When both national network and local markets are purchased, the local buy is often referred to as a "spot buy."

Traffic

1. As a verb, it refers to the process of moving the ad throughout the agency or station as it goes from the buy through production and finally to billing.

2. As a noun, it refers to the department, the process, or the people who are in charge of this process.

Avails

Times available (hence, avails) for radio or television ads. Once the avails are booked for the day, there are no more. Sometimes, advertisers are bumped from a pre-set time. If the advertiser is willing to be bumped or willing to take any time within the daypart that is available once the set time requests are filled, the ad rate will be reduced.

Run of Station (ROS)

Placement of ads whenever the station (radio or television) has time. An advertiser will get a reduced spot rate if he is willing to place his ads run-of-station.

Public Service Announcements (PSAs)

These ads for non-profit organizaitons are run free of charge by broadcast stations. The ads run whenever the station has available time. Broadcast stations usually allot a certain amount of time for PSAs.

Grid pricing system

Broadcast rates may be set on a grid pricing system that is designed to allow for discounts at light times of the year, less desirable times of the day, or early decision buying.

Thus, if an advertiser is willing to commit to a number of spots well in advance, he may receive a good discount for this decision. Prices go up as avails become scarce.

Optimum Effective Scheduling (OES)

This system is computer-generated and figures the best possible set of schedules for an advertiser based upon his individual needs and budget.

OES allows the sales rep to customize a rate package for each advertiser rather than use the standardized grid system.

Yield management

A broadcast pricing technique that matches and adjusts price levels to demand. It involves having accurate demand projections to forecast optimum rates for the maximum yield possible for that date and time.

The concept is similar to the techniques used by the airline and hotel industries which enable them to know how many discounted tickets or rooms should be available for times when demand will be lower. Prices for high demand times are priced accordingly.

Arbitron

A service that measures radio listenership and television viewing in all markets. Arbitron comes out twice a year.

Advertisers may rely upon Arbitron for rating stations within a market, primarily looking at: demographic mix, size of audience, and the audience match with advertiser needs.

Some stations use other rating services, such as Nielsen (TV) or Accu-Ratings (radio) to provide additional data for use in advertising presentations.

Area of Dominant Influence (ADI)

Geographical designation by Arbitron for broadcast.

Television stations are assigned to only one ADI, which is their primary area.

RADIO TERMS

Drive time

Time of day when commuters are in their cars driving to and from work. This is the time of heaviest radio use and the most expensive time or daypart for radio advertising.

Tag or "Live Tag"

1. Often, the last ten seconds or so of a radio spot are left blank for a Tag. This Tag is usually some sort of promotional information, ranging from location to special sale events.

2. The line identifying the advertiser on the commercial. Also referred to as "tag line," it is present in almost every ad.

Donut

Refers to the space left in the middle of a commercial – usually some sort of jingle – for announcer copy.

May be used in radio or television. Often, the "donut" is localized copy done by the station. A donut may also have a tag.

ID

Can refer to either:
1. Station identification
2. Short 5 or 10 second spot

Remote

A broadcast done from an area outside the station itself.

It is often a program broadcast from an advertiser's site as part of a promotion.

Live read

The on-air announcer reads the script on the air.

Stock, "Needle Drop," or Library Music

This is music purchased by the station for use in commercials and other promotions. Usage payments may be included in the purchase price, as part of an annual license fee, or each time it is used.

Though most of this music is now on CD, the original "needle-drop" term originated from the practice of a payment being due each time the needle was "dropped" on the record.

OUTDOOR TERMS

Out-of-Home

The general term for the category, it refers to all forms of outdoor advertising. Kiosks, clocks, bus shelters, airport terminals, taxi tops and painted walls are other common types of out-of-home advertising.

Showing

Measurement that indicates level of exposure to an outdoor board in one day. A showing of 100 means that the number of people exposed to the advertisement in one day was equal to the number of people in the market.

This measurement makes no distinction between reach and frequency.

Allotment

A group or showing of panels offered by a plant operator.

The number will vary by market size. Generally, larger markets offer more panels to deliver a certain showing.

Billboard

A very large sign with an advertising message or other information, generally placed on busy roads or highways where a large number of people will be exposed to the message. There are two standard types of billboards – posters and bulletins.

Bulletin

Most measure 14 feet high x 48 feet wide. Almost all are illuminated. Most painted bulletins are rotary panels, or "flex" vinyl which can be moved to different locations.

Poster

Standard 30-sheet posters measure approximately 12 feet high x 24 feet wide.

The pieces or "sheets" are pre-pasted and applied in sections to the poster panel's face at the location.

Bus Card, Car Card, Transit

A sign that is placed in or on the outside of buses.

These are also placed at subway stations where they are visible to those in the vehicle and in the station.

8 Sheet

Small billboard or poster. Sometimes known as "junior panels." An even smaller poster is a "Two Sheet."

Extension

Refers to any part of a billboard or poster sign that goes beyond the basic rectangular shape.

Rotation

The process of "rotating" the billboards through different locations.

Facing

The direction of a billboard face relative to the traffic flow. A south facing can be read by north-bound traffic.

DIRECT MAIL TERMS

Direct mail advertising

This refers to advertising, such as mailers and catalogues, delivered by mail. It has been a fast growing segment of the market. With changing lifestyles, it is far easier for many people to shop by mail or telephone – particularly with certain specialized categories of merchandise, or individuals far removed from most stores.

A major value to the advertiser is the ability to target likely prospects with customized messages and to measure response to individual ads. Direct mail generally refers to ads or catalogues sent via mail to a specific target group.

Direct response advertising

This may refer to any ads designed to get a response – with coupons or telephone numbers placed in magazines, newspapers, on late-night television, or in some other way.

Lists

These are the names and addresses of either prospective customers or active or inactive past customers.

Lists may be generated through actual company business, or may be purchased from another business, or from a "list house" which is in the business of generating lists of names for specific client needs.

Database marketing

Use of a database which gives customer names, addresses, past buying behavior, income, and a number of other parameters to enable a retailer or manufacturer to select those customers to target for a promotion or other sale.

Merging and purging

Refers to major list management activity. Merging means pulling together several lists for one database. Purging refers to removing duplicates or names that are not suitable.

Return policy

This is an important aspect of direct mail or direct response marketing and advertising. Since customers cannot see the actual goods being purchased, a reliable return policy adds consumer confidence.

800 Service

Another important aspect of direct mail and direct response business is a toll-free number for order placement.

This is an incoming number which begins with the prefix 1-800. It allows the customer to call free of charge.

Service, Shipping, and Handling

Some companies include shipping and handling in the order price. Others charge extra.

Today, more and more companies are providing second-day air or some other kind of quick service to customers as a part of their service.

SIX. Terms You'll Use...

YELLOW PAGES TERMS

Heading

The category description within the Yellow Pages.

Listing

The basic type of Yellow Pages advertising – name, address and telephone number.

In-Column Informational Ads

These appear alphabetically among listings and are set apart in a box surrounding listing information plus a copy line. They range between one-half and three inches. A second color is usually allowed. Artwork is usually not allowed.

Trade Items

These are items listed alphabetically under the name of the trade or brand name.

Trade Name Ads

Ads that consist only of the name of the trade or brand name. Separate listings are indented underneath for each business purchasing a listing.

Trademark Ads

These display trademark or brand name with limited information pertaining to that brand. Captions appear beneath the ad with individual business listings.

Display Ads

These appear separately from alphabetical listings and in-column informational ads. They are placed with the appropriate heading.

Co-op Advertising

Programs where manufacturers subsidize dealer Yellow Pages advertising that meets certain requirements.

Consumer Directory

Yellow Pages with listings specifically for consumers.

Business Directory

Yellow Pages with listings specifically for business users.

Keying

The use of some sort of identifier within an advertisement or coupon that permits responses to be tracked to a specific ad or medium.

7.
RATES
AND
CONTRACTS.

*"Business without profit is not business
any more than a pickle is a candy."*

Charles F. Abbott

A s a Sales Rep, you must become completely
familiar with your rate card and contract terms.
You must also know what sorts of discounts you are
authorized to offer on the spot and where those limits are.
Let's cover the basics of rate cards and contracts media by media – starting with newspapers, through radio,
TV, and all the way to Yellow Pages.

NEWSPAPERS

Newspaper rate cards give the cost (per inch) for contracts of differing sizes and lengths.

Stated Discounts and Policies

Discounts for frequency or volume buys are stated, as are costs and discounts for supplementary publications, such as the TV Book, for photos, for color, for multiple page buys, for repeat advertising, for special services, artwork and production.

Rate cards also state policies for deadlines, closing schedules and mechanical requirements.

Minimums

Rate sheets may also give minimum depth sizes for different column-width ads.

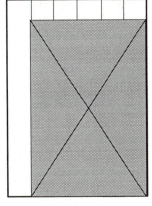

For example, many papers discourage advertisers from trying to dominate the page while saving a few dollars by buying an ad only 5 columns by 19 inches in depth on a six column page of $21^1/_2$ or $22^1/_2$ inches by charging for the full page.

The remaining space on that kind of buy would be virtually impossible for the paper to use – like the example on the right.

Column Inches and SAUs

Newspaper rates are sold by the column inch or by the Standard Advertising Unit (SAU). SAUs are priced as a whole and advertisers need only stipulate the size by the SAU number.

Many national and regional ads are sold in this format because it enables agencies to make up and send the same size ad to all newspapers.

Broadsheet papers are 6 columns wide for advertising copy layout and billing purposes. Standard newspaper pages are $21^1/_2$ inches in depth and $13\ ^1/_2$ inches wide.

Allowing for the side, top and bottom margins, a standard page offers 126 inches of advertising space.

Some papers figure their pages at 22 inches deep, giving a total of 129 inches of space to sell.

Classified Advertising

Classified pages are often sold in a 9-column format, producing more classified inches per page.

Classified rates are set by the line and number of times placed. Rates for the general public may be less than those for regular classified users, such as those who run employment, real estate, or automotive ads.

Classified display space is sold on a similar basis to other display sales.

Local Advertising

Local ads are likely to be sold by the column inch, which is measured as one inch in depth by one column wide.

Calculating ad sizes

Standard columns are $2\,^1/_{16}$ inches in width, although there are papers with columns of slightly less or more width.

No matter what the width of the column, a column inch is still 1 inch deep by 1 column wide.

To calculate the number of column inches in a newspaper advertisement, multiply the number of inches deep by the number of columns.

Example: a 3-column by 8-inch ad would be a 24-inch ad. If the charge per column inch was $36, the cost of that ad would be 24 x $36 or $864.

The basic newspaper space contract is for one year and may be based upon frequency (number of inches placed on a weekly basis) or volume (amount of space placed overall within the contract time). Volume may also be referred to as bulk.

Weekdays, Sundays, and Holidays

Ads placed on Sundays generally cost more than those on weekdays due to the higher level of circulation on Sundays for most papers.

Some readers buy weekend-only subscriptions.

Because Thanksgiving is such a heavy advertising day, some papers charge Sunday ad rates, but also deliver the paper to all subscribers (all-week and weekend) that day. This concept is called the "53rd Sunday."

Many papers charge separately for weekdays (Monday-Friday), Saturdays, and Sundays.

These rates are based upon the differing levels of circulation on these days.

Frequency Contracts

Because frequency contracts imply that a certain level of advertising will be placed per week, there is a premium charge per inch for contracts that run fewer times.

For example, using our basic charge per inch of $36, we may find that there is an additional 60¢ charge per inch for contracts that run 26 weeks. The 24-inch ad would then be $878.40 instead of $864. Usual time periods are 13, 26 or 39 weeks.

TMC

Many papers offer a total market coverage, or TMC, product to reach the audience living within the circulation area that does not subscribe to the paper.

Rate cards may reflect a price per inch for the regular paper and for the additional printing and distribution of the same ad in the extra total market coverage product.

This is usually a small newspaper with some key features and local news reprinted from the regular paper. If the TMC product is in tabloid format, ads are reduced proportionally.

Repeat Rates

There may also be a reduced charge available for placing a second ad within the same week. (Weeks run Sunday through Saturday.) For the second ad, the paper will save the original material and "strip" (place) the ad into the later paper.

Dates and prices may be changed by the advertiser, although the "repeat" rate may only be valid if 10 percent or less of the ad is changed.

This policy encourages advertisers to place more ads per week. Running the same ad again does not require nearly as much work as a new ad, so everyone benefits.

Same Size, Different Rates

Some rate cards, then, may provide several different options and levels of inch pricing for contracts of the same level – depending upon the other options chosen.

Thus, some rate cards would give a basic inch rate ($36), an inch rate with TMC included ($42), a repeat rate for another weekday without a TMC option ($25) and a repeat rate that includes TMC ($28).

FREQUENCY EXAMPLE

Black and white rates based on an annual contract:

Per Week	Weekday	Saturday	Sunday
2 inches	28.00	28.54	32.30
4	27.60	28.30	32.10
6	27.40	28.00	31.80
15	26.90	27.60	31.30
63 inches	25.10	26.40	30.25

The contract continues to levels up to four pages or 500 inches at continually decreasing rates.

Bulk or Volume Rates

Some advertisers do not want to run every week.

This may be due to seasonal demand or the need to concentrate advertising dollars in several short periods of time – similar to "flighting" on television.

For these advertisers, the bulk or volume rate is most appropriate. Under this kind of contract, a discount is given based upon the total amount of advertising guaranteed under the terms of the contract. The larger the space commitment, the more favorable the inch cost.

Additional Discounts

Most advertisers fall well within average rate card ranges, but for the very largest advertisers, such as department and grocery stores, special discounts may be constructed.

A special contract and discount structure is developed for this kind of advertiser; these large advertisers account for nearly three-fourths of all ad revenue for large newspapers.

Short Rates/Back-Billing

If advertisers sign a contract for a certain amount of inches (space) for a given time period and then fail to place enough advertising, the paper applies a short rate or back-billing policy.

This charges the rate per inch according to the level of advertising that was actually placed.

If the advertiser is very close, but not quite at the level of advertising in the contract, it could actually end up costing him more money for the inches he used than it would have for the full contract.

For example, if a contract was for 8000 inches a year at $43 per inch, but only 7960 inches were placed, a bill for the cost of the next lowest bulk contract level of 6,000 would be sent. The advertiser would then have to pay an additional 75¢ per inch, or $5970, for failing to fulfill his contract.

As we'll learn in the service section of this book, a good sales rep keeps a running total of the percentage of the ad commitment that has been met and should warn any advertiser who is in danger of falling short so that he can plan additional advertising to make up the difference.

In the example above, it would have only cost the advertiser $1720 to place the extra 40 inches – and he would have had the benefit of the extra advertising as well.

Standard Rate Sheets

Most newspapers print standard rate sheets, which means that the same information is available in the same place on the rate sheet for all papers. For example, Section 5 on all standard rate sheets shows Black and White rates; Section 15 gives mechanical requirements.

All standard rate sheets are also in 8 $\frac{1}{2}$ by 11 inch format, making it easy to insert the sheets into a notebook or folder. Standard formats were developed after advertisers requested them.

Regional and national advertisers may deal with many different papers. For example, one grocery store chain may be placing several pages a week with as many as 60-80 papers. For this kind of advertiser, easy comparisons and standard ad sizes are essential.

"One-Stop" Buys

Regional and national advertisers can now make one-stop shopping buys through national rep firms and many State Press Associations.

These organizations place multiple buys for advertisers, negotiating the rate and sending only one bill for the entire buy. The organizations check to be certain the ads have run as specified.

On the next few pages is a typical example of a Standard Rate Sheet and a Retail Advertising Agreement for a newspaper (Courtesy the Charlotte Observer).

Review these materials, and then we'll try our hand at calculating rates.

The Knight Publishing Company
RETAIL ADVERTISING AGREEMENT

☐ Full Run
☐ Regional

Charlotte, N.C. 19_____

This agreement authorizes Knight Publishing Company to publish retail display advertising for the undersigned as indicated:

( ) A. A minimum of _____to be published within_____
    in The Charlotte Observer from the effective date below

( ) B. Advertisements in the Sunday Charlotte Observer TV Week for a minimum of _____ weeks within a 12-month period from the effective
    date below.

During the remainder of this contract, The Knight Publishing Company shall be referred to as "KPC."

Advertiser agrees that this agreement is based upon the condition that Advertiser use the minimum space agreed upon during the contract term; and that, if the contract amount is not used as agreed, the charge for space shall be determined by KPC's regular schedule of rates.

Advertiser agrees to furnish copy and pay for its publication at the rate for the agreed minimum usage stated in the schedule of rates in effect on the day of publication. Each rate schedule now in effect or subsequently established is or will be printed and entitled "Retail Advertising Rates." The current rate schedule dated _____ is attached and made a part of this agreement, and each revised rate schedule will be substituted for the existing rate schedule and become part of this agreement.

Advertiser agrees that KPC may change terms, conditions, or rates in this agreement 30 days after mailing to Advertiser a copy of a revised rate schedule or other change. KPC agrees that, in the event of a change, Advertiser may terminate this agreement on the date the change becomes effective by giving written notice to KPC prior to the effective date of said change; and that termination by Advertiser under the conditions stated in this paragraph shall be without penalty to Advertiser provided Advertiser performs all obligations to the effective date of termination.

Advertiser agrees that bills for the previous month's advertising are due and payable on or before the 20th of each month unless KPC chooses to render bills weekly and require payment within seven days, or require that advertising be paid in advance. Advertiser agrees that, if an invoice is not paid when due, KPC may refuse to insert further advertising and this agreement may be canceled without further notice; and that if a contract is canceled, charges for advertising published prior to cancellation shall immediately become due and payable at the rate earned according to KPC's regular schedule of rates for retail display advertising. Advertiser further agrees to pay a reasonable attorney's fee of 15% as by law allowed on the balance due if it becomes necessary to place for collection any bill incurred under this contract.

Advertiser agrees that this agreement shall continue for _____ from_____19____ and shall automatically renew for successive like periods and conditions unless either party notifies the other in writing at least 30 days before the expiration date of its desire to terminate, in which event this agreement shall terminate at the end of the then current term.

Advertiser agrees that KPC may revise or reject advertising deemed objectionable because of subject matter, illustration, or phraseology. Advertiser agrees that tax levied against advertising will be added to the advertising charge.

Advertiser and KPC agree that this agreement shall cover ONLY THE ADVERTISING OF THE FIRM SIGNING THE AGREEMENT.

Advertiser agrees that, in the event of an error by KPC in an advertisement, KPC will furnish Advertiser a letter explaining the error and shall be otherwise relieved from responsibility.

Advertiser agrees that, to assure publication, KPC's schedule of copy and proof deadlines must be observed. Advertiser agrees that proofs, when submitted, will be for typographical corrections only; that changes of original copy will be charged for based on the time occupied in making such changes; and that a composition charge will be made for canceled copy already composed.

Advertiser agrees that, if publication is interrupted for any reason, or if advertising ordered to be published is omitted for any reason, KPC shall not be held liable for failure to publish advertising under this contract.

Advertiser agrees that advertisements and charges shall not be invalidated by insertions in other than requested position.

For value received, Advertiser assigns to KPC all rights, title and interest to all layouts of advertisements which represent the creative efforts of KPC and/or utilization of KPC's own illustrations, labor, composition, or material. Advertiser agrees that, without KPC's written consent, Advertiser is prohibited from authorizing for use in other publications photographic or other reproductions of any advertising layout appearing in KPC's publications. KPC agrees that Advertiser is not, however, precluded from supplying to other publications similar or identical material or information for production of advertisements by such publications or from suggesting the content or form of such advertisements.

Advertiser and KPC agree that if war, fire, civil commotions, labor strikes, freight embargoes, shortage of material, floods or other acts of God, action of a governmental authority, or other causes beyond its control cause either KPC or Advertiser to be unable to perform its agreements under this contract, then the party unable to perform its agreement shall be excused from such performance during the continuation of such inability except to the extent that mutually acceptable performance is possible and agreed upon.

NO VERBAL AGREEMENTS RECOGNIZED

Approved: The Knight Publishing Company
    RETAIL DISPLAY ADVERTISING

Customer Phone_____

By _____ (Advertising Manager)   By _____

Salesperson _____   Address _____

Advertiser _____   _____ Zip Code _____

1995 RETAIL RATES

Rate Book No. 9
Effective January 1, 1995

The Charlotte Observer

600 S. Tryon St., P.O. Box 32188, Charlotte, N.C. 28232

3　TERMS AND CONDITIONS

Knight Publishing Company mails bills the last day of the month; Advertiser agrees to pay within 20 days.

Advertiser agrees to claim allowance for errors within 15 days after publication.

An advertiser rescinding an order to publish an ad agrees to pay at cost for type set and engravings made if the advertising is not published within 30 days.

4　GENERAL RATE POLICY

1) Advertiser agrees that KPC has the right to revise or reject advertising.

2) Advertiser agrees that KPC may at its discretion place ads resembling news stories within hairline rules and include the word "Advertisement" or the abbreviation "ADVT" at the top or bottom.

3) Advertiser and KPC agree that if war, fire, civil commotions, labor strikes, freight embargoes, shortage of material, floods or other acts of nature, action of a governmental authority, or other causes beyond its control cause either KPC or Advertiser to be unable to perform its agreement, then the party unable to perform shall be excused from such performance during the continuation of such inability except when mutually acceptable performance is possible and agreed upon.

4) Advertiser recognizes KPC's rights, title and interest to all layouts of advertisements which represent the creative efforts of KPC and/or utilization of KPC's own illustrations, labor, composition, or material. Advertiser agrees that, without KPC's written consent, Advertiser is prohibited from authorizing for use in other publications photographic or other reproductions of any advertising layout that is the result of KPC's creative efforts.

5) The Charlotte Observer accepts no multiple advertiser sections, pages, or features containing local advertising except those sold by The Observer.

6) Automotive & Real Estate advertising are handled through Classified Advertising. For more information see the Classified Rate Book.

5　BLACK AND WHITE RATES

STATED SPACE CONTRACTS

Stated space affords the advertiser — small or large — the opportunity to run a consistent campaign less expensively then with bulk rates. The space can run any day of the week.

Per-Inch Rate For 48 of 52 Weeks

	Sun	Sat	Sat Repeat	Weekday	Weekday Repeat
1 inch	$63.71	$53.19	$42.55	$51.77	$41.42
2 inches	62.57	52.03	41.62	50.65	40.52
4 inches	61.23	51.32	41.06	49.96	39.97
8 inches	60.32	50.64	40.51	49.29	39.43
17 inches	59.87	48.80	39.04	47.50	38.00
32 inches	58.30	47.64	38.11	46.38	37.10
1 page	57.17	46.48	37.18	45.24	36.19
1 1/2 pages	56.25	45.78	36.62	44.56	35.65
2 pages	56.04	45.34	36.27	44.13	35.30
3 pages	54.24	43.69	34.95	42.53	34.02
4 pages	52.90	41.85	33.48	40.74	32.59

(Minimums are per calendar week Sunday through Saturday)

Observer contracts also may be signed for these time periods:

- 36 of 39 weeks ....48 of 52 rate plus 15¢/inch
- 24 of 26 weeks ....48 of 52 rate plus 30¢/inch
- 12 of 13 weeks ....48 of 52 rate plus 60¢/inch

ANNUAL BULK CONTRACTS

Linage on bulk space contracts may run all at once or over a 12 month period. Advertising in excess of the contract earns rebates and lower rates.

Per Inch Rates

	Sun	Sat	Sat Repeat	Weekday	Weekday Repeat
Open	$75.67	$65.02	$52.02	$63.29	$50.63
50 in.	65.74	55.74	44.59	54.25	43.40
100 in.	63.26	53.19	42.55	51.77	41.42
200 in.	62.36	51.55	41.24	50.18	40.14
400 in.	61.23	51.32	41.06	49.96	39.97
800 in.	60.32	50.64	40.51	49.29	39.43
1,400 in.	60.10	50.16	40.13	48.82	39.06
2,000 in.	59.87	48.80	39.04	47.50	38.00
4,000 in.	58.30	47.64	38.11	46.38	37.10
6,000 in.	57.85	47.42	37.94	46.15	36.92
8,000 in.	57.17	46.48	37.18	45.24	36.19
12,000 in.	56.04	45.34	36.27	44.13	35.30
20,000 in.	54.70	44.65	35.72	43.46	34.77
30,000 in.	54.24	43.69	34.95	42.53	34.02
40,000 in.	52.90	41.85	33.48	40.74	32.59

Repeats. Advertisers may qualify for repeat rate on any ad that publishes more than once in a seven-day period. Multiple insertions may earn additional discounts — check with your Observer sales representative. Changes are restricted to timing, coupon identification, and/or out-of-stock merchandise; and are limited to no more than 20% of total ad space. *Theatres, concerts, sporting events, amusement parks, plays, shows, and other profit-making events charging admission qualify for one repeat rate per week based on a combination of one Sunday and one weekday insertion.

The Thanksgiving Day newspaper is delivered to the weekend circulation base and advertising that day is charged at the applicable Sunday rate.

MULTIPLE PAGE DISCOUNTS
Within The Same Issue For A Single Advertiser

4 standard pages/8 tab	10% discount per page
6 standard pages/12 tab	20% discount per page
8 standard pages/16 tab	30% discount per page
10 standard pages/20 tab	35% discount per page

Discounts are given off applicable contract rate. Linage counts toward contract fulfillment.

ZONED ADVERTISING

City Zone Advertising — Limited ROP space is available every day for advertisers wishing to reach only local subscribers. Since space is limited, reservations are first-come, first-served. Color cannot be scheduled for city zone advertising. Ads of one or two columns are acceptable in any depth up to 19 inches; such ads exceeding 19 inches must run full depth (22 1/2 inches). Ads of three, four, or six columns are acceptable in any depth up to 11 inches; such ads exceeding 11 inches must run full depth (22 1/2 inches). No five-column ads are accepted. City Zone linage does not accrue toward stated space and annual bulk contracts. For more information, contact your Observer representative.

	Per Inch
Weekday	$30.20
Saturday	31.03
Sunday	36.35

Mecklenburg Neighbors — This news section published Wednesday and Sunday features four separate editions delivered in south, east, north/northwest and central Charlotte. For additional information, call Arden Valalik, 704/358-5301.

Regional Publications — Available in neighboring counties. For additional information, see your Observer representative or call Greg Ward, 704/358-5284.

MISCELLANEOUS RATES

Sunday Plus (TMC)	$ 6.17/inch
Break (pick-up rate)	8.01/inch
Standby	50% off applicable contract rates

Civic Rates for charitable, civic or fraternal organizations.

	Weekday	Saturday	Sunday
Per inch	$44.13	$45.34	$56.04

CO-OP ANNUAL BULK CONTRACTS

Linage on bulk space contracts may run at one time or over 12 months, permitting seasonal and promotional advertisers the advantage of contract rates. Advertising in excess of the contract earns rebates and lower rates. For information on free services available to you, contact Shirley Brown, 704/358-5424.

	Sun	Sat	Sat Repeat	Weekday	Weekday Repeat
Open rate	$69.38	$59.08	$47.26	$57.51	$46.00
100 through 799 inches	66.85	56.91	45.53	55.40	44.32
800 inches or more	65.71	55.74	44.59	54.25	43.40

Repeats. Same guidelines apply as those listed under Annual Bulk Contract Repeats.

TV WEEK RATES

		Unit Costs				
Size	Open Rate	6 Times	13 Times	26 Times	39 Times	52 Times
Full page	$2,780	$2,578	$2,493	$2,388	$2,251	$2,116
1/2 page	1,467	1,365	1,320	1,259	1,190	1,114
1/4 page	811	759	727	697	697	613
1/8 page	463	432	417	402	371	356
1/16 page	270	250	243	219	205	190
1/32 page	139	129	121	113	106	99

Advertisers with both ROP and TV Week contracts earn a 10% discount off applicable TV Week rates if both contracts are fulfilled.

Full-page advertisers earn an additional 10% discount.

TV Week Color Premiums

Black plus one color	$ 631
Black plus two colors	808
Black plus three colors	1,049

1 9 9 5   R E T A I L   R A T E S

TV Week Printing Variations

	Columns-by-inches
Full page	4 Col. (8 5/8") x 11"
1/2 page	2 Col. (4 1/4") x 11"
	4 Col. (8 5/8") x 5 1/2"
1/4 page	2 Col. (4 1/4") x 5 1/2"
	4 Col. (8 5/8") x 2 3/4"
1/8 page	2 Col. (4 1/4") x 2 3/4"
1/16 page	1 Col. (2 1/16") x 2 3/4"
1/32 page	1 Col. (2 1/16") x 1 3/8"
Full Double Truck (No Bleeds)	8.5 Col. (17 3/4") x 11"

Camera-Ready Color Ads. For ads smaller than full page, advertisers and agencies should submit veloxes in widths and depths stated above. However, for full-page and double-truck color ads, veloxes should be submitted in these sizes:

Full Page	8" wide by 10 3/16" deep
Double-Truck	16 1/2" wide by 10 3/16" deep

PREPRINT RATES
Cost Per Thousand

Number Of Pages	Open*	6 Per Year*	13 Per Year*	26 Per Year	52 Per Year	79 Per Year	96 Per Year	110 Or More
4 std/8 tab	56.18	54.08	49.88	39.38	38.33	37.28	34.65	33.60
6 std/12 tab	56.18	54.08	49.88	42.53	41.48	40.43	36.75	35.70
8 std/16 tab	56.18	54.08	49.88	44.63	43.58	42.53	38.85	37.80
10 std/20 tab	56.18	54.08	49.88	46.73	45.68	44.63	40.95	39.90
12 std/24 tab	56.18	54.08	49.88	47.78	46.73	43.05	42.00
14 std/28 tab	58.28	56.18	51.98	50.93	49.88	48.83	43.05	42.00
16 std/32 tab	58.28	56.18	51.98	50.93	49.88	48.83	43.05	42.00
18 std/36 tab	58.28	56.18	51.98	50.93	49.88	48.83	43.05	42.00
20 std/40 tab	60.38	58.28	54.08	53.03	49.88	48.83	43.05	42.00
22 std/44 tab	60.38	58.28	54.08	53.03	49.88	48.83	43.05	42.00
24 std/48 tab	60.38	58.28	54.08	53.03	49.88	48.83	43.05	42.00

*Full-run preprints earn $2/thousand discount.

SINGLE SHEET RATES
Must be inserted in full-run circulation or must include TMC zip codes to qualify for the following rates:
Cost Per Thousand

Number Of Pages	Open Times	6 Times	13 Times	26 Times	52 Times	79 Times	96 Times	110 Times
8.5" x 11"	$20.00	$19.00	$18.00	$17.00	$16.00	$15.00	$14.00	$13.00
11" x17"	36.00	35.00	34.00	33.00	32.00	31.00	30.00	29.00

Mini Tab Rates. Mini tabs (flexies) of 40 or more pages will be billed at the equivalent tab-page rate.

1) Part-run preprints may be purchased Mecklenburg County only or by zip codes within Mecklenburg County.
2) Target Area Preprints (TAP) partial distribution can be purchased outside Mecklenburg County by using truck routes or zip codes in The Observer weekday and Sunday. Distribution breakdown is available upon request from your advertising sales representative.
3) To calculate price, multiply appropriate CPM by Knight Publishing Company circulation requirements for distribution requested. Your advertising sales representative has up-to-date paid circulation and preprint quantity requirements.
4) Select or total market coverage is available by using direct mail or Knight Publishing Company Distribution in conjunction with newspaper insertion or by themselves. Direct mail or KPCD rates are available upon request from your advertising sales representative.
5) Deadline for receiving preprints is 12 days prior to distribution date. Delivery address: Knight Publishing Company, 621 S. Poplar St., Charlotte, N.C. 28202.
6) Opportunities for preprint distribution on days other than Wednesday and Sunday are limited and are subject to a handling surcharge. Please check with your sales representative for specific information and dates. Minimum distribution is Mecklenburg County. Preprints are manually inserted or "topped" by individual carriers.

PREPRINT LINAGE ACCRUES TOWARD CONTRACT FULFILLMENT
Linage from preprinted inserts in The Charlotte Observer will accrue toward ROP contract fulfillment. Accrued linage is calculated by taking the amount of revenue charged for preprint distribution and dividing by the appropriate daily or Sunday contract inch rate. This linage is not rebateable, but does accrue toward reaching higher contract levels. (Only ROP inches will be rebated.)

7   COLOR RATES & ROP COLOR PREMIUMS
Single Unit
Every effort will be made to meet advertiser's request for color. Under unique circumstances, it may become necessary to change the requested color or, because of mechanical limitations, cancel requested color. In these instances KPC will consult with the advertiser to explore alternatives. All requests for color are accepted under these conditions.

	Sun	Sat	Sat Repeat	Weekday	Weekday Repeat
1 COLOR					
1 time	$899	$872	$698	$849	$679
2 COLORS					
1 time	1,320	1,290	1,032	1,256	1,005
3 COLORS					
1 time	1,862	1,851	1,481	1,802	1,442
Double Truck					
1 COLOR					
1 time	$1,352	$1,283	$1,026	$1,249	$999
2 COLORS					
1 time	2,003	1,926	1,541	1,875	1,500
3 COLORS					
1 time	2,780	2,775	2,220	2,701	2,161

1) Only color ads run during each calendar month qualify for color performance discount.
2) In order to qualify, ads need not be same size or content.

MINI COLOR may be available on a space-permitted basis when other color is published on the same day. No plate charges or advance deadlines are required. Maximum size accepted is 12 inches, and ads must run 100% color using available color on the press. Color frequency discounts do not apply. Mini color rates:

Weekday Observer	$217
Saturday Observer	223
Sunday Observer	224

10   SPECIAL SERVICES
CAMERA/PLATEMAKING

Square halftone, line, ad reprint			
Through 8x10	$5.20	Larger than 8x10	$12.20
Outline halftone, reverse			
Through 8x10	6.95	Larger than 8x10	23.45
Benday, surprint			
Through 8x10	11.15	Larger than 8x10	37.40
Fluoro, combination, reverse benday, specialty screen			37.40
Line blow-ups			25.60
Negatives			6.00
Transparencies (includes one color key)			98.35
Color comics, flat color (includes one color key)			76.10
Transparency with flat color (includes one color key)			168.70
Extra color key			19.70
Plate charges (each plate charged separately)			
Standard or two tab			35.20
Doubletruck			70.40
Camera/platemaking charges subject to N.C. sales tax.			
Labor per hour			31.05

NOTE: ALL HALFTONES MUST BE 65-LINE SCREEN

PRODUCTION CHARGES
Composing room. The time charge is $16 per hour in units of a half hour with a one-hour minimum. This includes composition and handling costs for chargeable revisions, "held 30 days" ads, and ads set but not published.
Excessive proof revision. Incurred when an Advertiser makes excessive changes on a proof.
Art services. No charge is made for art and borders selected from art service books. Customized artwork created at the request of the Advertiser or Agency will be chargeable at the rate of $25/hour with a quarter-hour minimum. Outlines and minimal touch-ups will be chargeable at the rate of $16/hour, with a quarter hour minimum. The Charlotte Observer Creative Services Department will help you increase the effectiveness of your advertising dollars. For free speculative ad designs, please contact your sales representative.
Original logo design: $25/hour with minimum of $50.
Plate charges. Plate charges are incurred when an Advertiser makes changes after proof corrections have been released to the newspaper.

12   R.O.P. DEPTH REQUIREMENTS
Minimum Sizes

1 column	1 inch deep	4 columns	4 inches deep
2 columns	1 inch deep	5 columns	5 inches deep
3 columns	3 inches deep	6 columns	6 inches deep

Ads more than 19 inches deep must be full 22 1/2 inches deep. All ads must be at least as many inches deep as columns wide except strip ads and 2 column by 1 inch ads.

13   CONTRACT & COPY REGULATIONS

Revenue Contracts
Opportunities exist for advertisers to earn additional rate incentives by committing to minimum yearly dollar expenditures. Call Gordie Cherry, 704/358-5278, for information and qualifications.

A. Charges
1) Advertiser agrees that KPC may revise contract rates on 30 days written notice and other rates at any time.
2) Advertiser agrees to pay a rate adjustment when not fulfilling consecutive time orders and contracts are not fulfilled.
3) Advertiser agrees to pay time charges for changes that deviate from original copy.
4) Advertiser agrees to pay a composition charge when canceling copy already composed.
5) Advertiser agrees to pay taxes on advertising and services.

B. Insertions and Cancellations
1) Advertiser agrees that KPC assumes responsibility only for insertions, cancellations, or corrections received in writing prior to deadlines as printed in this rate sheet.
2) Advertiser agrees that forwarding an order construes acceptance of KPC rates and conditions; that failure to make an order correspond with this rate sheet will be regarded by KPC as a clerical error; and that KPC will without notification publish and charge for such ads according to this rate sheet.
3) Advertiser agrees that, if publication is interrupted for any reason, or if advertising ordered to be published is omitted for any reason, KPC shall not be held liable.

C. Position
1) Advertiser agrees that ads cannot be scheduled for special positions and will appear in available positions.
2) Advertiser agrees that no adjustments, reinsertions or refunds will be made because of departure from requested position.

D. Proofs
Advertiser agrees that proofs, when submitted, will be for typographical correction only, and that other changes will be charged at the rates specified in the production charges section.

E. Errors
1) Advertiser agrees that, if KPC errs in an advertisement, KPC's liability shall not exceed the charge for the portion of the ad in which the error occurred, and that KPC will furnish Advertiser a letter explaining the error and shall be otherwise relieved from responsibility.
2) Advertiser agrees that KPC is not responsible for incorrect materials supplied by another newspaper unless Advertiser requests changes in writing.
3) Advertiser and/or his Agency agree to hold KPC harmless against claims asserted because of an ad or its contents.

14   CLOSING SCHEDULES

Final Copy Deadline For Proof	Space Reservation Deadline	Final Copy Deadline No Proof	Proof Out	Corrected Proof Released By
Monday Insertion				
Wed. 4 p.m.	Thur. 1 p.m.	Thur. 4 p.m.	Fri. 8:30 a.m.	Fri. 5 p.m.
Tuesday Insertion				
Fri. 4 p.m.	Fri. 1 p.m.	Fri. 4 p.m.	Mon. 8:30 a.m.	Mon. 1 p.m.
Wednesday Insertion				
Fri. 4 p.m.	Mon. 1 p.m.	Mon. 4 p.m.	Tue. 8:30 a.m.	Tue. 1 p.m.
Thursday Insertion				
Mon. 4 p.m.	Tue. 1 p.m.	Tue. 4 p.m.	Wed. 8:30 a.m.	Wed. 1 p.m.
Friday Insertion				
Tue. 4 p.m.	Wed. 1 p.m.	Wed. 4 p.m.	Thur. 8:30 a.m.	Thur. 1 p.m.
Saturday Insertion				
Wed. 4 p.m.	Thur. 1 p.m.	Thur. 4 p.m.	Fri. 8:30 a.m.	Fri. 1 p.m.
Sunday Insertion				
Wed. 4 p.m.	Thur. 1 p.m.	Thur. 4 p.m.	Fri. 8:30 a.m.	Fri. 4 p.m.

Proofs not released by the appropriate proof release deadline will be considered correct and will be released for publication. Double trucks, color and surprints deadline 24 hours earlier than ROP on all schedules (daily, advance, special sections, etc.). Tuesday color deadline with proof is previous Wednesday at 4 p.m.

COPY SUBMISSION DEADLINES — Deadline times refer to the hour due in newspaper office.

SUBMISSION OF COPY — Includes all ad components such as printer's layout, typewritten copy, finished art and necessary photos.

ARTWORK — Orders for producing art are not considered submission of copy. Producing art requires at least 24 hours. Art must be completed and submitted by the time advertising copy is due.

COPY SUBMITTED IN ADVANCE OF DEADLINES will be processed as soon as practicable, but without committing to delivery before normal proof schedule.

CANCELLATIONS
Notification must be received prior to the appropriate no-proof deadline and/or the space reservation deadlines listed.
NO CANCELLATIONS ACCEPTED SATURDAY OR SUNDAY.

ADVANCE DEADLINES
All holidays have advance deadlines. For exact deadlines, contact your Observer representative.

Tuesday color . . . . previous Wednesday 1 p.m.

Wednesday Food Section
Space Reservations . . . . Friday 2 p.m.
Deadline for proof. . . . . Friday 4 p.m.
Deadline, no proof . . . . Monday 1 p.m.
Proof release . . . . Monday 1 p.m.

Saturday Home Section
Deadline for proof. . . . . Monday 4 p.m.
Deadline, no proof. . . . . Tuesday 4 p.m.
Proof release . . . . Wednesday 1 p.m.

Sunday Carolina Living Section
Deadline for proof/no proof . . . . Monday 4 p.m.
Proof release . . . . Tuesday 1 p.m.

Sunday Arts/Travel
Deadline for proof. . . . . Monday 4 p.m.
Deadline, no proof. . . . . Tuesday 4 p.m.
Proof release . . . . Wednesday 1 p.m.

Sunday Observer TV Week
Space reservations . . . . Tuesday 1 p.m.
. . . . (13 days before publication)
Deadline with or without proof . . . . Wednesday 4 p.m.
. . . . (12 days before publication)
Proof release . . . . Friday 1 p.m.
. . . . (10 days before publication)

15   MECHANICAL REQUIREMENTS
STANDARD PAGE
6 COLUMNS BY 22 1/2 INCHES

Widths in	1 Col	2 Col	3 Col	4 Col	5 Col	6 Col
Picas	12.5	25.7	38.9	51.11	65.1	78.3
Inches	2 1/16	4 1/4	6 7/16	8 5/8	10 13/16	13

R.O.P. DOUBLE TRUCK
Available in 13 columns by 22 1/2 inches only: 161.2 picas wide by 135.6 deep.
Inches: 26 3/4 by 22 1/2. Billed at 12 3/4 columns.

SCOTCH DOUBLE
Available in 11 columns by 22 1/2 inches only: 134.9 picas wide by 135.6 deep.
Inches: 22 3/8 by 22 1/2. Billed at 11 columns.

TABLOID PAGE
Five columns (65.1 picas) x 13 inches deep.

New Standard Advertising Units
Accepted but not mandatory.

18   COLOR COMICS
There are three marketing opportunities available to advertisers within the comic pages in the Sunday Charlotte Observer:
• Display advertising
• Spadea wraps
• Press inserts
Contact your Observer representative.

20   CIRCULATION
PUBLICATION
The Observer: Seven days a week. The Observer is a member of the Audit Bureau of Circulations. Audited circulation can be found in the ABC reports issued each six months.

11/14/95
Quantity: 3500

TIPS FOR SOLVING RATE PROBLEMS:

1. Calculate the number of inches per ad by multiplying column inches by the depth of the ad in inches.

EX: A 2-column by 8-inch ad contains 16 inches of space.

2 X 8 = 16

2. Check to see if the contract is less than annual or 52 weeks in duration. If so, find the appropriate level of extra cost per inch for that shorter time period.

EX: Ads cost $36 per inch on an annual contract for the frequency the advertiser wants. Since he only wants a 26-week contract, there will be an additional charge of 60¢ per inch.

NOTE: Add the extra .60 to the $36 before you do any other calculations. If you add the extra cost in at this point, you will avoid any problems by forgetting it when you do the final calculations.

3. See how many ads are wanted per week. Figure the number of inches per week. Then multiply that figure by the number of weeks in the contract. This gives you the number of inches for the entire contract.

EX: The 16-inch ad will be placed twice a week for 26 weeks. This gives you a total of 32 inches a week.

Multiply 32 inches x 26 weeks for the number of total inches. For this problem, the number of inches is 832.

32 X 26 = 832

4. Multiply the cost per inch by the total inches.

EX: 832 inches by $36.60 per inch.

Total cost of contract is $30,451.20.

832 X $36.60 = $30,451.20.

1. Client's contract is 17 inches a week for 24/26 weeks. Now the client wants to place a 3-column by 5-inch ad in a Wednesday paper.

What is the cost per inch? _____

What is the cost of the ad? _____

What is the cost of the contract if ads run for only 24 weeks?

_____

2. Client's contract is 40,000 inches a year to be used on Sunday. He wants to place an ad 4-columns by 12 inches.

What is cost per inch? _____

What is the cost of the ad? _____

What is the cost of a repeat ad on the following Tuesday?

_____

3. Contract is for 1 page a week for a year to be placed on Tuesdays with TMC coverage for the following Wednesday. A full page in this paper is 129 inches.

What is the cost of one full page ad? _____

What is the cost of TMC coverage the following day?

_____

4. Client wants to place two 2-column by 4 inch ads per week, both to be run in Thursday's paper for the next 12 weeks.

What size contract does this client need? _____

What is the cost of one of these ads? _____

What is the cost of the entire contract?_____

5. You have a client who wants to run a 4-column by 8-inch ad each Sunday and have that ad repeated on Thursdays. He wants to place these ads every week for the entire year.

What is the cost of one ad? _____

What is the weekly cost? _____

What is the total cost for this contract?

_____

6. This client wants to run 1400 inches a year. If the ad is 2-columns by 6-inches, what is the cost?

_____

7. We have a client who wants to sign a bulk contract. He plans to run a full-page ad three times a month, but does not want to be committed to a frequency contract.

For what size contract is the client qualified? _____

What will be the cost per inch if he advertises Sundays only?

_____

SEVEN. Rates & Contracts.

OTHER RATES AND EXAMPLES

Preprint Rates

Preprint rates are charged in a different manner. Because these ads are not printed in the regular newspaper, the space cost is not figured per inch, but by the number distributed, which is rounded out to thousands.

The advertiser decides how many preprints need to be delivered and whether they will be inserted into every single paper (full-run) or only in newspapers going to a certain area (or combination of areas) in the circulation zone.

Advertisers then pay for each thousand inserted and delivered in the papers.

For example, suppose the full-run circulation figure for a large newspaper is 300,000 and a part-run package for a city-zone insert goes to 180,000 homes.

If the cost per thousand inserted was $36, the advertiser would pay $10,800 for the full-run delivery and $5480 for the part-run delivery.

For an example, look at the section marked preprint rates in the retail rate sheet on the previous pages.

Calculating Preprint Rates

Here are two ways to calculate the cost of these preprint delivery rates:

1. Because the cost is per thousand, you have 300 thousands for the full run and 180 thousands for the part-run.

Thus the calculations are:

300 x 36 = $10,888
180 x 36 = $5,480

2. Multiply the entire circulation by the cost per thousand for inserting and delivery and divide the dollar total by 1000:

300,000 x 36 = 10800000/1000 = 10,800
180,000 x 36 = 5480000/1000 = 5480

Again, there are discounts. The more preprints you insert per year, the less the cost per thousand.

Credit for preprint placement

Advertisers who want to use preprints as part of their advertising mix may be reluctant to also sign a large contract with a newspaper for regular advertising.

To make it easier for advertisers to put together the best package of newspaper advertising for their needs, papers allow a credit against the regular bulk or volume commitment for preprint advertising.

It's actually simple: Advertisers receive credit toward their contract commitment for the amount they spend in preprint insert and delivery costs.

Everyone wins because the paper is also able to convince the advertiser to buy a larger contract than he otherwise might.

Because the advertiser feels he can assure flexibility in the type of newspaper advertising he can buy, he is more confident in signing his annual contract.

Here's how it works:

Client A has a contract for 40,000 inches a year to be placed on Sundays at a cost of $49.91 per inch.

In addition, he decides to run six 8-page tab preprints for the full circulation of 300,000 at a cost of $51.50 per thousand (cost per thousand is a discount from the open rate of $53.50).

The total cost for one of these preprint insertions is $51.50 x 300 or $15,450.

For the six inserts, then, the total cost is $92,700.

This advertiser receives credit not in absolute inches (preprint inches and R.O.P. inches are not comparable), but for the number of inches the $92,700 would have bought in the regular paper.

At $51.50 per inch, this comes to 1800 inches.

The 1800 inches is subtracted from his 40,000-inch contract as though he had run this advertising in the regular paper.

If he had run none of his regular inches, his contract obligation would now be 38,200.

This kind of credit gives the advertiser flexibility in deciding how to place ads – R.O.P. or preprint – and the paper can encourage him to sign the bulk contract at a high level.

Credit toward contract reduces the risk for everyone.

Here's another example:

Suppose an advertiser has a contract for 12,000 inches to be run during the week. Cost per inch is $41.63.

The advertiser now wants to run a series of three preprint ads (single sheet), but only to a zoned section of 50,000 readers.

The single sheet cost per thousand (8.5 x 11 sheet) is $17. The cost of that preprint run three times is 50 x $17 x 3 or $850. His credit would be $850/$41.63 or 20 inches.

SEVEN. Rates & Contracts.

PROBLEMS FOR YOU:

Try your hand at these…

1. This advertiser has a contract for 40,000 inches a year to be placed in the Sunday papers.

He plans to run six 12-page "tab" (tabloid) sections as inserts on some of the Sundays. He will do the inserts' full-run circulation, which is 300,000.

What is the cost of placing one of these tab sections?

What credit will this advertising get toward his regular contract for the entire preprint placement?

2. This advertiser has a contract for 20,000 inches a year to be placed in the weekday papers.

She has decided to place 13 4-page tabs as inserts during the year. They will run on Sundays and she wants them to reach 240,000 of the circulation (full-run is 300,000).

What is the cost of one preprint?

How much credit toward the contract will this advertiser get for one preprint?

How much credit will he accrue for the entire year of preprint placement?

ANSWERS TO PROBLEMS

RADIO AND TV

Spots and Frequency

Radio and television time is sold in "spots" – 5, 10,15, 20, 30 or 60-second time slots spread throughout the contract period.

Frequency and repetition are important components for advertising success in broadcast, particularly for radio.

Reaching the designated target audience often enough for the message to be effective is a primary goal.

The Grid and Dayparts

As you examine the sample rate sheet, you will see that the cost for radio time depends on daypart, with the most expensive times during drive time, when radio has the largest audiences.

The grid, which shows prices for different times of day also shows prices based upon expected time availability.

Pricing and Discounts

Time of day discounts are built into the rate card or "grid."

When demand for radio ad time is high, the times available are more expensive. When demand is low, discounts can be quite high. After all, unsold time is gone forever.

While newspapers can – within limits – print extra pages for additional advertising, radio has a fixed number of advertising minutes – or avails – per hour.

Thus, the cost for radio and television time is a function of demand and availability – as well as the level of audience listenership or viewership. Cost is also a function of the contract in terms of frequency – as always, larger advertisers get lower rates.

Although the radio grid provides basic prices for different daytimes and levels of demand, broadcast pricing for both radio and television time is largely a matter of customizing a rate plan based upon customer need, demand for the time wanted, and the amount and frequency in the contract.

Early Contract Commitments

Advertisers are rewarded for making early decisions and contract commitments by getting the optimum lowest prices for the time of day and amount of time agreed upon.

An early contract commitment assures the station that the time is sold. Time bought later is then at a premium and can be priced higher.

Here's an example of a Radio Grid Sheet for spot radio rates:

SAMPLE GRID SHEET - WWWW-FM

Sample Rate Card - Effective 3/15/95

Grid Levels	I	II	III	IV
AAA	45	41	37	30
AA	39	35	31	28
A	22	20	18	16

Maximum Reach Plan
$1/_2$ AAA, $1/_4$ AA, $1/_4$ A

Daypart Plan
$2/_3$ AAA, $1/_3$ AA

Daypart Times:

AAA	Monday-Friday	6:00 AM - 9:30 AM
		4:30 PM - 7:30 PM
	Weekend	8:00 AM - 5:00 PM
AA	Monday-Friday	9:30 AM - 4:30 PM
		7:30 PM - 11:00 PM
	Weekend	5:00 PM - 11:00 PM
A	Monday-Friday	11:00 PM - 6:00 AM
	Weekend	11:00 PM - 8:00 AM

"ADDED VALUE"

There are additional ways to make a buy on your station appealing. They're ways to "add value" to the media buy.

While primarily used by radio stations, each of these types of "added value" programs has some parallel in television.

Bonus Spots

One way of maintaining the official rate card and utilizing the full amount of time available on the station is through the use of "Bonus Spots."

These are additional spots on your station – usually during less popular time periods.

Sometimes 10" ID's are also used as Bonus Spots.

Sponsorships

Sponsorships of certain segments of programming, such as the Traffic or Stock Market Reports, are another way to add value.

These add on-air mentions, either by the announcer or through a pre-recorded set of "bumpers," short bits of audio (or video) that go on the front and back of the mini-program. Often, there is also a full commercial during the program.

So, for example, the Traffic Report could have an opening 15" bumper, one minute of Traffic, a 60" commercial, one more minute of traffic and a closing bumper.

There would be two additional sponsor mentions in this program, plus you could guarantee a certain number of additional "brought to you by..." mentions during the day.

Remotes

Remote broadcasts from a retail location add value two ways.

First, they generate a high level of publicity for the retailer through on-air mentions during the remote broadcast as well as during a period leading up to that broadcast.

Second, the remote itself can generate traffic to that location as people come to see their favorite radio personalities.

Promotions – a two-edged sword

Call-ins, contests, concerts... radio promotions are almost a world in themselves. They're one of the key ways radio stations add value.

It's a two-edged sword – too many promotions can get in the way of each other and clutter up the station format, each bit of "added value" demands a certain amount of time and station resources and overuse can cheapen your product.

Promotional ideas could fill a book in themselves.

And, in fact, you can get a number of books full of promotional ideas from Radio Ink Magazine and other specialists.

Television Promotions

Generally, local television stations have done less in this area than radio stations, but that is changing.

Locally-originated programming is particularly adaptable to this type of involvement, utilizing local broadcasters as part of the advertising. However, when those broadcasters are also news people, this can be a problem.

Nationally, networks are doing more promotional programs with key sponsors. Cable TV is also becoming more active on both a national and local level.

PROBLEMS FOR YOU:

Here are some broadcast examples.

1. Client wants to run 20 30-second spots per week split between drive time and late night. Contract will run for six weeks. He is buying early, so you are able to give him III level pricing.

Using the grid as a basis, what is the cost of this contract?

2. The same client has decided to upgrade the program to 35 30-second spots in the same time frame. The client wants a better price, but avails are scarce and you're having a hard time finding space.

You offer a custom plan off the grid.

You base it on Level I prices for the extra 15 spots, but give a 10 percent discount.

Is this a good deal for the client?

Is it a good deal for the station?

ADDITIONAL BROADCAST CONCEPTS:

Here are two helpful approaches to maximizing the income potential of a broadcast property – Yield Management and OES.

Yield Management

Broadcast sales utilizes a form of yield management in setting rates and estimating demand.

Prices for time are set by a combination of demand, customer need and competition within the market. Airlines and hotels use yield management to set prices all the time.

Thus, prices go up when demand is high. Because all three of these industries have an inventory of time that will be lost if it is not bought, prices may go down at the last minute if some of the flights, rooms or radio spots are not bought.

Those stations that use yield management techniques to predict demand and set prices are able to respond more quickly and more effectively to changes within the market – both those generated by advertisers and those generated by the competition.

Pricing levels can be set by the predictions of demand and sales based upon past history. Adjustments can be made as demand shifts or competitive activity increases or decreases within the market.

Although the grid format has been traditionally used as a way of showing advertisers differences in costs for different times of day and levels of demand, it is generic in nature.

Sales reps have always calculated custom plans and pricing schedules based upon the needs of the client.

Optimum Effective Scheduling (OES)

Many stations are now moving to OES – Optimum Effective Scheduling. It's an important way to sell radio and a good way to use radio.

It's a system for figuring out the number of commercials needed for an effective schedule on a radio station.

The formula to figure out a station's Optimum Effective Schedule (OES) is the station's turnover multiplied by 3.29.

True OES uses all days and dayparts and reaches about 45% of a station's cume effectively.

Advertisers who use OES, generally have better results from their advertising.

Here's a sample OES Schedule.

Customized Radio Buy Plan for June 1995

Client: A
Spots per week = 49
Spots per 4 week period = 196
Target Audience: Adults 25-44
Strategy: Distribute across all dayparts. Emphasize drive time.

	MON	TUE	WED	THU	FRI	SAT	SUN	Total
AMD	2	2	2	1	2	2	2	13
MID	1	2	2	2	1	2	2	12
PMD	2	1	2	2	2	1	2	12
EVE	2	2	1	2	2	2	1	12
Total	7	7	7	7	7	7	7	49

Reproduced with permission of National Broadcasters Association

RADIO CONTRACT CONDITIONS

In radio, contract forms vary widely.

The Front of the Contract

The front will normally cover the buy itself.

It will indicate the client, and outline the number of spots, the length of spots, and, often, when they will run.

Much of this information will also show up in your station's Confirmation – a form sent to clients on a regular basis.

Some will actually have a grid with the schedule indicated.

Some stations are going to a Yield Management System, with a computer grid delivering the latest rates.

Many stations use DARTS or Columbine – software programs that keep station logs, provide affidavits and confirmations, and also do invoicing.

Basically, the contract will confirm the approved schedule. It will also indicate amount due and, often, terms of payment.

There are places for a station representative and a client, or agency representative, to sign.

The Back of the Contract

A contract is a legal document. Radio Station contracts usually cover some or all of the following areas:

Payment and Billing

This part of the contract deals with terms of payment, invoicing, and billing procedures.

Many stations include other payment policies, including those related to the payment of commissions.

Performance (proof that the spot ran) may also be included in this part of the contract.

Terminations and Renewals

This may be one section or two.

It spells out the rights of both parties, usually with time limits for cancellation on the part of the client.

Materials and Approvals

This covers how materials are to be submitted and when.

Often, there is some specific time limit, i.e. "Copy must be in Station's hands by 4:00 PM, two days previous to broadcast."

There may be some approval mechanism or a general clause "All programs and Advertiser's copy must conform to Station's standards."

Breaches of Contract

The Station reserves the right to cancel if bills are not paid.

If the Station does not perform relative to the terms, the Agency or client may cancel the contract.

There is often a clause dealing with what happens if the station does not broadcast.

Substitution of Programs of Public Significance

As part of their license, stations have duties to the public and also governmental obligations.

Stations retain "the right to cancel any broadcast or portion thereof covered by this contract in order to broadcast any program which, in its absolute discretion, it deems to be of public significance."

There are provisions for notifications and "make-goods."

Rates and Charges

There is usually a section covering standard procedures related to rates, i.e. "The station reserves the right to increase rates, but no such increases shall be applied to broadcasts under this contract, or renewal thereof, until three months after notification in writing to the Agency and acceptance by the Agency including specific rate revisions affecting the contract."

There may be an indication of areas where additional payment is necessary, such as talent and remote charges.

Other matters affecting frequency discounts may be covered.

General

There are a number of other areas which may be covered.

The primary one relates to – **Liability.**

This covers a number of areas, from possible libel to temporary interruption of transmission due to equipment problems.

Other Contracts

A station may have other types of contracts, as well.

Most stations have some sort of **Trade Contract.**

This sets terms and conditions for the exchange of goods and/or services from a client for air time from the station.

For example, meals at a restaurant in exchange for commercials for that restaurant.

(This is covered in more detail on page 276.)

OUTDOOR

Outdoor contracts may cover only placement and rotation or they may include the production of the outdoor "board."

Production can range from painting the board – or even a wall – to state-of-the-art computerized reproduction.

Generally, the plan is presented and, if approved, is then prepared as a formal estimate.

Upon receipt of signed approval, estimates are translated into formal contracts.

Reconciliations

Billing after contracts may involve some reconciliations – particularly if the buy is for multiple markets.

For example, if damaged posters are found, cash credit or make-goods (additional postings) should be requested.

Companies in every market have paperwork procedures designed to cover these contingencies.

YELLOW PAGES

Yellow Pages Contracts are annual contracts.

Usually, the client pays monthly.

Contracts may be for a single directory or for multiple directories.

DIRECT MAIL

Direct Mail is a discipline unto itself.

It can range from small customer mailings for local retailers to huge national mailings involving the coordination of huge databases, custom laser printing, and sophisticated response tracking.

There are five basic cost areas in Direct Mail and each can range from the simple to the complex.

1. List and Database Management

Organizing, coordinating, and keeping track of the data is

key to an effective program.

One of the basic truths of Direct Mail is "you're as good as your list." Mailing to the right people is key.

A related necessity is keeping track of their responses.

Direct Mail depends on precise measurement of response percentages – particularly for large programs. The difference of a percentage point – or even a fraction of a percentage point – can mean the difference between profit and loss.

2. Creation and Design

The crafting of the message and the graphic presentation are also key. Creative effectiveness creates great "elasticity" in the Direct Mail dollar.

An effective message can perform two to ten times more than an ineffective message. For this reason, it is also common to invest in the testing of appeals and creative approaches.

3. Printing

Many pieces are printed. Even though the cost per piece may be 25¢ or less, a small amount of profit per piece printed can total to a lot of money.

Likewise, inefficient bidding or poor planning can take the profit out of a job.

In Direct Mail, the contract is usually the result of extensive bidding on the front end.

It is also common for much of the profit margin on a job to be built into the print production costs, so it's a critical area.

4. Postage

This is usually a large portion of the cost of direct mail.

It is critical that the weight of the piece be taken into consideration and that even aspects such as zip code sorting are done to minimize postage costs.

When you're sending tens of thousands of pieces, saving a penny apiece postage adds up to substantial dollars.

5. Mechanical & Handling

The folding, stuffing and sorting of thousands of pieces of direct mail is a task all by itself. Each physical act, stuffing a piece in an envelope, attaching a label, sealing an envelope, etc. has a cost attached to it.

It is critical that each specific physical or mechanical process is indicated and the cost accounted for.

6. The Contract

Properly done, the contract is the result of a detailed planning and bidding process.

Still, there are many instances (such as handling responses) where it is impossible to make a precise bid since the level of returns is indeterminate.

Contracts range from large formal documents and proposals to simple letters of agreement to perform services.

THE VALUE OF CONTRACTS

Contracts provide security for both you and the client.

With a contract commitment, the client is eligible to receive a discount based upon the level of advertising specified.

Without a contract, the advertiser would have to pay the open rate, which assumes the ad is a one-shot placement and therefore the highest rate available.

Even the smallest contract provides some kind of price break for the advertiser.

For the media business, the contract provides an assurance of steady cash flow. Calculating the number of and duration of contracts also enables the sales rep to know how much space is still available so they can plan their own time and sales calls.

It also means the ad dollars are committed to your medium and not to someone else.

A record of contract sizes and timing also provides the media business with key information for planning and, particularly in the case of broadcast, for pricing according to estimated availability.

The contract provides both the security of knowing how much advertising is coming in – and therefore the commission – but also specifies the number and type of ads wanted, facilitating better ad development and client service.

For example, if a sales rep knows the advertiser has a commitment for a six-month radio contract, he is able to suggest a series of ads that will work well together for the client to receive the most effective impact for the ads placed.

GOOD PLANS = GOOD CONTRACTS

Whatever it may say on the contract, if the program fails to achieve some measure of success, all bets are off.

Almost all contracts have some form of cancellation clause. It is your job in developing the plan to put together a program that minimizes this possibility.

The Integrated Plan

Developing rate plans that work means basing the plan on

client needs. This is the first step in selling as a marketing partner.

Here are key steps you should go through in developing effective rate plans for clients:

• Review client goals – specific articulation of what clients want the advertising to do for them.

• Review client expenditures – number and types of ads, sizes, budget and how the budget is set.

• Review client impressions of past ads and of past media used, including your own.

These will all help you develop a plan that is truly based on client needs.

YOUR GOAL

Your goal is to develop a plan that integrates all of the media the client has or should use.

You need to look at all media expenditures – not just the expenditure on your medium. Naturally, you may well have a bias in this regard, but to sell as a marketing partner, you must help the client look at his total program.

The integrated plan should take the client goals and past advertising history into account.

Everything in the plan should be placed there for a reason – and this reason should be articulated to the client.

In other words, you should be able to justify and explain all the choices that the plan represents – even if it isn't in your medium.

On the next page is a worksheet for developing a plan.

PLAN WORKSHEET

Targets:

Primary target market for this business

Secondary target markets for this business

Background:

Advertising history

Advertising in your medium

Advertising in competing medium

Each medium as percentage of total ad budget past year

SEVEN. Rates & Contracts.

Goals & Budget:

Client goals for this advertising period

Emphasis of this campaign

Budget available for this campaign

Schedule:

Weekly frequency or seasonal emphasis

Placement for each week/month of the contract period

Time of week or time of day

Complete campaign placement with explanation for time and date choices

Cost:

Total cost of package

Projected effectiveness of package in reaching goal

MINI-CASE STUDY

Ferguson's Tires

Ferguson's is a family-owned tire store located in a city of 250,000. The main store is near the city center, and there is a new branch in a recently developed outlying area near a major new mall.

Ferguson's carries all the major lines of tires and prides itself on superior service, both in speed and quality of product. In fact, Ferguson's provides a shuttle service to the nearby mall so that customers can shop while their tires are being replaced.

The store feels service and the quality of their products are the major selling points they have.

There is competition, particularly from discount auto service shops. One of these stores is located just four blocks from the new branch and is even closer to the new mall, and this is one reason why Ferguson's provides the shuttle service.

The ad budget has been $6000 a month in recent years with the major metro newspaper and local radio splitting the ad dollars.

Yellow Page or directory advertising comes from a separate ad budget.

Ferguson's manager, Jim Allen, is vaguely unhappy with the ad plan, but the pressure at work keeps him too busy to think about it.

For the past three years, he's kept the same contracts and just signs up for them when the reps come around. The print and broadcast campaigns aren't very connected since each of the reps has individually developed one for their own medium.

Jim knows he could get more impact. "Next time," he says, "I'll have more time to rethink the effort."

Ferguson's is a case where ad placement decisions are based too much on past history.

With new competition coming in, Jim needs to think about what he wants his ads to do.

Even if he stays with the same budget distribution, he should do it deliberately after establishing goals and thinking through the plan rather than just signing up for what he's always had before.

Discussion Questions:

(Discussion in italics)

What are some options Jim might consider here?

Newspaper and radio are good vehicles for his advertising, but are they doing a complete job?

Does the radio format match his audience?

What about direct mail?

With this kind of business, it would be easy enough to develop a customer database.

Jim could also target nearby neighborhoods, and might consider some kind of introductory deal.

The mall might be open to some kind of cooperative promotion effort as well. If Jim or a sales rep approached them before any competitors did, both might benefit.

Finally, how can the advertising efforts be unified?

Jim can keep using the newspaper for price information and illustrations of the differing products. He might even want to start a service theme within those ads, using some of the space for a column or tips about auto safety.

Radio can serve as reminder ads. But Jim needs to think about using some ad dollars for direct mail and for promotions as well.

And, what about that shuttle service?

MINI-CASE

Bamboo Restaurant

The Bamboo Restaurant is located just off a busy shopping street in the downtown area of a city with 100,000 population.

The original owner, Mr. Lee, has been overseeing the day-to-day operations of the restaurant ever since it opened 11 years ago.

Advertising has been sporadic with print placed in the daily newspaper (circulation, 35,000), some radio spots, and flyers sent to nearby businesses.

Lee estimates he spends about $800 a month on advertising (not counting coupon redemptions).

There's a monthly magazine available that is free in all the hotels as well as other locations such as drug stores and the mall. Bamboo has never advertised in it.

Lunch business is good, as many people who work nearby come in for the lunch specials and buffet. But the restaurant would like to attract more dinner customers, particularly families, and out-of-town visitors.

Lee is just about to give some of his duties to his son, Shen, who has just graduated from college and is anxious to go to work as the restaurant manager.

It was the son, in fact, who called your small agency and asked for a meeting. His exact words to you were *"We need to know more about advertising. Either we're going to do it right or we're going to save the money. I don't know much about it, but it seems our money is wasted."*

With the past history of this restaurant, it seems to you that the first discussions should focus on ad placement. Creative can come later.

Discussion Questions:

What would you suggest to the two Lees?

Is the magazine an option?

Radio? Newspaper? Promotions? What kind of ad goals should they set?

One of your first tasks in working with these clients should be to set goals and consider percentages of budget to be spent on different media to reach those goals.

You should find out what promotional offers they are prepared to make on a regular basis – as high-value promotions may be necessary to generate trial (remember, this can add value to your ad budget).

You'll also need to talk about budget commitment and the amount needed to reach goals.

Right now, you need some kind of game plan for the meeting. What is it?

THINK BEYOND THE SHORT-TERM

Put the campaign approach to work for local clients

Our final point in this chapter isn't about the details of contracts, but about the underlying principle that makes the contract good and the relationship successful – good planning.

Sound planning and a long-term campaign approach is the basis for contracts that get renewed.

And, as we've discussed, long-term clients are essential for a successful career in media.

That means that local businesses – and local clients – need to plan campaigns in the same way agencies and national clients do.

And you're the person that has to help them do it.

Thinking beyond the contract period

It necessitates thinking beyond the contract period.

In the long run, it pays off.

The campaign approach gives the client a unified advertising plan, provides confidence in signing a contract, and saves time throughout the whole period of the contract.

For most local clients – and for many sales reps in all media – the idea of thinking through all the ad executions for the whole contract period is new.

Many local clients develop ads "on the spot" in response to store needs or outside circumstances.

Chris Lytle likes to talk about the appliance store that

turned an ice-storm into a sale event.

But unlike the weather, most clients know when the ads will be placed.

It's just that they often do not know what will be in them.

Campaign thinking can be a lot of work at the front end.

Ads may still have to be changed to respond to changing conditions, but having a series of ads finished and ready to run takes the pressure off throughout the year and unifies the ad message.

The campaign approach puts much of the planning in first and provides a stronger ad message.

Good campaigns make for good contracts

For the sales rep, the campaign approach encourages the client to make a commitment.

The client cannot help but be impressed by the time and effort put in on his behalf.

This in itself can often help sell the contract.

The client can modify or change the ads, of course, but the impact of having a year-long plan for both media use and creative execution is clear.

And, once people are thinking long-term, signing at least a short-term contract becomes both obvious and necessary.

8. STAYING ORGANIZED.

This section isn't called "Getting Organized," it's called "Staying Organized."

In a job like Media Sales, where you are continually on the move, you have to be organized at all times.

For the world around you may be very disorganized.

Often, new clients (or potential clients) will need a lot of help sorting out basic business issues on the way to developing the right advertising plan.

That's what becoming a marketing partner is all about.

Helping your client succeed means success for you as well.

But you can't do it if you aren't organized.

Here are some tools you'll need.

THE CALENDAR – A PLANNING TOOL

Use a calendar when you are working with and planning for a client account. This calendar should have a list of all major shopping dates, such as special sales, local events and holidays.

You also need a past history of advertising for the client – seasonal sales and promotional periods, anniversaries and other specifics. This may mean you need as many as three years to build your calendar – last year, this year and next year.

Some events, such as Christmas shopping, and back to school, may be the same for many clients on your list.

Other dates and events, such as Earth Day or Chinese New Year, may be important for only a few of your clients.

Make a Master Calendar

Before you make individual client calendars, first make up a master calendar showing all the major events for your area. Be sure to include special local events such as SpringFest, a canoe race, or a jazz festival – anything that merchants might want to use as a trigger for a special promotion or sale.

Customize a Calendar for each of your clients

Then, customize a calendar for each of your clients.

Computer calendar software can make it easier for you to note comments from last year and generate ideas to increase or change advertising for the coming period.

Talk about the important dates with each client.

Note opportunities for ads that could generate additional store traffic or calls because they are tied into a relevant event for this type of store.

For example, the opening of the baseball season is an important date for a sports store – so is an upcoming bicycle race. For a children's clothing store, Back to School sales still bring big profits.

There are less obvious events as well. For example, every store is entitled to an "Anniversary Sale."

It's up to both the sales rep and the client to take advantage of known opportunities and develop new ones.

Calendars are Planning Resources

Developing a customized calendar can be an excellent focus for a planning meeting. Together, write down as many events, or possible events, as you can. Then prioritize them and choose the ones that can bring the biggest return for you.

Reps should try to keep a calendar for each client.

Businesses should keep one for themselves – this is particularly useful in helping retailers stay organized.

Notes from past years, as well as previous calendars, can become valuable planning resources.

RECORD KEEPING – WHAT YOU NEED

The more detailed your records, the better you can assess how differing ad campaigns and media mixes worked in the past and the more effectively you can plan for the future.

Planners

You will need some sort of "Planner," a combination calendar and phone book, usually with extra pockets and places for business cards and notes – often with a few pages devoted to each important client.

They can be expensive, leather-bound and elaborate or very basic and inexpensive. Whichever you choose, your own detailed planner should include:

- Your own appointments: day, week and month
- Reminder dates to call clients
- Client preferences for day and time for calls
- Important dates
- Notes on competitive activity
- Ideas for advertisers
- Notes on background articles of interest to your clients
- A list of cold calls to make – including new businesses that are coming into the area
- Market Resources – start collecting a list of suppliers who can help you do your job: event organizers, printers, premium suppliers, potential tie-in partners. As you build your network of relationships, they will help you add value to your programs and execute them more professionally.

This information can be kept in a pocket calendar, a large notebook planner or in computer files. The most important thing is that the material be accessible, pertinent, up-to-date and easy to use.

Computer Software

Today, we all need to take advantage of the productivity benefits offered by a computer.

For database management, correspondence, making presentations, and keeping track of finances, a computer does a lot of work for you. There are even programs specifically designed for the needs of salespeople.

But, whatever software programs you get, there are two important points that apply to any and all of them.

Two Important Points

First, make sure you have plenty of back-ups and a hard copy – just in case.

Computers crash, hard discs go bad, programs bomb. This can be particularly true when a small database program, common in most scheduling software, becomes loaded with names.

The longer you are dependent on one program, the more you need to be sure you are backed up. And, the longer you use this program with no problems, the less prone you are to back up regularly.

Don't wait for disaster. Get in the habit of backing up regularly and keep a hard copy of everything you've done since the last time you backed up.

And maybe you'll keep that hard copy longer. People talk about "the paperless office," but the reality seems to be that, as computers allow us to put out more paper than ever, we have more paper than ever to deal with.

Second, try to develop a smooth interaction between your computer-based program and your planner.

Some programs offer special printing formats and even special paper that fits in most common planners. Try to find a smooth relationship between your computer-based program and the planner you use.

If you don't, you'll find your computer and your planner each carrying little items that aren't in the other. Suddenly, you'll need something and you won't be able to find it.

Try to keep both your computer and your planner up-to-date with each other.

TYPES OF PROGRAMS

The world of computers changes so quickly that it's hard to offer advice that isn't immediately obsolete – but here are some types of software packages you can use.

In some cases, we'll mention brand names, but, again, with the speed of change, brand-specific information may already be completely out-of-date:

Integrated Programs

These combine word processing, database management, graphic, and spreadsheet functions. They may not be terrific at any one of them, but they're often enough to do the job.

As computers get faster and memory gets larger, these types of programs are getting better. Two of the most popular have been Microsoft Office and ClarisWorks.

Word Processing Programs

You should know how to type well. You should also become comfortable with some sort of word processing program to help you with your correspondence and draft presentations.

Even in this world of voice mail and e-mail, letters and memos can still be powerful tools.

There are many good programs of this sort.

Two more helpful hints:

1. Try to develop formats for letters, call reports and memos that you can customize quickly.

2. Develop a file-naming system that you understand – so you can easily find an important file from six months ago.

Scheduling Software

There are a number of these calendar-type programs. ACT, Shortlist, Datebook, and InControl are examples.

Most are good if you use them consistently.

Try to develop a system to keep your computer information up-to-date. Often, the "hard copy" printout becomes the place where you write down important notes and numbers – or staple on business cards.

Be sure that information gets into your program!

Spreadsheets

Lotus or Excel have been the two most common programs to date.

Often, you will be asked to do some type of spreadsheet-based budget as part of your presentation.

Some of this can be handled with the small spreadsheet programs included in the integrated software mentioned previously.

Other times, you may want a more flexible and more powerful program. Often, there will be someone at work who is familiar with one of these programs.

We recommend that, all things being equal, you choose the program that someone else in your office is familiar with.

An experienced user is better than a user's manual.

Presentation Software

Again, there are a number of programs that can produce good-looking slides and overheads. New programs even allow you to add multi-media elements, like broadcast commercials or video bites from focus groups.

Here, the technology is changing very rapidly, and we cannot predict which will be best for you.

However, we will repeat our advice that you find someone already experienced with a program of this type and use that person as a resource as you develop your skills.

DeskTop Publishing

Quark and PageMaker are two examples of desktop publishing (DTP) programs that have revolutionized the way ads, brochures, and presentation booklets are made.

EIGHT. Staying Organized.

Whether or not you become a desktop publishing expert, you should develop at least one good-looking format you can use for presentation booklets.

PageMaker uses a "Style Sheet" that allows you to set typographic standards for your presentation. Develop a style sheet you like and then copy it for your presentation. This book was done on PageMaker.

For designing ads or posters, Quark is usually preferred, primarily due to its approach to type manipulation.

Word processing programs are developing more and more desktop publishing-style features, and many allow you to add charts and spreadsheet data.

Sales Management Programs

There is another type of program you might want to explore – software specifically designed for salespeople.

Sometimes, they're called "contact managers" or "contact management software."

They usually combine database programs for leads, with a built-in follow-up function, word processing for correspondence, and spreadsheets for expenses.

These same features are often combined in "integrated" programs. These types of programs work well for some – not for others. Don't believe everything you read in the ads.

Again, you might try to get some hands-on experience with a colleague who has discovered a particular favorite.

Whichever you choose, if you can, try before you buy.

Notebook Computers and PDAs

Smaller computers and PDAs (personal digital assistants) are providing more and more power and portability.

This is good news for the profession of media sales.

There will probably always be some limitations with screen size and brightness and the interface between the electronics and hard copy on paper will remain a logistical problem.

Today, something on a computer screen is still no match for a piece of paper that a client can hold in his or her hand.

However, this equipment may become as vital as the planner and will provide the computer-smart sales rep with an additional marketing and management resource.

E-Mail, Modems, and On-Line

You'll probably want a modem and e-mail as part of your computer set-up. More and more people have these services and it can be a handy way to send documents or stay in touch.

Instead of "phone tag" and voice mail, you can just place a document in a client's mail box.

As for the Information Highway as a media opportunity – well, the highway may be here, but traffic is still a problem.

In some ways, it's too heavy, with phone lines being over-taxed trying to move large amounts of information over ordinary phone lines. It works for text, but for graphics or video, it can be a problem.

In other ways, traffic is too light – the number of people actually visiting any single Web site is often quite small.

The larger on-line services are offering some advertising opportunities and, for certain types of advertisers (such as flowers by wire), it already makes some sense.

In general, however, you should get an e-mail address and a mail box, get on-line, and see what's happening in this exciting new world.

RECORD KEEPING

Your "Future Book"

Sales reps and businesses should keep a "Future Book" of events of particular importance, people who should be contacted, and other calendar events for the future.

Reminders about yearly or monthly events and notes about important happenings, successes or failures should all be part of this important organizational tool.

Records about Clients

For each client's business, you should have:
• Target audience
• Amount of ad budget
• Past advertising history – each medium, including yours
• Clip file of all print ads – for the business and for the competitors – often these are filed by category
• Name of contact locally (plus name of decision-maker if decision-maker is not same person as contact)
• Other pertinent material about the business such as length of time in the area and length of time manager has been in the area

Another example would be articles on that particular industry (trade magazines such as *Advertising Age* usually touch on each industry once a year)
• Correspondence, if any

Before making any sales call, you should review all this pertinent information. And, at the very minimum, carry it with you in your briefcase or car.

You will probably develop your own filing format for clients (some items you will file by category – such as "automotive"), but it should accomodate the information you need in a sensible and orderly way.

PROFITABLE HABITS

A few more habits that will pay off for you in the long run.

Keep an Automotive Log

Your car will be an important part of how you make your living – and it will be a major expense, particularly at the beginning of your career.

Keeping track of mileage and expenses is one thing you can never do too well.

Keep Your Receipts

Keep them and find a way to keep them organized and under control. Set aside a regular time to keep things up-to-date.

Use your Planner to confirm expenses.

You don't want to be sitting up all night on April 14th, the day before your taxes are due, trying to remember what you did fourteen months ago, in February of the previous year.

FOLLOW-UP

One of the reasons you need to stay organized is that you seldom make that sale on your first call. That means you need to be able to follow-up regularly and consistently.

Regular Follow-Up

You need to have a reason to make a follow-up call.

Sometimes new news, or a new opportunity with your medium can be the reason.

If you are genuinely interested in the business, that can be a reason. Many marketing research resources, such as the RAB, continually provide important pieces of industry data. Bringing these to a potential client's attention can be a good reason for a follow-up call.

Remember, most clients are in the sales business themselves – if they weren't selling something, it is doubtful they would advertise. People in sales respect other people in sales if they do it well. Positive, informative, and regular follow-up is one way to earn that respect.

So, while your medium must be sold on its merits, your efforts at marketing your medium may well be viewed as part of the added value. It's one way you have an opportunity to act as a marketing partner.

And staying organized is critical for a consistent and professional program of follow-ups.

Sales follow-up

Another big part of client services is the work after the contract is signed and the ads are finished.

The job is really never over.

As you'll see in the section on continuing client service, it is the rep's job to maintain an ongoing relationship with each client.

That involves reviewing the ads, the placement and the evolving business goals and target market on a regular basis. It also involves keeping in touch both in person and by phone. The client should know he is important to you.

Your job as a sales rep is to make the product tangible for the client through good ad ideas and development.

And that means consistent well-focused follow-up.

That means Staying Organized.

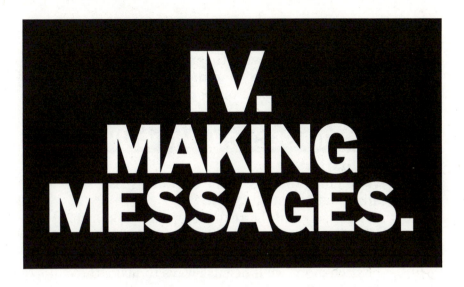

IV. MAKING MESSAGES.

"Advertising is a team sport."

Bruce Bendinger

*I*n this section, we'll cover one of the most enjoyable, complex, frustrating and exhilarating parts of your job – developing the message for your medium.

The Media Rep – a critical player

Whether it's a newspaper ad, a radio commercial, or an outdoor board, the media rep is often the critical player on the team that makes it happen.

Sometimes you help others get the job done.

Sometimes you have to do it yourself.

Some assumptions

For the rest of this section, we'll assume you have a minimum of help, though, naturally, that won't always be the case.

Often, an agency or an in-house ad department will do the job. Usually, other professionals at your station or newspaper will be on hand to handle all or part of the job.

We'll also assume that you need to create a new message – which also won't always be the case.

Sometimes message development may only involve taking a client's existing message and adapting it for your medium.

But, sometimes it will all be up to you.

This is particularly true with new clients who may not have advertised in your medium before. And that's often when it's most critical to figure out what the message should be.

So... the better you understand the whole process of message development, the better you'll do – whatever role you happen to play.

HOW THIS SECTION IS ORGANIZED

9. Getting Started
First, we're going to cover some overall issues.
We'll talk about "creativity."
We'll address some of the realities of the workplace.
And we'll talk about the use of "spec ads."

10. Getting Connected
In the next chapter, we'll discuss ways to make the connections you need to develop that message.

We'll touch on formats for developing Strategies, and talk about Positions, Propositions, and Promotions.

We'll show you some ways to plan it out and some ways to do it when you have no time at all.

We won't be able to teach you all you need to know – but it will be a good solid beginning.

11. Getting It Done
Finally, we'll discuss producing that message with tips for working in various media – primarily newspaper and radio.

Again, we can't cover every medium in detail, but we can introduce you to a few of the basics.

9. MESSAGES. GETTING STARTED.

*I*n the very earliest days of advertising, advertising agents merely sold space – and took a commission. Then, around the turn of the century, Albert Lasker discovered a new definition of advertising, "Salesmanship in Print."

The business of advertising wasn't merely selling the space – it was selling what was <u>inside</u> that space.

Ever since, the key competitive factor has been how well that space is filled – the better we fill that space, the better our clients will do and the better we will do.

THE NEED FOR "CREATIVITY"

A primary consideration in developing messages is what we generally call "creativity."

In our industry, this refers to the complex mental process involved in creating a message.

Types of Thinking

Creativity actually includes a wide range of thinking processes. It includes idea-generation and analytic, inductive, deductive, strategic, empathic and artistic thinking.

• **Idea-Generation** – this is the most pure creative thinking. You develop ideas – usually by making new connections. An idea is, as James Webb Young defined it, *"a new combination of two previously existing elements."* However, this is just one of the types of thinking you use in the creative development process.

Let's review the others.

• **Analytic Thinking** – analyzing the parts of a complex problem – you look at each element.

• **Inductive or Deductive Reasoning** – looking for "clues" to help solve a problem or understand the customer better. Here, you look for insights.

• **Strategic Thinking** – determining strategies by deciding which problem to solve and which factors to emphasize – and deciding the best way to accomplish a task.

• **Empathic Thinking** – learning to craft a message from the customer's point-of-view. Unlike many other types of communication, advertising is receiver-driven.

• **Artistic Thinking** – this involves aesthetic factors, often having to do with design and visualization.

This may also include audio or audio/visual design. Sometimes this has to do with creativity, other times it relates to other areas of "taste" such as proportion or current graphic or musical styles.

All of these types of thinking are part of what we call "creativity." It's not just one way of thinking. It's many ways of thinking.

When it's done well, creativity adds distinction and memorability to any ad. Basically, it makes the message more effective – which makes the media budget more effective.

When it's done well, the impact of creativity on effectiveness can be quite substantial.

One more important point to remember

Even though we call it "creativity," we don't judge it on how "creative" it is, but rather on how effective it is.

CREATIVITY = EFFECTIVENESS

So, even though we may call it "creativity," we are still measuring effectiveness and – ultimately – sales.

This can be confusing for young people in the business – they are encouraged to do one thing, "be creative," and then judged by a somewhat different criteria.

But even if the result is an uncreative (but sensible) message – like "On Sale! 50% Off!" creative thinking techniques are still often used to develop that message.

Creativity in the larger sense may be a complicated mystery, but there are some simple underlying principles that everyone can keep in mind while creating effective advertising messages.

There are many other books and resources that will be able to help you in more depth.

If you really want to get good at developing messages, you'll need to keep studying and keep working at it.

If you work at it, you'll get better at it – no matter how "uncreative" you are.

General Considerations

Here are some of the other things that will be a part of developing your messages.

Consideration #1. Making the most of your abilities.

Creating selling messages that work is one of the most satisfying aspects of the media business.

It's a terrific chance for you to develop your writing skills and your "empathy" skills – which will help your selling skills.

They all depend on an ability to connect with the person on the receiving end of your message.

Whatever the circumstances, as you develop the basic skills necessary for making messages for your medium, you'll also become a better salesperson.

If you work for a newspaper, you'll learn to write headlines and copy and know the basics of layout and production.

At a radio station, you'll learn how to write and produce a commercial that keeps your audience tuned in through the entire 30 or 60 seconds.

At a TV station, though there will be many other skilled technical people around, you'll become familiar with the many aspects of television production.

Outdoor, which many see as quite basic, is actually one of the more challenging creative mediums, since the demands for simplicity and impact are so severe.

Whatever medium you work in, the better you know what it takes to create an effective message, the better you'll be able to sell it.

Consideration #2. Making the most of small budgets.

Many local budgets are small. And today, virtually every ad budget is too small to do all the things a smart marketer would like to do.

That's all the more reason clients need smart, consistent advertising programs – what we call the "campaign approach." And all the more reason you have to be a marketing partner.

You need to help make that budget work as hard as it can.

Locally, that usually means you have to make your creativity work within the discipline of limited resources.

Smaller budgets make creativity in these ads even more important. Creativity adds distinctiveness and memorability to any ad. This can give them more impact. The impact can be even greater on the local level where it is so rare.

Consideration #3. Making the most of opportunities.

Successful advertising is often about opportunity.

An effective message is often one that makes the most of opportunities in the marketplace – consumer needs, competitive strengths, and unique appeals that can add up to extra persuasion.

After all, an effective message is one that the consumer translates into an opportunity to buy.

One "opportunity" you will consistently face is the "opportunity" to do something on "Spec."

"Spec" is short for "speculative advertising." It's the opportunity to do free work in the hope of making a sale.

SPEC ADS – HOW TO USE THEM

"Spec" or speculative ads can be a very important part of both creating winning, selling messages and communicating with the client.

A sales rep develops spec ads to show the client what ads for the business would be like.

Remember, clients are usually not used to thinking about advertising in the same way those in the advertising or sales end of the business do.

Seeing ideas in print or hearing them on tape gives clients a much more realistic and concrete idea of what the campaign will look like and what it can do.

Spec Ads – Pros & Cons

We could spend a lot of time debating the pros and cons of "spec work." It's expensive. It's time-consuming. It's a lot of work with no guaranteed pay-off.

But, if you want to make a sale, showing some ads in the hope of getting some business can be a good way to do it.

It's pretty much that simple.

Of course, it's also much more complicated than that.

In any business, when you give something away, the perceived value is diminished. Nonetheless, there are times when a free sample is the best way to sell something.

Ask any fudge shop owner. Free samples keep fudge shops in business. Even P&G does sampling to generate trial.

When a client sees or hears his or her very own name in an advertisement, it makes advertising in your medium a more appealing and persuasive idea than it would ever be without that piece of spec advertising.

It's human nature. And clients are, for the most part, only human.

At the same time, you may enjoy it so much that you'll always look for an opportunity to craft a great message – even when it's on "spec."

One successful General Manager helped build his sales career by writing one spec spot per day before going to bed. The next day, he always had something specific to sell.

Getting Ideas for "Spec Ads"

While ideas for spec ads come in the same way as other ad ideas, the first idea usually isn't about the ad – it's about the advertiser.

The first idea is usually "this company should be advertising in my medium." A good start.

Next, you need to know something about the business – either from talking to the manager or from observation or both – and developing advertising particularly for that business.

The points we've made earlier about "street smarts" and "keeping your antennae tuned" also apply.

Often, a new opportunity in the marketplace generates an opportunity for a spec presentation.

WAYS TO USE "SPEC ADS"

"Spec" can be used for businesses that are regular clients or for potential clients.

For either, they demonstrate an interest in the business itself and a commitment to service.

1. Cold Calls

For cold calls – calls on businesses that have never advertised with you or are new in town – spec ads can be a good way to open a conversation about the advertising that would be ideal for that client.

Even if the prospective client doesn't feel the ads are right for the business, your interest and the time you've spent show that you are a person willing to work to develop the right ad campaign.

In general, it's better to learn more about the business first, but in some situations, it's a luxury you don't have.

The ads themselves give you something to talk about and you'll learn more about the business than if you had come in to talk with nothing to show.

If you do use spec for cold calls, be sure you know as much as you can about the category – even if you won't know as much as you'd like about the individual business.

2. Regular Clients

For regular clients, spec ads are a way of introducing a new campaign or discussing a new contract year.

Here, too, the ads are a spark for discussion and for learning more about the client's thoughts.

By asking your client to react to the ads, you learn a lot about what he or she is really thinking about the future direction of the advertising.

By incorporating the client ideas and modifying them, you provide a higher level of customer service.

Spec ads may be in print or broadcast, with radio being the most likely broadcast medium for a spec ad for a local client.

Spec TV can be presented as a storyboard or key frame or with a similar commercial done in another market.

In print, spec ads are generally fairly big – 10" by 15" is a usual size. Sometimes, presenting the idea in a larger space can be a good way to set it up.

It can also be helpful to paste a copy of the ad onto a page of your publication so the client can get an even better feel as to how it will look in the marketplace.

Radio ads are usually 30 or 60 seconds and may be produced and presented on an audio cassette, though, at the initial stage, they're more commonly presented in script form.

3. Major Presentations

The most important use of spec is as part of a major presentation to an important client – new or old.

The message you develop for this presentation will represent the distillation of the marketing problem.

It will be a message that will connect that market to the marketer – a key component of our "4 M's."

The message may take some time to develop – since you will need time to make the right connections.

But if you do it right, it will not only connect your client with the market – it will connect with your client.

PROSPECTING FOR SPEC

Spec for similar clients

Sometimes you have very similar clients.

For example, you may have two or three men's clothing stores, five pizza parlors, and three restaurants on your prospect list.

You need to differentiate – and the key to differentiation is to develop unique positions for each client.

The trick is to position each in a way that dramatizes their individual attributes and sets them apart.

Differentiating positions provides these advantages:

• Each client has the best chance to attract customers who would appreciate what that business has to offer.

• Each client is set apart from the competition and the best points for that particular business are spotlighted.

• It helps you to think about every client as an individual business. This is essential for good client service.

Hopefully, having competing clients will become a problem. For when you are successful marketing one client in a category, it will attract other clients in that category.

Differentiation is key to giving all of them the service that each one of them deserves.

Next, we have to make the right connections.

10. MESSAGES. GETTING CONNECTED.

As we craft our message, the 4 M's of Media – Market, Marketer, Message and Medium – all come together.

The Importance of Connections

Essentially, we use Messages in our Media to connect Marketers with Markets. The message development process is about determining the best ways to make those connections.

This short chapter contains practical advice about some of the other connections you'll have to make in the process – connecting with the right people, the right information, the right strategy, and, finally, the right Selling Idea.

CONNECTING WITH A SELLING IDEA

Is it craft or art? Well, it's probably both.

Few of us could paint a museum-quality work of art. Most of us could paint a room.

While few of us could write the very effective original Volkswagen campaign, most of us can write the very effective "Gas. Next Exit."

Sometimes it's pure genius.

Sometimes it's just plain common sense.

Sometimes it's an idea that's "out there."

And, most times, it's based on some insight into your audience that helps you generate a Selling Idea.

At the core of your message, you need a Selling Idea.

What about "The Big Idea?"

Many excellent advertising people will speak very persuasively about "The Big Idea." They will show you excellent creative campaigns that were effective in the marketplace based on that "Big Idea."

The only problem is "Big Ideas" are generally only recognized in retrospect – that is, after they become "Big Ideas." And, often, there are many other factors in the marketplace that contributed to that business success.

That's why it's quite often hard to know at the beginning whether or not that nice idea is a "Big Idea."

So, while we're always looking for a "Big Idea," we're more comfortable with the term "Selling Idea."

Why do you call it a "Selling Idea?"

Because, no matter how big or small the idea becomes in the marketplace, we can all make some sort of judgment as to how well an idea "sells."

This also helps combine the two factors we talked about earlier, creativity and effectiveness. You want a creative idea, but you want an effective idea.

If it's a "Selling Idea," chances are it's both.

There are no guarantees, but it puts you on slightly more solid footing as you evaluate ideas.

How do you know?

You don't. Advertising is only one part of the whole marketing process. All you can really do is apply your best abilities and judgment against the problem.

If it tends to be easy to understand why you should buy, and if it tends to inspire more ideas that are both compatible and effective, that's usually a good sign.

As Leo Burnett said, *"Great copy and great ideas are deceptively simple."*

When your Selling Idea connects with other ideas, this is also a good sign. Does it inspire a promotion? Does it inspire PR?

In these days of "integrated marketing communications," the factors that make ideas sell effectively in a variety of ways and a variety of media are usually those that typify a good "Selling Idea."

Only time will tell how "Big" it is.

CONNECTING WITH THE RIGHT PEOPLE

You need good judgment and talented people.

That's why another important thing you can do is get the best people you can find to help.

Can you do it yourself? Sure. There are plenty of ads, direct mail pieces, and even commercials that were essentially put together by one person. Sometimes you don't have a choice.

But, most of the time, you'll do a better job (and have more fun) when you involve others with special skills – they can help make your message better.

For good message development, you usually need three kinds of partners.

1. Thinking Partners
2. Design Partners
3. Production Partners

Each can help you along the way.

Let's briefly review their contributions.

1. Thinking Partners

These are people who can help you "think through" a problem. Sometimes they're fellow reps or friends in the business. Sometimes it's your boss, sometimes it's your husband or wife or "significant other" and sometimes it's the client.

In every case, they're people whose experience and opinions can help enrich the mix of ideas and hypotheses as you work out your message.

Often, they're the people you'll be talking to – consumers.

Try to discover their "Sweet Spot." Find out what's important to them about the category and find out what the client's "brand" means to them.

Try to see the world through their eyes and listen through their ears.

Whether it's a "BrainStorming" session specifically called to generate ideas on a certain problem, an informal "let's kick some ideas around" get together, or just a chat with some customers, you can benefit from a second opinion.

2. Design Partners

Whether it's art or craft, every medium has an "aesthetic" – certain artistic standards that typify the best in the field.

Whatever medium you work in, you need to develop good relationships with people who have skills in the crafts associated with that medium.

For newspapers and other print media, you want to know good art directors and graphic designers. For radio, you want to know good voice talent, audio engineers, comedy writers and maybe some musicians.

Television needs good art direction, as well as producers, directors and technicians. And for other specialized media, like outdoor, you will often find art directors and designers who are particularly good in the medium.

3. Production Partners

Finally, there are other skilled people who can help you get the job done – at art studios, recording studios, video editing facilities and photographic studios.

Each may play a role in creating the finished message.

As your career progresses, you will want to develop the relationships and resources necessary to create the finest work for your clients.

To do that, those are the people you have to connect with.

Now let's talk about the process that helps you build the connections your message is based on.

STRATEGIES & PROPOSITIONS

The Nature of Strategy

Your message will be based on a strategy.

A strategy is an hypothesis about the best way to persuade.

Aside from the fact you usually have less time and fewer resources, developing strategy for local accounts is pretty much the same as developing strategy for national accounts.

So let's take a look at how big companies do it.

The Strategic Triangle

The Strategic Triangle (or Strategic Triad) consists of three elements: business (or product), customer (or audience) and competition (or category). Your strategy will be the result of some unique interaction of these factors.

First, think about the business itself and about what is distinctive and appealing about it.

Then, think about the audience. What does the audience see? What do they need? What do they want? What can the business or service offer that meets those needs?

How can you talk to the audience in a way that will make them see this business as a place they would like to shop?

Finally, how can you position this business and service so that it stands out in the target audience mind as different from and a better choice than other competing businesses?

It is important to position each business – within its category, against competition, and within the consumer's mind.

Both your competitive advantage vs. the competition – and the benefit you offer your audience – are often parts of a strategy. They're all based on the relationship of these three elements – the Strategic Triad.

Strategy, Message, and Creative Development

Guidelines for creative development generally begin with the process of first developing a strategy for the message (what you're going to say) and then some sort of theme or "proposition" (the best way to say it).

These stages are related to each other and it's often hard to know where one stops and another begins.

The fact is, you're often doing all of them at once.

As you think of message approaches, you're also thinking of creative advertising ideas and the best sales strategy – all at the same time.

You're using, *"that ultimate non-linear processing tool, the human brain."* (Kenichi Ohmae said this in *The Mind of The Strategist*.)

However you do it, wherever it leads, at each step of the process, the key is making the right connections.

Three Ways to Make Connections:

Here are three useful systems that can be used by major marketers as well as local marketers.

They help you make the connections that develop strategy and turn them into effective messages.

They might even help you be "creative."

Each of these systems offers a helpful approach to developing your message and you should become familiar with each of them. They are:

1. The 5 P's

This is a simple checklist that accomodates all the things you need to develop an effective local campaign.

It combines both short-term and long-term factors in campaign development – including the need for promotion.

2. The GE Focus System

This is a very effective way to develop messages quickly.

It is an unusual but very effective sequence of thinking.

It was first developed many years ago by General Electric's Advertising and Sales Promotion Division.

3. The Three-Part Strategy Statement

This is a format used by many clients and agencies.

It's one that will be recognized as a professional approach by most marketers and, even though you should spend a lot of time developing a strategy, it can be done on the run.

THE 5 P'S

This worksheet approach integrates five good ways to think about advertising: Problem, Position, Proposition, Promotion, and Plan.

Each one represents a discipline in itself, but by connecting them together, you can organize the basic elements you need to build a successful program.

In some ways, it serves as a check and balance system – if they are all compatible with each other and work together, chances are you have a solid program.

Remember, when you're thinking right about advertising, things tend to work together.

These five P's help you get focused on those basics.

Each is stated as a question – a "Q."

1. What's the Problem?

What is *"The Problem the Advertising Must Solve?"*

The client, his problems, and the competitive environment will all be important elements as you set objectives.

Remember, clever ideas that do not relate to the business and counteract the competition are just that – clever ideas.

What you need are creative ideas that also *sell* for your client. And, chances are, if you do that, you will indeed be solving a problem.

Consumer Problems

Even though it involves a client's *business* problem, it must be stated as a *consumer* problem – from the consumer's point of view.

As a consumer, you don't care one bit if all the stores on the street want to sell more – in fact, you probably assume it as you walk on by.

As a consumer, you have a limited budget and very specific needs. So, that store's problem must be served up in a way that solves the consumer's problem.

This is easier said than done. To do this well, you need to get into the problem-solving mindset before you begin to write.

The client is often willing to tell you his problem (not enough sales, traffic, etc.), but the consumer is seldom around to tell you the problem from their perspective.

But that's what you have to discover – the Problem.

Tracking down the Problem from the consumer's perspective is often the first part of good message development.

Strategic Problems

An understanding of the problem is inherently strategic.

A statement of the problem to be solved usually includes aspects of the product, the consumer, and the competition. You're often using all three parts of the Strategic Triangle.

Think about the Proposition *You Deserve a Break Today.* Notice how it addresses a Problem in a memorable way - this works off a Consumer Problem.

Pepsi-Cola's *The Choice of a New Generation* works off of a Strategic Problem.

2. What's Your Position?

To do Positioning well, you need to check out the competition – what kinds of ads run for businesses that compete with your client?

Could prospective customers confuse your ads for others in the same kind of business. If the ads are too much alike, your client may be spending money to sell a competitor's goods and services!

You have to develop a unique position within the mind of the consumer. Understanding how the competition fits in the consumer's mind is part of that.

Simply put, there are four Positioning options:

#1/BEST – This positions you as the category leader

AGAINST – This positions you against #1 in the category

NICHE – This positions you as #1 for a certain reason – or attribute

NEW CATEGORY – This establishes a #1 position by redefining the product category – and placing your client at the #1 position.

This is the second P – you should have a clear idea of the position you want to achieve in the mind of the consumer.

To find out more, you should read two books by Jack Trout and Al Ries, *Positioning, The Battle for Your Mind* and *The 22 Immutable Laws of Marketing.*

3. What's the Proposition?

Why buy? What's the Benefit?

What are the "Factors That Motivate Purchase Behavior?"

Most important, how do you turn all of the things you want to say into a single MEMORABLE PROPOSITION?

There are many variables, but we do know this...

Your Proposition should be based on a Selling Idea.

Alka-Seltzer delivering a benefit is turned into the Proposition *Plop! Plop! Fizz! Fizz! Oh, What a Relief It Is!*

It will be a set of words that you use over and over.

Here's where you really need to write a great piece of copy! Here's where you really need to sell.

Ads that sell are ads that put your Selling Idea into a memorable set of words – words that give the prospective customer a real reason to be interested. That's a proposition.

Giving that customer a reason to come into the store is an important part of retail advertising.

Often, the Problem and the Position can work together to help you write an effective Proposition. Like Apple Macintosh – *The Power to be your Best.*

Many good propositions tie the product name into the benefit (or the solution to the problem). *Dirt Can't Hide From Intensified Tide.*

Sometimes there are a number of needs and benefits, sometimes there is only one. Whichever is the case, your proposition should be a memorable presentation of how your client meets the consumer's need.

A Proposition is inherently strategic.

As Rosser Reeves, developer of the USP (Unique Selling Proposition) stated, *"Each advertisement must say... buy this product and you will get this specific benefit."*

In today's market, it can often be difficult to provide a benefit that cannot be provided by many competitors – other grocery stores have groceries, other car dealers have new cars – so it becomes even more important that your proposition is a memorable one that connects with the consumer.

Some very successful creators of advertising, like the Leo Burnett Company, often build distinctiveness for their brands through a unique ownership of the generic benefit in the category – a memorable and well-executed proposition containing what Leo Burnett calls *"inherent drama"* can do that.

Tony the Tiger demonstrates the taste and food energy in Frosted Flakes with the dramatic line, *"They're Gr-r-reat!"*

Your Proposition should work in all media.

It's important that all advertising efforts be integrated across the media used – the campaign approach.

Thinking with a campaign approach may help you develop themes, logos, and copy ideas that translate well in print, broadcast, and promotions in all media – the more simple and relevant the better.

Recognition builds over time. The simple, relevant ideas are the ones your client can live with – and benefit from – for several years. *Just do it.*

Pick something that is distinctive and that your client can claim for his very own. Be wary of cliches.

If it comes to you easily, it may be that it comes so easily that it is used by everyone else in town – or, it may be just the opposite. There are no hard and fast rules.

Our best advice is look for a distinctive piece of language that you can own. If it can include your client's name, so much the better.

4. What's the short-term Promotion?

What can you do to "blow the doors off?"

Even strong Positions and memorable Propositions need an appealing Promotion to drive traffic, improve distribution or get in-store display.

It takes a Promotion to get things in motion.

Both you and the client need to understand that while a good ad can build awareness for the long-term, building traffic short-term depends on offering today's market-savvy consumers a dramatically attractive reason to visit.

It may be dramatic savings; it may be something else.

Years ago Myer-Emco, a Washington DC stereo store, became the #1 audio retailer in the market with a high-service strategy that included regular turntable clinics – and only one sale a year!

Hardly anyone uses a turntable any more, but there are still many types of in-store activities that can build traffic.

Many retail ads ask for immediate action of some kind. But some do not.

We suggest that most advertisers in most retail categories should offer some incentive in their initial advertising.

After they are well-established, pure "image" advertising is often a wise way for retailers to advertise, but, at the beginning, anything to stimulate traffic should be considered.

Different Audience – Different Reactions

Remember, audience reactions to the very same ad may be quite different.

Your ads will simultaneously reach those who are ready to buy, those who may be interested in the future, and those who are already regular customers.

But, for all of these groups, a promotional incentive can still serve to stimulate retail reactions.

For those ready to buy, it will help them select that store. For those interested in the future, it may help some of them advance the purchase date. And for regular customers, it may cause them to return sooner than they would otherwise.

A strong advertising schedule in your medium should be matched with strong promotions at the store level.

5. What's the long-term Plan?

This is a point we will make early and often.

Every piece of advertising should be part of a long-term program – one with a plan.

Each ad should contribute to an on-going sales and information message from the business.

The strategy for your local client should include the same kind of overall plan, perhaps on a less grand scale, as for any client anywhere. In planning the advertising, you'll need to act as marketing consultant, media planner, and creative director all in one.

So you'll need to keep the business, the audience, the media choices, and the actual creative strategy and execution all in mind. It's more work up front, but it pays off in continuity and cumulatively provides stronger ad messages.

Remember, it's not an ad – it's a campaign! Have a vision and a mission. Keep it up. And keep planning ahead.

PREPARING THE 5-P'S

It's fairly straightforward. You can do it in a work session with the client or alone in your office.

You may find that the first "P," the Problem is the one that you'll have to spend a lot of time thinking about.

Many clients will give you a long list of problems. But you will quickly find out that, quite often, it's the same list! Not enough sales. Not enough traffic. New competition. And so on.

The key is to find a way to turn those problems around so that you see the situation from the consumer's point of view.

And then create a campaign that: solves the consumer Problem, establishes a good Position in the marketplace, communicates a memorable Proposition, with a traffic-building Promotion, all as part of a long-term Plan.

Here's an example:

EXAMPLE: FRANKLIN'S

Problem.

Many newcomers to the market are unaware of Franklin's unique selection and service tradition. (Note how Franklin's problem is stated as a consumer problem – it's their problem that they don't know about this excellent store.)

Position.

Franklin's is #1 in the local market in terms of length of time and service in the community. They may also be #1 in selection of traditional styles.

Proposition.

In this case, we have two possible propositions for our meeting. Each is based on a marketplace reality. This will give the client a chance to get involved with our program, offer some input and make some decisions.

Our two choices are…

1. "Style that doesn't go out of style."

This proposition is based on Franklin's traditional selection and history in the market. A survey of styles offered in the store and some conversations with customers indicated that this was the approach to style favored by the people who will be the best Franklin's customer.

(Note that this leaves other differentiated fashion positions open for other men's clothing retailers.)

2. "Nobody fits you like Franklin's."

This is a proposition based on Franklin's unique service of providing size records as well as their overall service tradition.

Remember, it's not bad to have two good ideas. This way the client gets to choose. And, once they're involved in making the choice between one theme and another, they've already moved past the issue of whether or not to advertise. Now they're dealing with which ad to choose. This is progress.

Promotion.

Seasonal Sales. Item Specials.

If "Nobody fits you…" is chosen, suggest something related to size records.

For example, FREE RE-ALTERATIONS. Franklin's will re-alter something you purchased somewhere else when you buy a new item at Franklin's.

If "Style that doesn't go out of style" is chosen, prepare a calendar that highlights Franklin's tradition – the anniversaries of other events, famous birthdays, local celebrations, etc.

Long-term Plan.

Develop a schedule based on seasonal sales events with "image" advertising between events.

Look for high-margin sales opportunities (i.e. See the new Fall Line-Up). Too many retailers promote only low-margin sales (Clearance, etc.). Help your client maintain margins as best as possible.

Tie in with a local outdoor company for a rotating billboard that features the new theme – see if you can get some co-op money for this from a fashion vendor.

Implement an ongoing direct mail campaign targeted at people who move to town along with a relationship-building program for current customers.

Build a calendar with seasonal events alternating with the long-term customer recruitment program.

You might also want to set a goal – to achieve a certain number of new accounts – represented by a new size card. This might also inspire other complimentary programs – like direct mail and internal sales contests – all aimed at achieving that goal.

THE GE FOCUS SYSTEM

This three-step process helps you work through message development in a very useful sequence.

Here's how it works.

1. Focus on the Target

After determining your audience demographically, try to understand this audience as a person.

Remember, the same person can shop at both a hardware store and a gourmet deli. Even though they're the same person, they can be very different consumers in each store.

Talking to current customers or Heavy Users of the product category can often be a good way of getting to know that person in depth.

2. Focus on the Proposition

"The Proposition relates what we know about the product to what we've learned about the Receiver." The proposition is a strategic statement, not necessarily a headline, though if you had to set it in type and run it tomorrow, it would be useful.

Your proposition tells the customer that if you use this product (or shop at this store) you will get a certain benefit.

This proposition also relates to The Problem the Advertising Must Solve and your client's Position.

3. Dramatize the Proposition

Now it's time to get creative – find a way to communicate that proposition in a dramatic way.

Most of the ad themes you remember are propositions.

And don't forget that your dramatization can also have a visual (or audio) component to make it more memorable.

Legendary ad man, George Lois (originally an art director) looks for *"words that bristle with visual imagery."*

A Quick Exercise

Write down some ad themes you remember (like *You Deserve a Break Today*) and restate them as simple propositions (a meal at McDonald's is a pleasant change-of-pace).

This can help you learn to work the other way around.

Three Kinds of Thinking

The Focus System involves different kinds of thinking:

1. Thinking about the Receiver uses analysis and insight.

2. Thinking about the Proposition uses strategic thinking.

3. Dramatization of the Proposition usually involves some type of creative thinking.

EXAMPLE: FRANKLIN'S

Let's take a look at our friends at Franklin's again, this time using the GE Focus System.

Focus on the Receiver

The Franklin's target is male. There is a wide age range, but they tend to be concerned with being dressed appropriately.

Through interviews, you discover that Franklin's current customers appreciate the high level of service and, for major purchases such as suits and sport coats, they find the size file to be not only convenient, but to represent that they are important to Franklin's.

Dramatize The Proposition

Here, a case can be made for each proposition (Style that never goes out of style/Nobody fits you...), since both factors are important to Franklin's target.

A legitimate standard for judgment could be which Proposition can be best dramatized.

For creative development, a small amount of money could be budgeted to have two free-lance teams address both propostions.

Notice how the GE System provides a sequence for evaluation and development – by understanding the Receiver first, you can judge the Proposition against your knowledge of the Receiver.

Having agreed upon a basic proposition, you can then focus on making it as dramatic and memorable as possible.

Client Approval

It is also possible to get client approval at each stage.

For "difficult" clients, this can be a way to make the process more efficient and effective.

A first meeting might involve developing a shared understanding of the Target.

The second meeting would involve agreeing upon a basic selling proposition. At this stage, it won't matter if the language is awkward, and you can get the client to clearly state the benefit he offers.

Finally, at the third meeting, you can focus on dramatizing the proposition that has already been agreed upon.

THE 3-PART STRATEGY STATEMENT

Here's a standard way of stating a strategy that can be done quickly. Clients and agencies have been known to spend many months writing strategy statements in this simple format – but you might not have that luxury.

You might even have to write it while you're meeting with your client – to get agreement on the next step of your program.

The format has three parts:

An Objective Statement

A Support Statement

A Tone or Brand Character Statement

You should try to use objective and somewhat neutral language in writing the statement – i.e. "Peter Paul offers a choice of candy bars" – <u>not</u> *Sometimes you feel like a nut.*

Try to avoid executional phrases in the statement – a strategy is a guide to advertising, not an ad.

Here's how it goes...

1. The Objective Statement

The Objective Statement is a simple sentence that links the Target Audience, the Product (or Store) and the Benefit.

It is usually stated this way.

"Advertising will convince (Target Audience) that (Product) will (Benefit Statement)."

2. The Support Statement

The Support Statement provides the "Reasons Why" the Benefit is delivered. It is often done with bullet points, that list Support points in order of importance.

Generally, the most important Support point is always used and others are used as the situation warrants.

It usually begins this way. "Support will be…".

3. The Tone or Brand Character Statement

Here, we either want to describe the appropriate attitude for the advertising (Tone Statement) or the basic Position or personality of the Brand (Brand Character Statement).

There are no hard and fast formats for this part of the statement, though they often start "Tone will be…" or "(Name of Brand) will be portrayed as…".

This can be helpful in getting up-front agreement as to what kind of advertising is right for the brand.

EXAMPLE: FRANKLIN'S

Let's say, after much difficulty, you have been able to schedule a meeting at Franklin's.

They discuss their business with you and after listening and taking notes, you write down a three part statement that reads as follows…

Advertising will convince Adult Males that Franklin's offers the right fashions and the right fit (at the right price).

Support will be:

• Franklin's wide selection of traditional styles (which won't go out of style).

• Franklin's "dedication to the right fit" including a personalized record of your exact measurements.

• Name brands and good values.

Tone will be personal and service-oriented (and will avoid extreme fashion trends).

Note the use of parentheses. Sometimes you want to make an implicit point and sometimes there will be something that you do not want to say all of the time.

In this case, (at the right price) communicated that you would talk about prices when appropriate.

The other two parentheses, set the stage for a possible "Against" position against newer "trendier" competitors and also serves to signal any creative group that Franklin's fashion personality should emphasize traditional fashions.

It may be possible to get some level of agreement – or at least an agreement that allows you to prepare some "spec" work for a subsequent meeting. You can now go ahead with some common agreement.

WHICH SHOULD YOU USE?

At different times, each of these formats will be useful.

In addition, your newspaper or radio station will often have formats and worksheets.

Some of them may also have a place for useful information, such as budgets, due dates, and legal requirements.

You will also find that all three formats we have reviewed have a quite a lot in common.

Each has a place to analyze the business problem.

Each has a place to talk about the Target Consumer.

Each has a place to list the Benefit or the Proposition.

Pick the one that works for you – or make your own.

Becoming familiar with a good work plan will give you a place to organize the necessary information you need to develop messages that work in the marketplace.

MESSAGE DEVELOPMENT EXERCISE:

This is a good time to try a Message Development Exercise. Use each of the formats to develop your message.

For this exercise, select a current or prospective client where you already know a good deal about their business and their target – so your time can be spent on the actual development of the message strategy – as opposed to the initial groundwork necessary in developing marketing background and Target Customer information.

Fill out each of the three formats. Usually, you'll find them consistent with each other.

But, you might find that one of the formats provides you with a new insight – because it caused you to make a new and different connection.

11.
MESSAGES.
GETTING IT DONE.

Now let's talk about some of the basics you'll need to know to craft the best possible message in your medium.

In this chapter, we'll cover some basics on Propositions and Selling Ideas, copywriting principles and a bit about design – all designed to get you started with the right habits.

Then we'll give you some beginner's tips on working in the various media forms.

MORE BASIC ASSUMPTIONS

As we've mentioned, you will probably do better if you can team up with skilled message crafters – designers, engineers, editors, etc.

But, for the purposes of this chapter, we'll still assume that you're pretty much on your own.

We'll also assume you need to develop a message based either on the strategy you developed in the previous chapter or on a similar piece of information – like an advertising approach currently running in another medium (i.e. a radio ad for a potential client who's running newspaper).

In this chapter, we'll skim the surface of a number of topics related to crafting that message in the various media forms. We won't turn you into a polished professional, but we'll help you get started with the right habits.

At the end of this book, we've listed other resources where you can find out more about crafting messages for your medium.

PROPOSITION BASICS

A proposition is a proposal. Your ad will essentially make the proposition, "use this product and you will receive this benefit."

Your proposition will most likely be an involving expression of the benefit.

Theme, Slogan, Selling Idea...

Whatever you call it, your message needs a focus.

We believe that this focus should be some sort of selling proposition – a statement about the product that communicates a benefit to the consumer. Better yet, it should be an "involving statement of the benefit."

This can be direct or implied.

Direct or Implied Benefit Statements

Propositions can be a direct statement of benefit (*Brown's Chicken – It Tastes Better*) or it can be an implied benefit (*We're #1*).

Now, on the face of it, telling someone you're #1 might not seem like a benefit. But customers are very good at reading benefits into these types of statements.

Think of what #1 implies. It means more volume – which means possibly a better price due to quantity buying or lower margins. Better selection is also implied by a #1 claim.

And, whether true or not, consumer satisfaction, service and knowledgeability are also implied by this statement.

So, while it may be true that "#1 is not a benefit," it's also true that implied benefits can be easily derived from certain types of propositions.

Your proposition can state a benefit directly, or the benefit can be implied.

Facts and Feelings

Many ads contain both facts and feelings. Propositions can be based on facts – Big Mac, fries and Coke for $1.99 – or they can be based on feelings – *You Deserve a Break Today*.

A good proposition connects with the right facts and the right feelings.

The Need for Campaigns

The proposition should also work in all media.

That's why, even though you may be working in just one medium, you should become somewhat familiar with all of them – and learn the strength of each.

Many clients think first about the print ads and then try to fit the print ads into radio – and sometimes television.

Many times the same ads that were effective in print do not translate well into the other media. Yet, if the only thing the ads have in common is the store logo, cumulative impact is lost and there is no real campaign.

Whichever medium you work for, work to make the advertising as strong as possible across differing media.

This makes for better advertising and helps make sure that all ads come from the same basic market thinking.

For the sales rep, this also means better control of the account – whatever medium you work with.

We call it "The Campaign Approach."

FINDING THE SELLING IDEA

As you look for the right Selling Idea for your campaign, you might find this section of the book a bit frustrating. You want answers, and this area is one where the right answers are critical.

At the same time, all we can offer you are some general approaches used by people who solve these problems regularly. They are useful and have been proven effective – but the rest is up to you.

Any idea, including a Selling Idea, is "a new combination of previously existing elements." Once again, it's about making the right connections.

Here are two interesting approaches to making those connections, "The Sweet Spot" and "Triggering Events."

"The Sweet Spot"

In her book, *Hitting The Sweet Spot*, Lisa Fortini-Campbell talks about this combination in terms of insights – an insight into how the consumer thinks about the brand or category and an insight into other aspects of the consumer – which can often be combined into a powerful message.

This "Sweet Spot" contains a "truth" that consumers recognize as being true for them – and they read themselves into the message. It can be as rational as looking for the best price on a car battery or as emotional as worrying about being stranded with a dead car battery.

And, of course, it can be both.

Alamo Rent-a-Car combines feelings about the open road *(The Miles of Alamo Country)* with the fact of free mileage *(where all the miles are free).*

Look for the right combination of facts and feelings as you build your message. And try to hit that "Sweet Spot."

"Triggering Events"

Chris Lytle, at The AdVisory Board, recommends looking for "triggering events." This is a smart, effective, real-world way to develop insights into effective selling.

Simply put, try to discover the events in a consumer's life that trigger a purchase decision. For example, that sound your car makes when it needs a new battery – or, worse yet, no sound at all. This is a triggering event.

To discover that event, you might want to ask customers why they're here today instead of yesterday or tomorrow.

Look for recent stories based on customer behavior. Ask the sales people or the store manager – always a good source of this information.

You might want to build your Selling Idea on that event – perhaps "you deserve a break today."

Once you have your idea, you need to turn it into an ad or commercial – you need to write it with style.

BASICS ON WRITING STYLE

This is covered at greater length in newer books like *The Copy Workshop Workbook*, or in classics like *Tested Advertising Methods*, by John Caples.

Here are some basics of contemporary copywriting style (excerpted from *The Copy Workshop Workbook*).

1. Short simple sentences
"Make it simple. Make it memorable."
Leo Burnett said that. It's good advice.
Get to the point quickly.

2. Active verbs and a positive attitude
Make your message active and upbeat.

3. Parallel construction
Consistency of construction helps make it easier for people to understand what you say.

Consistency of construction helps organize the information in your message.

4. Alliteration, assonance and rhyme
This has to do with the sound of words.

Alliteration comes from similar beginning sounds of words. Like *"Let it be Lowenbrau."*

Assonance comes from similar internal sounds of words. Like *"Invest in Karastan."*

Rhyme, of course, comes from similar sounds at the end of words. Like *"For all you do, this Bud's for you."*

Repetition creates both alliteration and rhyme in *"Plop. Plop. Fizz. Fizz. Oh what a relief it is."*

Good writing sounds good.

These memorable lines also have one more thing....

Rhythm

All good copy's got rhythm.

Most good copy has a rhythmic flow that organizes your message in a clear, upbeat way.

The reader or listener moves with you.

Whether read aloud or silently, your copy should have a strong, natural, easy-to-follow rhythm.

Relevance

Good copy speaks the language of the consumer.

Even though it's one-way communication, it seems to create an involving dialogue with the reader or listener.

When asked about their favorite ads, consumers may say things like, "It talks to me." Or, "It seems like they know me." Or, "They understand where I'm coming from."

Or, simply, "It interested me." As Howard Gossage said, *"People read what interests them; sometimes it's advertising."*

Whatever the technical aspects of your writing, in the final analysis, it will be judged by the reaction of the audience.

In virtually every case, we are most interested in consumers reading themselves into the message – as individuals.

Because when people read themselves into your ad, that's the real breakthrough.

Write your message with the receiver in mind.

An Example

Here's a good example of a proposition –

"Choosy Mothers Choose Jif."

Now, it's clear that this is a Selling Idea, but let's take a quick look at it. First, the Benefit is implied. Obviously, there will be some reasons why "choosy mothers" will choose the product, but it is not directly stated.

Second, it is a rhythmic and memorable set of words. It has both rhyme and alliteration. And it most certainly has rhythm.

Finally, it has relevance.

Peanut butter is a category that mothers control – it's food.

Nutritional content is important. Mothers (the target) know this – so the meaningfulness of the statement is clear.

Direct or Implied, Fact or Feeling, your proposition should have characteristics that make it worth repeating.

HEADLINE HINTS:

Anyone who writes copy should take a look at John Caples' book, *Tested Advertising Methods*. (If you're in direct response, it should probably be mandatory.)

Here are some hints on headline writing from this classic.

News Headlines

1) Begin your headline with the word "announcing"
2) Use words that have an announcement quality
3) Begin your headline with the word "new"
4) Begin your headline with the word "now"
5) Begin with the words "at last"
6) Put a date in your headline
7) Write your headline in news style

Headlines That Deal With Price

8) Feature the price in your headline
9) Feature reduced price
10) Feature a special merchandising offer
11) Feature a reduced payment plan
12) Feature a free offer
13) Offer information of value
14) Tell a story

Use Key Words in Headlines

Begin your headline with the word(s)

15) "How to"   19) "Who else"
16) "How"   20) "Wanted"
17) "Why"   21) "This"
18) "Which"   22) "Advice"

Other Effective Headline Approaches

23) Use a testimonial-style headline
24) Offer a test
25) Use a one-word headline
26) Use a two-word headline
27) Warn the reader to delay buying
28) Let the advertiser speak directly to the audience
29) Address your headline to a specific person/group

Naturally, no set of rules or hints is perfect, but you may be surprised at how often this time-tested advice is useful.

MORE TIPS

"Copy Chasers," which specializes in business to business writing for *Crain's*, also has a few good tips:

- **Invite the Reader**
- **Promise a Reward**
- **Back up the Promise**
- **Have a Logical Sequence**
- **Talk Person to Person**
- **Be Easy to Read**
- **Reflect the Company Character**

Many other excellent books offer tips of their own – take a look at the Resources section in back.

THE BASICS – TYPE

Next, let's cover the way your words are translated onto the printed page – type. Here's a quick introduction to the language of type and typography.

Typefaces – Fonts & Families

Typefaces are also called **fonts.**

Many fonts are organized into families, which include regular, *italic* and **bold** versions of the same typeface. Sometimes there is also a light version of the face.

There may also be a condensed version of the typeface, which allows more words per line, as well as *italic condensed* and **bold condensed** versions.

Though most people do not automatically think of typefaces when they think of memorable ads, a good type choice can be quite important. Or, more to the point, a bad one can be quite harmful.

Typefaces convey the style and tone of the ad.

They give visual clues to the reader.

They can make your message more formal, more classic, more casual, or more modern.

While there are many typefaces, only a relative few are used on a regular basis.

Unusual fonts, generally only used in headlines or logo treatments, are sometimes called **display faces.**

Here are some other typeface terms to know:

Serif

This is the kind of type used in most books and much copy. Serif type has a tail or extra strokes on each letter.

Many experts think serif type is the easiest to read for longer copy – some of the easiest-to-read are called "reader faces." The tail strokes lead the reader to the next letter and the next word.

In the United States, we learn to read with letters and words that have this detail. Times, Century (Century Schoolbook is a similar face) and Garamond are some common serif typefaces.

This book was set in ITC Century.

This is Times. Note how the letters are slightly more condensed.

This is Garamond. The letters have a slight bit of sculpting and a different proportion for a slightly more elegant look.

Sometimes a client wants to pick a typeface that no one else is using. As long as it is readable and appropriate for the business, this can work well and create a distinctive look.

One example of this choice is United Airlines which picked *Bookman Italic,* a typeface rarely used, for its logo and headlines. A fast rule, however, is that body copy must be easily read.

Sans Serif or Sanserif

Quite simply, this kind of type does not have a serif.

The subhead copy in this book is a sans serif face.

It is **Franklin Gothic.**

Sans serif fonts tend to be more modern looking, and can convey more of a news feeling – many newspaper headlines are set in some form of sans serif (or sanserif).

Sans serif type can work well in headlines and subheads, but can be very difficult to read in longer body copy.

Here are some popular sans serif faces.

Futura Light. Futura. **Futura Bold.**

Here's Helvetica. **Helvetica Bold Condensed.** *Helvetica Black Italic.*

This is set in Helvetica Condensed. See how more words fit?

Type sizes

Points refer to vertical size. Type sizes range from 5-point to 72-point – and even larger.

Most body copy in ads ranges from 10 to 14 points.

This book was set in 12 point type. (Actually, it's 11.5.)

This is 14 point.

This is 10 point. This is 8 point.

This is 6 point – sometimes called "mouse type." It's about as small as you can go.

Leading

Leading (pronounced "ledding") is the space between lines of copy. Thus, you may specify copy that is 10 over 14 (10/14) referring to the basic space (14 points deep) and the size of type (10 points) that will be placed in it.

This book was 14/16 – 14 point type with 16 points of leading.

By the way, the word originates from the early days of hand type-setting. To add space between lines, the typesetters would insert strips of lead. Thus, leading.

A "Rule of Thumb"

One rule of thumb is to never use more than two typefaces – or type families – within one ad.

Many ads have only one with possible differing sizes and "weights" (italic, bold or plain) co-existing.

This book has a "display" face, **Franklin Gothic,** and a "reader" face ITC Century.

Vertical and Horizontal – Points and Picas

There are 72 "points" of type in one inch.

Again, these are vertical measures.

The horizontal measure is "Picas."

There are six of these to an inch.

Computer-based typesetting

The craft of typography was once controlled by a whole system of typehouses – typographers were skilled craftsmen, schooled in the art of producing readable and well-designed information.

Today, we can each set type with the computer sitting on our desktop. There's good news and bad news in this.

The good news is that sophisticated print production resources once only available to large advertisers and pubications are now available to virtually everyone.

The bad news is that much type is being handled without the skill and craft that makes it most effective.

Computers merely do what we tell them to do – and, all too often, we are not skilled craftsmen.

Work to learn the basics of typography.

And, for the overall type design of your campaign, try to involve knowledgeable people – so that your client benefits from the best type design.

Good typography pays off in improved readability.

THE BASICS – DESIGN

The importance of design

Visual communication is a larger and larger part of the job that must be done in all print media – as well as television. And it's a skill that demands much in the way of time, talent and tools.

Good design also involves issues like proportion, balance, contrast, and visual flow. And good designers know how to use these tools.

To be a good design partner, you need to know the basics.

Design is an important aspect in projecting client image. It is the way to visually organize all the elements in the finished ad so that they all come together.

We all know that an ad with lots of white space and script writing would probably work better for a classic French restaurant than for a simple family diner – or a pizza parlor (unless, perhaps, they were introducing gourmet pizza).

Design must follow simply from the client type and purpose. "Form follows function."

While it is true that an ad should first grab attention, all parts of the design must work together.

Four Basic Design Principles:

The Non-Designer's Design Book, by Robin Williams (Peachpit Press) is an excellent introduction to the basics of design. The four basic principles of design organization are:

Proximity. How near things are to each other.

Grouping related elements together, helps organize your information visually.

When a number of elements are organized together into one element (like a picture of an item, its price and descriptive copy), they are perceived as more of a single unit.

Often, retailers want to feature a number of items in one ad. This principle is key to organizing all of that information.

Alignment. When things are lined up with each other, this also helps organize the page visually.

Elements should have a visual connection with each other – invisible lines that help organize the page.

Aligning left or right margins can help, as can aligning things in the center.

Repetition. This is another way to say "consistency." The repetition of certain visual elements – type size, for example

– also helps pull a design together. It both unifies the design and adds visual interest.

By repeating design elements (like type sizes or bullet points), you help organize the information for the reader.

Contrast. This is an important way to add visual interest.

Don't make everything the same weight and the same size – use contrast to show the reader what's important.

In addition to adding interest, contrast also helps to visually organize the information on the page.

In the design of an advertisement, you will find these design principles extremely helpful. As you learn, it's a good idea to learn by working with a good graphic designer.

And be sure to look for Ms. Williams excellent book to understand these principles further.

SIX PRINT DESIGN ELEMENTS:

Generally speaking, there are six parts to a local retail ad – though not all six are present in every ad.

You will often have to decide how to use these elements in the ad you are planning and designing for each of your clients.

The six elements are:

1. **Headline** (and subheads)
2. **Visual or graphic**
3. **Body copy** (and bullet points)
4. **Client logo or identification** (or slogo)
5. **Border or definition**
6. **White space**

Let's talk briefly about each of these elements or parts.

1. Headline

The headline is like a book title.

Along with the visual or graphic, it should be an attention grabber. While it can be very short, particularly if the ad is very small, it should give the reader an essential piece of information (fact or feeling) that draws them into the ad.

If the headline doesn't work, the reader most likely won't go any further. Set an objective for the headline – to get the attention of the reader you want as a customer.

Subheads

You can also use subheads effectively. In essence, subheads tell more bits and pieces of the story and help organize the ad.

Subheads sustain reader attention and help the reader iden-tify new information.

This is particularly important for retailers offering multiple items, or items with multiple benefits or sales points.

A good use of headline and subheads can tell a fairly complete story – even without reading the body copy for all the details.

2. Visual or graphic

Along with the headline, this is the other important element in drawing the reader into the ad.

Visuals for local ads may be anything from line drawings to photographs – many local retail ads show the product itself.

This can be very effective as a draw for getting people to come in and ask for a specific product and to reach people shopping for that specific product.

Tires and batteries are good examples of this use of illustration. Though they aren't particularly unique or interesting as visuals, they help identify the item for those in the market at the moment – they connect with those "triggering events."

But you should work to expand the range of visuals and visual techniques you use and, of course, make them appropriate for the client and relevant to the customer.

For example, a cartoon can work well for a pizza parlor and an art photograph for an exclusive clothing store. Choose the graphic style carefully – you'll want to continue it throughout the campaign.

Consistency is another important factor in developing the cumulative power of a campaign.

3. Body copy

Here's where you tell your story.

Often, there is not much body copy in a local ad.

But what there is should make the reader even more interested. Body copy in local ads usually gives very specific information – selection, size, price, etc. And, of course, location information, such as the address and phone number. This type of information may be very important to a customer trying to decide whether or not to get in the car and drive to the store.

Remember that local ads often want immediate action as a result. Write to achieve that goal.

• **Bullet points**

• Sometimes bullet points take the place of narrative copy. They list benefits, features and other appropriate information in a way that is easy for the reader to understand.

4. Client Logo or identification

This is one of the important ways you build recognition for your client. The client may already have a logo or, in some cases, you may have to design one.

A logo should distinguish that client from all others in the local market and particularly in the same store or business category. A logo must be something you can use from now on, so the choice of logo design is critical.

"The Slogo"

The logo unit may also integrate into its design a long-term campaign theme, or slogan. Some people call the integrated logo and slogan unit, "The Slogo."

5. Borders

Borders are not used in every ad.

But there must be some technique to set the ad apart from those adjoining it or your client's message will merge with those around it. Borders can help give impact to the ad.

Naturally, they should be appropriate.

6. White space

White space is the element most people forget.

It's the part of the ad that doesn't have anything in it. There may be only a little. Or there may be a lot.

You can use white space to make other parts of your ad more important – whether you're working on a 1-column by 3-inch ad or a full page in a newspaper.

White space helps you make more effective use of the other elements in your ad.

Layout pointers

Still assuming there's no one around to help, a good way to begin is to outline the space on a plain piece of white paper.

There are two basic ways to approach the design of an ad – words first or pictures first.

For some people, looking at space allows them to begin to design the elements in their minds.

Then they can begin to transfer that overall image to the paper (or computer) and adjust it.

For others, digging right in with a pencil or pen or typing away at the computer works better.

Ask yourself if you are a person who thinks of the headline or body copy first. If so, you are a more word-oriented person.

If you see the visual or the whole ad design first, you are a more visually-oriented person.

These orientations may dictate the way in which you begin your ad design. Words first or pictures first.

Computers

As mentioned, many local ads are designed and written on computers. There are many good packages for both DOS and MAC systems that allow the designer and writer to produce professional, camera-ready ads.

Basic design principles still apply. Remember, the computer only does what you tell it to – but you can produce a variety of choices for the client in a relatively short amount of time.

Graphic Designers

While many papers and local magazines have graphic designers to produce ads for clients, smaller organizations may not.

You may find an investment of time in learning a computer design program will pay off in big dividends for you and for your clients as well.

Two other helpful approaches:

1. Develop some basic design solutions that work well – a few type and layout solutions that you know how to implement.

2. Have a professional design a format for your client.

You'll pay more for the first few ads, but after the format is developed, you can often change the ads in a relatively straightforward manner – one that you can handle.

The photo, headline and copy may change but the logo elements and the overall design, proportion and typography will stay the same.

This allows you to combine good design and continuity for your campaign in a cost-effective way. Remember to prepare your client for the fact that the first layout may be costly.

The most important thing

The most important thing about layout is that the reader is led naturally and easily through all the elements.

The purpose of the layout is to make it easy for the reader to get the information in the ad.

Some very talented designers may suggest interesting and "challenging" design solutions. For some types of advertising and advertising problems, they can be quite effective.

But if the ad seems a bit hard to read, inappropriate for your audience or not relevant to the product or the product category, you are entitled to question some decisions.

Sometimes the designer has made good decisions and once you understand their approach (they should be able to explain it to you), you may agree.

If you do agree, remember – their explanation may also help you sell the design to the client.

Sometimes, the designer was just bored with doing it the same old way and that's not usually a very good reason.

As time goes by, you will become better at working with these talented contributors to your clients' success and you will find you work with some very well.

When you are doing your layout, experiment with different size visuals. While it may seem risky to use a large visual in a small ad (or vice versa), it works for some clients.

Generally speaking, the simpler the layout the better.

The most usual layout for local ads is headline on top, followed by visual, body copy and logo. The visual may be on one side with the body copy next to it. The size of the ad dictates the kind of layout you can do.

Now it's time for some tips that are more media-specific.

BASICS FOR NEWSPAPER

News

The newspaper is about news.

That includes product news.

For the most part, your newspaper advertising should project some sort of immediacy.

Continuity

Continuity is also important, since many customers are only in the market for products infrequently. Holding to a regular and recognizable look and positioning theme can be helpful in establishing your client in the consumer's mind.

Then, when the day comes that the customer is in the market, your client will have the advantage.

Information

Whether it's a store address or price information, this is also important to the reader.

Even if it's set in small type, useful purchasing information is one of the things that make newspapers such an important and effective medium.

Make sure your client's newspaper campaign delivers in these three dimensions – news, continuity and information.

Impact and Image

There's another important use of the newspaper for all advertisers – to make an impact in the marketplace.

Handsome full color image ads for the holiday season, bold editorial-style ads addressing an important topic, and fresh, new, eye-catching ads introducing us to a new store, a new product, or a new service are other effective ways to use newspaper.

Display

Display ads often work to deliver impact and image.

For larger retailers, they also often work to convey a large amount of product information.

Small Space

Small, clever ads can be memorable and make a business stand out. A series of them (especially with a campaign approach in both layout and copy style) can translate into a cohesive package for the advertiser with the advantages of both reach and frequency within the target audience.

Print ads can be very small – 1 column by 3 or 4 inches – and still be very effective. Each ad should be complete in itself yet part of an ongoing series of messages about the business.

One simple message per ad times many ads can create a powerful message in the reader's mind.

Some small businesses may run two, three, or more ads per issue of a newspaper or magazine.

Seeing the same general layout and logo – many times in the same place – on successive pages can have a great deal of impact on the reader.

FEARRINGTON FARMS

Fearrington Farms is a village developed on an old farm about ten miles south of a college town of 50,000 people.

The development has won a number of design awards. It is a real village, with a village center that contains a market, post office, bookstore, bank, and a number of other features.

A few years ago, when the village was just developing, Fearrington ran a number of small ads to draw local people down to the market where there was a deli and small restaurant.

The ads were very small – 1-column by 4 inches. Three things made this campaign work well:

1) The design of the ads – they were distinctive and well-planned.

2) The placement of two to four ads on consecutive pages of the local newspaper rather than one large ad for the same cost.

3) The consistency of the campaign. They were easily identified, built recognition, and piqued interest.

The ads worked to build traffic and the quality of the experience built repeat business – with satisfied customers. These small ads were the catalyst.

Small can be beautiful

Ads don't have to be big to be effective.

In this case, the creative thinking and design planning that went into the beginning of the advertising effort increased effectiveness.

Repeating this quality design eventually saved far more than the extra time and money that was spent on the initial design work.

Other lessons to be learned are the power of a relevant logo and the payoff from consistency.

BASICS FOR RADIO

A good radio commercial can have impact, but repetition and frequency count as well.

Since radio is often a "background" medium, the message may need some repeating to sink in. Some information might not be picked up or remembered the first time.

The good news is that tighter radio demographics make it easier for you to repeat your message to the same audience.

Radio fits most local budgets and the combination of print and radio serves many smaller businesses quite effectively.

Some Sound Advice

Just as you develop a unique look in print, remember that all the things that create the individual sound of your commercial – announcer, music, and sound effects – are key to establishing your long-term brand image.

Time, Tempo, and Talent

As you write your commercial, think of a 60 second time line. How much do you spend at the beginning establishing context?

Where on that time line do you pay off your proposition?

Sometimes, looking at your commercial in this way can give you a better perspective on the structure of your spot.

How fast do you move along the time line? That's Tempo.

By controlling the tempo of your commercial, you can add distinctiveness. Try to develop a pace that's appropriate for the message you want to communicate.

Don't just rush to pack everything into those sixty seconds. Say too much and people won't remember.

Finally, look for the most talented people in your market – and at your station. The best people can take your words and make them more persuasive and pleasing to the ear. Sometimes it's not just *what* you say or *how* you say it. It's *who* says it.

Pitch, Situation, and Song

There are three basic types of radio commercial.

The Pitch – basically an announcer talking to you.

The Situation – some sort of mini-drama where the product plays an important part.

The Song – a jingle or other piece of music that often repeats the client's slogan.

And, of course, they're often used in combination.

For example, a local fast food franchise might use a nationally produced musical jingle and have a local announcer read special promotional copy over the jingle "bed."

A very interesting book with a 60-second title, *Effective Radio Advertising. A Guide to Winning Customers with Targeted Campaigns and Creative Commercials* (Lexington Books) offers some surprisingly useful advice.

The authors (Weinberger, Campbell, Brody) examine a range of successful radio commercials showing how different types of commercials work for different types of products.

For example, expensive "considered purchase" products respond well to fact-based commercials. "Fun" products, like snack foods, respond well to jingles and comedy.

So, even though there is a wide range of creative opportunity in radio, certain types of products can be sold more effectively with certain approaches.

And, in terms of what those approaches are, it's almost always some version of The Pitch, The Situation, and The Song.

Beds, Donuts, and Tags

The structure of some commercials has an announcer read over background music. That's a musical "bed."

Sometimes, there is a place for the announcer in the middle of a pre-recorded musical commercial. That's a "donut."

And often, there is a place at the end of the commercial to read localized copy. It may be a special promotional offer or a local store address. That's a tag.

Structure – Context, Content, Conclusion

Like so many other things, a good radio commercial has a Beginning, a Middle, and an End.

At the Beginning of a commercial, you usually need to establish Context – what the commercial is about – whether it's for oil changes or Oil of Olay.

In the Middle, you deliver the Content of your message.

At the End, your commercial should have a Conclusion, a Pay-Off, a Call to Action. This is the reason for the commercial – the point you are driving home.

The overall proportion of your commercial should let the structure develop naturally.

Linkage

One other aspect of radio that's much different from print also has to do with time – your listener can't go back and hear something he or she missed.

So your writing has to help the listener keep track.

Here's a technique that can help – we call it **linkage.**

It comes from *linking* the words in your sentences to the sentences before and after. Here's an example.

"When you write a radio commercial, it should be easy to follow. When it's easy to follow, it's easy to understand. And when it's easy to understand, chances are, you're linking the copy. That's what we call Linkage."

Listen and Learn

Those are but some of the basics of radio. As you work in this industry, one of your best resources will be the experienced people who produce great radio commercials.

Dick Orkin's Radio Ranch, and others, have demo reels of their best commercials. The **Radio Advertising Bureau** and **Interep** have reels of excellent commercials available.

Get those tapes. Listen and study. Commercials done by the best in our industry are a lesson in themselves.

As you begin, try to find the best people at your station to help you. As time goes by, you'll become more confident and more capable of writing radio for your clients.

CENTURY FORD

When Don Klemkowicz took over Century Ford in Rockville, Maryland, just outside Washington DC, he had two objectives.

First, he wanted to position himself within the Washington market as the Ford dealer that provided excellent service. He upgraded his service department and, with his agency, developed an image radio campaign with the theme, *"At Your Service."*

Second, he saw one more growing opportunity – trucks.

He looked outward, past the suburbs and all the way to West Virginia. He also selected a different set of radio stations and projected an entirely different image for their complete line of Ford Trucks.

They used a hard-driving country and western music track with the theme, *"The Best Truckin' Deal in Town."* The music included various length "donuts" to present information on their truck capabilities.

One of the things that made the whole package distinctive was the Niche Leadership position they staked out for themselves – many other dealers had trucks, but no one staked such an assertive claim in the category.

The memorable theme and the distinctive radio commercial, matched up with radio demographics, reached an audience with lots of potential truck customers for Century Ford.

Here's how it looks with our "Five P's."

The Problem. Nobody thought of Century Ford (or anyone else) as a truck expert.

The Position. A Niche Leadership Position. #1 for trucks – with Ford's complete truck line.

The Proposition. Best Deal, Best Trucks, Best Service. Very assumptive – again, no one else was doing much of anything at the time.

The Short-Term Promotion. The creative was structured to accomodate an on-going series of deal-oriented truck offers.

The Long Term Plan. Repetition of the Position and the Proposition would establish Century Ford as the leader in the truck category. It worked.

MUSIC INTRO

Roll on over, Climb aboard.

They got your truck at – Century Ford.

They got the best truckin' service,
      best truck line around

They got the best –
      truckin' deal in town.

LOCAL ANNOUNCER BED - 27 seconds

They got the best truckin' service,
      best truck line around

They got the best –
      truckin' deal in town.

LOCAL ANNOUNCER TAG - 9 seconds

MUSIC BUTTON.

The Seven Word Program

Chris Lytle of the AdVisory Board says you should ask yourself, *"What seven words do I want to PROGRAM into the people who won't buy this week?"*

Remember, radio is great for building up frequency with a narrow audience. Focus on what you want that audience to remember about your client – so when they are in the market, those seven words will come to mind.

BASICS OF TELEVISION

A/V – A to Z

First, the words and pictures should go together.

That's called audio-visual integration and it's still key to successful communication on television.

Second, the number of ways you can put words and pictures together are almost infinite. Television is a wonderfully creative medium and there is no way that this short chapter can tell you all there is to know.

But we would like to make a few useful observations.

Exciting Change – Exciting Growth

Creating television commercials has traditionally been complex and expensive. Low-budget commercials usually look like low-budget commercials. But this is changing.

With the growth of cable TV and computer technology, it's changing in two exciting ways.

First, with cable, television advertising is becoming more affordable for more advertisers. Audiences and production budgets may be small, but it's television – and it's affordable for more local businesses.

Second, with more computer processing capacity, previously expensive computer graphics and video editing can now fit on a large desktop computer – and there are more people who can do this editing and production work.

The result is local TV production using better graphics and better techniques. Every day, local advertisers, video production houses and media companies are finding creative ways to overcome production budget limitations.

Local Product Budgets

Your TV spot may be competing against expensive national commercials produced for hundreds of thousands of dollars.

Still, if done well, local audiences will respond to well-done locally-produced television commercials.

One of the first things to think about is how you can visually dramatize your Selling Idea. It's a good idea to look for cost-effective ways to generate the visuals you need.

Sometimes, good visual material is made available to you. For example, car dealers often have "stock footage" of new car models sent to them by the manufacturer.

Sometimes a little creative thinking will help discover a production partner who will help you create a great spot.

Local Production Partners

If you work at a station, there will be facilities and crew available – though you will usually have to share them with the local news, which takes top priority at the station.

Many cable operations have production staff and facilities – or arrangements with other suppliers.

Get acquainted with the resources available – local video camera people, video graphic artists, and video editors.

Sometimes, they're at your station and sometimes not. Wherever they are, they can be invaluable in achieving good television commercials at a reasonable cost.

Often, they are as interested as you are in maximizing the value of your local TV commercial – so you can get extra time and attention paid to your commercial without paying extra.

The production people will then use these examples as part of their presentation – to get more work with bigger budgets.

So your first step in writing a TV commercial may be finding those who can produce your TV commercial, and then discovering what they can do well.

Good advice

You can write the commercial first and then try to find the production resources to produce it. Or, you can get to know your production resources and then write a commercial that they can produce well.

For a beginning media rep and a small production budget, we think this is good advice.

ARCHWAY COOKIES

Jim Milan at WEWS (Channel 5) in Cleveland took a look at the sponsors of the Children's Miracle Network (CMN) Telethon. He saw that one of them was Archway Cookies, which had a large bakery in Ohio.

He contacted Archway Cookies to discuss a program that tied together Channel 5's CMN activities with some additional local opportunities.

Working with Archway management, he developed a program that included:

• A spot schedule during Archway's promotion.

• Coverage of Archway involvement at the Rainbow Children's Hospital (a CMN Hospital), which was used as part of their CMN promotional activities.

• A television commercial produced by the station

which featured one of their local talk show hosts.

Milan used existing station promotional activities to find additional sponsorship and billing opportunities. The video coverage was used as part of their regular programming – the station regularly covered events at Rainbow Childrens Hospital while promoting the Telethon.

Creating the message was easy – the commercial converted the national copy message into a local version, using Channel 5's talent.

Finally, a relationship was established. When another program sponsorship became available – which included a tie-in with a local milk company – Jim was able to use his knowledge of Archway's marketing to develop a program that fit their needs.

Starting with a small Telethon opportunity, he was able to add a regular advertiser to the station roster.

The Evolution of Media

Media guru Marshall McLuhan once observed that the content of one medium is the previous medium, (i.e the content of TV is movies).

In that sense, the content of The New TV (i.e. cable) is all TV. Your channel-changer contains virtually all TV – from Nick at Night re-runs to the latest MTV video.

More channels will evolve into even more opportunity.

Today, many of the marketing and promotional approaches that have traditionally been used by other media forms – such as tie-ins, subscription offers, and regional editions – are now becoming part of television's marketing repertoire.

A Tactical Medium

Outdoor is a tactical medium. It is very good at accomplishing certain specific things.

For example, at its simplest, **Directionals** can extend the location of a retail operation by indicating the store's location.

Outdoor is very good at reminding or reinforcing a campaign in another media. Look for creative ways to give a big local advertiser impact on outdoor.

Since people are on the road when they see most outdoor, it is particularly good for businesses that are a part of our commuter culture – autos, oil changes, car phones, radio and radio stations are good examples.

Visual Impact

Strong simple design is critical.

Outdoor is a visual medium – the visual often drives the message. It's a piece of art on the commercial landscape.

A cluttered message won't do the job for you.

Powerful visuals, beautifully done art, and extensions to add an extra 3-dimensional effect are other ways to increase the visual impact of your board.

Verbal Impact

You have to cut your message down to its essence.

Some say no more than five words. Some say no more than seven words.

The point is, your message must be dramatic and focused.

All type messages can also work in outdoor.

In this case, your words become the visual.

Subordinate messages, such as location or phone information, may be necessary, but try not to clutter up the layout.

The Need for Involvement

Recent research indicates that outdoor can be particularly effective when it is mentally involving.

A good example was a popular Yellow Pages campaign based on word play. The TV was already familiar.

By first putting up the visual, people were encouraged to guess what the latest Yellow Pages category was.

Since outdoor often builds up great frequency, you can work to develop extra involvement by offering a mental challenge with your message.

If they miss it on Monday, they can guess again on Tuesday – when they drive by again.

Study the Experts

Frequency helps in virtually every medium. So we'll repeat our point that you can learn a lot from the people in your industry who do it well. And since outdoor is a particularly good medium for building frequency, we'll repeat it again.

The Institute for Outdoor Advertising runs a national award contest – The Obies.

There are also international contests. Outdoor is a very important medium in many other countries and some of the artistic treatments are quite stunning.

Study these award-winners and see if you can't apply some of the lessons and artistic excellence to your local project.

Who knows, one of your boards may win one of those awards.

BASICS OF DIRECT MARKETING

Good List + Good Offer = Good Results

If you work for a company that specializes in direct marketing, your company will have a lot of information about what works and what doesn't.

In general, the better the list and the better the offer, the better your direct program will do.

This is true whether you have a high-end offer for a big ticket luxury item or a low-end offer for a local pizza chain.

One of your key jobs will be communicating this to your clients and then developing offers that deliver the results you're both looking for.

The Importance of Testing

Depending on the type of direct marketing services you represent, factors such as 800 numbers, credit card sales, Free Trial Offers, and pricing are often quite important.

So is the featured appeal in your solicitation.

That's why testing can be so important.

If possible, the beginning of your direct marketing project should involve testing appeals and programs to develop the one that's most effective.

Once you have a good one, that offer becomes the benchmark as you develop additional programs that try and improve on those results.

Direct Marketing, when done well, is a game where you're always "raising the bar."

Other Experts

John Caples' classic books, *Tested Advertising Methods* and *How to Make Your Advertising Make Money* are a great way to start.

Contemporary direct writers like Bob Bly, Bob Stone, and René Gnam will also help you improve your direct marketing skills. They're listed in Resources.

Today, virtually every marketer, from P&G and Mercedes-Benz, to your neighborhood dry cleaner and the local pizza parlor, is looking at some form of direct marketing.

That's why the field is growing across the board – from mass mailers like Val-Pak to those who sell specialized programs aimed at narrow targets.

YELLOW PAGES BASICS

Yellow Pages advertising directs consumers to the place of purchase. Other media help create desire and awareness for products and services, but when consumers are ready to buy, they often consult the Yellow Pages to find a place to purchase.

Who/What/Where

Directory advertising is based on the traditional Who/What/Where – it's simple, but there is little margin for error.

Unlike a newspaper ad which can be corrected or changed the next day, a directory mistake can take as long as a year to correct, so it is absolutely critical that good decisions are made and that everything is triple-checked for accuracy.

Memorable phone numbers, eye-catching visuals and spot color are some of the ways that you can "dress up" a Yellow Pages listing.

In many categories from auto rentals, to pizzas and plumbers, to locksmiths and window replacement, a high percentage of decisions are made over the phone.

For these categories, you may want to sell the extra benefit of a larger ad or an eye-catching second color.

As an added value, you may also want to help your client make his phone answering more creative – improved voice mail and message services as well as a short phone course for employees are ways that you can add creative value to even the simplest listing.

After all, you are the telephone directory expert. Use your knowledge to add value to the relationship.

THE CAMPAIGN APPROACH

This is a point we can't make too early or too often. We talked about it at the beginning of this chapter, in the middle, and we'll talk about it at the end of this chapter.

Local businesses – and local clients – need to plan campaigns in the same way agencies and national clients do.

One of the oldest agencies, NW Ayer, has a slogan we should all remember, *"Keeping everlastingly at it."*

The Power of Advertising

The power of advertising is cumulative and long-term as well as short-term. While clients have a right to expect some level of immediate results from their ads – the real power kicks in when a single-minded program builds over time.

It makes sense. With even the largest audience, only a certain percentage will be in the market for any product at any one time.

So the longer and more often you can put your message in front of that audience, the better your advertising will perform.

That was one of the reasons the Fearrington Farms campaign worked – they kept at it. Most new advertisers need to be reminded of the necessity to keep at it.

The campaign approach gives the client a unified advertising plan, provides confidence in signing a contract, and saves time throughout the whole period of that contract.

A New Way of Thinking

For most local clients – and for many sales reps in all media – the idea of thinking through all the ad executions for the whole contract period is new.

Many local clients develop ads "on the spot" in response to store needs or outside circumstances.

Most clients know when the ads will be placed on a weekly or contract basis. What most clients do not know is what will be in those ads.

Campaign thinking can be a lot of work at the front end – and ads may still have to be changed in response to changing conditions. But having a series of ads finished and ready to run takes the pressure off throughout the year.

The campaign approach puts much of the planning in first and provides a stronger ad message.

For the sales rep, using the campaign approach encourages the client to make a commitment.

The client cannot help but be impressed at the time and effort put in on his behalf.

The approach can sell the contract – and keep it sold.

The client can change the ads, of course, but the impact of having a year-long plan for both media use and creative execution is clear.

INTEGRATION

Today, more and more marketers and advertisers are talking about "Integrated Marketing Communications."

It may sound complicated, but much of it is simply common sense marketing.

It's choosing the most effective communications media – from a wider range. This includes sales promotion vehicles, publicity, event marketing, and direct marketing.

And it means making your messages work together.

For example, radio plus outdoor has been described as "poor man's television."

Now, new low-cost cable offers other opportunities that can be combined with more traditional media forms.

Look for opportunities

Your new ad campaign for a local retailer might be based on newspaper or radio, but it could also include:

• A letter to the customer list (Direct)
• A button and bumper sticker (Out-of-home)
• An incentive contest for employees (Sales Promotion)
• A kick-off event, complete with press kit and press party (Publicity and Event Marketing)

Do any or all of that, and you've done "Integrated Marketing Communications." Again, it's making connections.

On one level, it's new and exciting, using some of the latest technology. On another level, it's just common sense and "street smarts." It's knowing that your new client might be able to build some sales with an old customer list.

And, whatever you call it, it's your job to help that client make the right connections.

"Polishing" your craft

Creating messages is a demanding job all in itself.

You may find that you're quite good at it and want to do even more – writing a spec ad every night before bed.

Or, you may find more excitement bringing in a new client and letting your other team members produce the message.

Whichever part of your career you decide to emphasize, you will always be a part of making sure that the messages that connect your marketers to your market are as effective as possible.

That means staying in touch with the best in your industry. Study the awards books.

Learn from the best people you can find.

The more you learn, the better you'll be able to communicate the important principles of your medium to the people that craft the ads and the people that pay for them.

And, when you have to pretty much do it yourself, you'll be as well-equipped as possible.

A good media rep can make the difference between messages that miss and those that make the right connections.

A good media rep can show the client the best way to "keep everlastingly at it."

EXERCISES:

1. Using one of the completed formats from Chapter Ten, develop a Selling Idea – a set of words that states the Proposition in a memorable way.

2. Now, write three ads in your first choice medium (print, radio, etc.). The Proposition should be the same, but anything else can be different. Or similar. Your choice.

3. Now, pick two mediums that you're less familiar with and try to write ads using the same Proposition and any other elements from your first set of ads.

4. Call the ad club in the nearest large market and ask if you can have a copy of their latest ADDY awards book.

Often, this will not only show examples of some of the best work in your market, but it will identify some of the best people.

5. Tonight, write down a spec ad idea for a client or a new client. Do the same thing tomorrow night.

V.
FROM PROSPECT TO PRESENTATION.

"Plan the sale as you write the ad."

Leo Burnett

In this section, we'll put together some of the things we've been covering.
    Now that we know the marketplace, we'll hit the streets and make cold calls as we look for some of the best prospects for our medium.
    We'll talk about some of the necessities for staying organized – a job that never stops.
    And, once we find our prospects, we'll put together a sales presentation that makes the sale.
    It's a lot of work. But it can be a lot of fun.
    Let's get started.

12. HITTING THE STREET.

You have the basics and understand the business. It's time for you to get out on the street and sell. Here's what you need to do just that.

HOW TERRITORIES ARE ORGANIZED

There are two basic territory configurations: geographic and client-specific.

Once you reach a higher level in your job, you may be assigned to a client-specific category based upon amount of advertising placed.

And, of course, the higher level you reach in your job, the more likely it is that you will be handling the larger clients.

1. Geographic Territory

In this type of assignment, you'll be working with a specific area determined by geographic boundaries.

You'll deal with a number of different kinds of businesses.

The strong point of this kind of territorial organization is that you are close to all the clients.

So you can make many calls in the same area.

2. Client-specific organization

In this type of assignment, you'll be working with clients in specific kinds of businesses. You are more likely to be an expert and know more about that type of business.

For example, a large newspaper may have a department that specializes in furniture sales or in auto dealers.

Assigned to this kind of department, you'll be expected to be an expert in the concerns of these specific kinds of clients.

A large newspaper or broadcast entity is likely to use this kind of client-specific organization.

The list you are assigned is of utmost importance. Be sure to understand the background of each of the clients and the opportunities your own individual client list offers. Also be certain to understand the limitations.

Most beginning lists offer some good clients, but also some that are promising but inactive. Your ability to categorize these and to plan to deal with each kind effectively is essential.

This is known as checking out the clients.

CHECKING OUT THE CLIENTS

Getting to know your accounts

The basic rule for dealing with your accounts is "Be a friend."

Remember, you're working on a long-term relationship.

It usually takes at least five calls to make that first sale. And, since most beginning salespeople give up after the first two or three calls, most sales are made by a few dedicated salespeople.

One tried and true axiom is "Time is money." But this doesn't mean you'll be selling and closing accounts every minute of the day. What the axiom should mean to you is that everything you do should ultimately lead to selling success.

The time you spend getting to know your clients is time well invested. Spending time in the store or business, getting to know the daily routine and the personalities of the people who own and run the business, scoping out the people who shop – all of these are time investments that will pay off in efficient selling down the road.

You need to identify the decision maker.

One or two people in that business will be making decisions about media placement. It's essential that you know who they are and that you get to know them.

You need to identify their priorities and needs and work with them to show how your medium and your market plan for them will work to help them achieve success.

You also need to work as a team with your clients.

Because you are building a long-term relationship, you need to project – and deliver – client service. You are working together to be successful. You and the client are friends and business compatriots.

There are tactics for building trust.

Show that you can be relied upon to show up when you say you will.

Come up with good and specific ideas for the business and work within the constraints of the business.

These all help to build trust between you and the client.

What you want to achieve is that the client relies upon you for market and media judgment. Building this kind of trust takes time, but is well worth the effort.

No account list is static. Businesses close or move or expand. New businesses come to town. Businesses change media choices.

You need to keep up with all of this.

And you need to keep developing new business.

The Prospect File

Your ally in this is the Prospect File.

To be a good sales rep, you need to be aware of all the business movement in your town. You need to keep a prospect list and make calls on these potential clients on a regular basis.

Prospects should be:

1. New businesses

Those that move to town – or expand to new locations.

2. Businesses in your inactive file

Those who once advertised with your medium, but no longer advertise with you.

3. Businesses that have never advertised with your medium

Although they may be long-term in your town, they have no experience with your medium.

Now that you have your list, it's time to get out and make some calls.

And, since you're just starting out, you'll probably have to make some "cold calls."

"COLD CALLS"

"Cold calls" are client visits to the businesses listed above – those with which you have no regular contact.

Be Prepared

It may be called a cold call. But you can't go in cold.

You need to plan your calls to these people by doing the following:

1. Be prepared to talk about the strengths of your particular medium.

You should be able to talk about its place in the media mix of your locality and the benefits it offers this business.

2. Be prepared to "qualify" the candidate.
You might want to use the "Ten Questions" survey below.
3. Be prepared to talk about the business itself.
To do this, you must have done your homework about the business. Scope it out.

Visit the business and find out as much as you can from observation. In addition, find out what you can from others.
4. Check out the advertising that's been done.
You should know the advertising choices and types of ads the business has placed during the last several years.
5. Check out the business's financial stability.
You need to know if the business is worth going after before you put in the effort. That's why you need to qualify the client.

QUALIFYING THE CLIENT

You can't do "spec" for every prospect – you have to choose which prospects are most worth going after.

The following "10 Questions" can be a good start for identifying your best spec prospects.

10 QUESTIONS TO ASK

Here are some questions that can help you get the background you need for some "spec" work.

1. How long have you been in this business?

2. How long have you been in this location?

3. Who do you see as your primary target market?

4. Who are the secondary markets?

5. From how wide a geographical area do you draw?

6. Are you happy with the level and kind of traffic in your store? (Or business?)

7. Who do you identify as your competition?

8. What is your assessment of your business in comparison with that competition?

9. What is your advertising budget?

10. What is your usual advertising mix?

There may be other questions as well, but these are good starting points. After you have the answers to these important questions, you need to do a local credit check on the prospective business.

Sometimes, as promising as clients may seem, they will sign a large contract, but be unable to pay the bill. It is your obligation to check this out before you run any ads with the client.

AN IN-STORE SURVEY

Here's a survey checklist designed by The Advisory Board for radio sales people. Whatever media you sell for, it can help you get a feel for the business you're calling on.

Store Hours:
Monday-Friday: _____
Saturday: _____
Sunday: _____
Days open late: _____

Observations:
Plaques, awards, citations, founder's pictures: _____

_____
Featured item displays:_____

_____
Marked-down items: _____

_____
Other locations in coverage area: _____

_____

Customer Profile by Observation
Number of salespeople in store: _____
Number of customers: _____
Estimated ages:
❑ 18-24   ❑ 25-34   ❑ 35-44 ❑ 45-54 ❑ 55+
Percentage by gender/group
Men: _____
Women: _____
Teens: _____
Couples: _____
Other observations:_____

_____

Account Grading Worksheet

Yes No

- ❑ ❑ Can we sell this advertiser's products/services to our listeners?
- ❑ ❑ Does this advertiser want to make it happen?
- ❑ ❑ Does this advertiser regularly advertise on a direct media competitor?
- ❑ ❑ Is this a direct, local place of business?
- ❑ ❑ Is this advertiser a big newspaper user?
- ❑ ❑ If there is an agency involved, is it a local one?
- ❑ ❑ Is the advertiser being neglected by other media reps in the market?
- ❑ ❑ Does the decision-maker like our station?
- ❑ ❑ Is the business an attractive, well-run enterprise?
- ❑ ❑ Is the advertiser a prestigious one whose presence on our medium will make us more credible to other prospects?
- ❑ ❑ Does this advertiser have multiple locations in our coverage area?

Total Number of **YES** _____

Trade Magazine

Name of trade magazine: _____
- ❑ Read Table of Contents
- ❑ Skim the cover story

Write down 10 jargon words (or phrases)

1) _____ 6) _____
2) _____ 7) _____
3) _____ 8) _____
4) _____ 9) _____
5) _____ 10) _____

Key Issues

Note (or discover) three key issues/trends in the industry:

1) _____

_____
_____

2) _____

_____
_____

3) _____

_____
_____

TWELVE. Hitting The Street.

Advertising Ideas
Note (or discover) any obvious advertising ideas:

_____

_____

_____

Strategy for Next Call
Problem to solve:_____

_____

_____

Three reasons our station can help this advertiser:

_____

_____

_____

Approach: _____

_____

_____

WHY – AND HOW – CLIENTS BUY

Clients buy media for a variety of reasons.

First come first served
The worst reason may be because another media rep got to them first, but this is a common reason.

Convenience
One reason clients buy is because of convenience. They're busy and often don't have the time to make an in-depth study of their media options. An aggressive rep who will do much of that work will often be well-received by this type of client.

No agency
Many smaller and medium-sized clients do not work with an advertising agency. This means that the media rep has to provide the services that an agency would. It also means that you can gain more control over the account and develop a one-on-one relationship with these clients.

Other reasons
Other reasons include: a perception that the plan will get the best results, and a lack of any real long-term plan (when you don't know where you're going, any road will take you there).

And there are many other reasons – some good, some bad.

Building on strong fundamentals

Over the long run, you want to build your business with clients who advertise for the right reasons.

Your initial search should focus on discovering those who can derive the most benefit from your medium.

When the basic reasons for using your medium are sound, the results are more likely to be satisfactory and the relationship based on a more solid footing.

Fundamentally, we believe the best way to sell a client is:

1. Present a well-reasoned media plan.

2. Show that the plan is in keeping with the marketing needs and goals of that business.

You start with hitting the streets.
You succeed by hitting the target.

13. STREET SMARTS.

Whatever you learn about the technical aspects of media placement and selling will not be enough. You need "street smarts," too.

You have to learn to look and listen.

As I often tell students, *"I can tell you the techniques and give you the information, but I cannot turn you into a super salesperson in the classroom."*

Yes, you need the techniques and information. But there's still something missing. What's missing is "street smarts."

An ad director at a major metropolitan newspaper once told me about a brilliant woman he had hired with an MBA from a major university.

After one week on the job, she came to him and said, *"I can't use much of what I learned in school."*

She needed "street smarts." Here's what that means:
- Learn to listen to the client.
- Observe what is going on in the business.
- Look at the customers – listen to them if you can.
- Know the competition – both theirs and yours.
- Finally, develop a sense of what is needed and when.

Instinct as well as Intellect

It's instinct as well as intellect. But it can be done.

Some reps come by it naturally. Others take more time. It's a matter of style, common sense, and luck.

You can control the first two as you hope for a little luck.

As Louis Pasteur said, *"Fortune favors the prepared mind."*

You need to develop perseverance and flexibility. You also need to know when to give up or take a fall-back position.

Five or more calls

Common wisdom tells us that 80 percent of sales are made after five or more sales calls.

You need to be among the 10 percent of reps who make these final calls. That's perseverance.

You also need to be alert to changing client needs. Competition changes, spending patterns change, customer bases expand and decline. Awareness on your part gives flexibility. And you need that.

It's deadly to insist the client needs what you offer.

Set a goal for yourself and for your client and be prepared to offer differing game plans to reach your mutual goals.

Keep alert. Hang loose.

These are not opposing strategies.

Many management "gurus," such as Tom Peters, note the "loose/tight" aspects of successful companies.

SETTING YOUR OWN GOALS

Juggling

Selling is like juggling many balls in the air at the same time. Some may fall – then you need to adjust your strategy – and get more balls in the air. This is essential.

Set a goal for yourself and your medium for each client.

Keep track. And keep raising your expectations.

Jugglers start with just one ball. They learn the right moves, the right rhythms and the right habits. They drop a lot of balls along the way.

When you meet or exceed your goal, analyze why.

Do it again and improve. Practice makes perfect.

If you fail to meet a goal – and it will happen – do the same. Figure out a new game plan or keep to the old one. Or both.

Juggle.

Setting realistic goals

Try to set goals for yourself that stretch you a bit. They should be realistic, but just a bit ambitious.

Look at past sales achievements for others in your job and with your particular set of businesses.

For many successful sales reps the strategy is somewhere between stark realism and "no guts, no glory."

Be optimistic within realistic bounds.

MEDIA SALES MANAGEMENT

Manage Yourself First

To be successful, you first have to manage yourself.

Your own medium – and your own boss – will have certain norms you'll have to comply with.

But you should go beyond filling out the weekly "hit" forms (who you saw and how it worked) and keep track of your own goals in some kind of planner.

Develop a realistic – and workable – checklist system of your own. Here are a few prototypes:

CHECKLIST 1 – PROSPECTS

New Businesses

Business Name: _____

    Location: _____

    Type of business: _____

    Contact person: _____

    Competition: _____

    Current advertising (competition – from observation): _____

    Comments from others: _____

Non-Active Former Advertisers

Business Name: _____

    Location: _____

    Previous ad schedule with my medium: _____

    Reason for stopping ads in my medium: _____

    Contact person: _____

    To do: _____

Active Businesses

Business Name: _____

    Contact: _____

    Level of my goal met by this business: _____

    Plan for development for my medium: _____

Ideas for new campaigns: _____

_____

_____

_____

Immediate and long-range goals: _____

_____

_____

Assessment of my success _____

_____

_____

Cheerleader Needed

You also need to be your own cheerleader.

It's a tough job – often, with more rejection than success – certainly at first.

And you need to be honest with yourself as you come to grips with that rejection.

But you also have to manage that – and that means you need to do a little cheerleading.

If you tried, even though you didn't make the sale, give yourself an "A" for effort.

Know your own strengths and weaknesses.

When you succeed with a client, pat yourself on the back and give yourself a cheer. Enjoy the feeling.

If you fall short of your goal – and it will happen regularly at the beginning of your career – analyze why. Learn at least one useful lesson from each unmade sale.

Then congratulate yourself for learning that lesson.

At the beginning, the only person who you'll be able to count on to get yourself up for the next sale is you.

That's why you have to be your own cheerleader.

SAMPLE CHECKLIST 2 – GOALS

Goal for [Month/Year]

    Goal for major account #1: _____

        Percentage of goal met: _____

        Times visited [dates/results]: _____

_____

_____

        Strategy for immediate action: _____

_____

        Strategy for continuing action: _____

_____

        Problems: _____

_____

    Goal for major account #2: _____

        Percentage of goal met: _____

        Times visited [dates/results]: _____

_____

_____

        Strategy for immediate action: _____

_____

        Strategy for continuing action: _____

_____

_____

        Problems: _____

_____

_____

    Goals for other accounts: _____

_____

    Goals for cold calls: _____

_____

_____

_____

My Overall Monthly [or Yearly] Goal

Strategy: _____

_____

_____

Percentage met: _____

_____

Percentage yet to achieve: _____

_____

My numbers for each account from last period:

_____

_____

_____

My numbers for each account for present period:

_____

_____

_____

New accounts – numbers to be achieved:

_____

_____

_____

My own best attributes in selling/working with clients:

_____

_____

_____

Things I need to improve:_____

_____

_____

_____

Overall assessment of my performance this month/year

_____

_____

_____

Winning

It's a great feeling when you win in this business.

When you achieve your goals, win new clients (and client trust), and when you see your ideas and your clients in print or on broadcast – you receive daily rewards.

And this is a job where you can win every day.

Keep track. You can chart your wins as you go along.

Setting and meeting goals not only makes you feel like a success, but is also financially rewarding.

You can do this.

You'll help yourself, you'll help your clients, and you'll help the medium you work for.

It's win/win/win.

YOUR PROFESSIONAL PERSONA

Being a sales rep means you are always on call. And it means you need always to be ready to be interrupted and to have answers for each client on hand.

As we mentioned, developing rapport and understanding with the client gives you the tools to think effectively about each client's business and each client's needs.

It means you are in the position to be a consultant, a business person and a friend – all at the same time.

You need to develop your own professional persona.

A study conducted by Learning International showed the top three reasons people buy had nothing to do with price, but related directly to the quality of the sales force.

Those reasons were:

- **Business expertise and image**
- **Dedication to customer**
- **Account sensitivity and guidance**

These characteristics need to be an intrinsic part of the way you do business.

Your personal style

Think carefully about the ways in which you feel most comfortable talking and working with a client. The more you bring your own personal strengths into the process, the stronger and more sincere you will appear – and be.

Having a professional persona also means having a code of ethics that you adhere to – and it should include keeping client confidences, being honest about client needs and treating clients fairly.

There is a fine line between pointing out that a client may need more ads to remain competitive and succeed in his or her business plan and telling a client the advertising strategy and business plan of their biggest competitor.

If you are running your end of the business right, clients will tell you a great deal about their plans, successes, and problems. And that means they need to be able to trust you and talk with you in confidence.

Your habits

Being professional means you are prepared by knowing all the facts available. It also means you are able (and willing) to analyze them and to respond to both general and specific questions (and to check the facts to make sure your answers are right), find the answers if you don't know them readily, and alert the client if there is some change you know about.

It also means you should be forthright about policy.

Don't promise things to get a contract signed when you know the chances are slim to none that you can follow through.

Being professional is very much about follow-through.

It involves calling back, keeping track, making and keeping appointments, faxing or delivering information and proofs.

Today, with cellular phones and fax machines, you're better able to keep in touch with clients than ever before.

It also means they are able to get you almost anywhere – but the more available you are, the more sales you can make.

Being professional means putting forth your best effort for every client every day.

Your look

You'll have to develop a professional wardrobe as well – working as a sales rep means looking professional on the job.

Here's a good piece of advice given to our class by a student who recently graduated; *"Don't ask for fun stuff during your senior year. Ask for professional clothes for every gift-giving occasion. Make sure your family knows you are getting ready to get out in the world and that having a professional wardrobe is just one of the tools."*

Some other things you'll want to acquire once you have the job are practical necessities: a couple of umbrellas (leave one in the car), flashlight, maps, and a cellular phone.

Many clients will become friends with whom you'll have a great working relationship, but you can't be casual about the professional nature of your relationship.

THIRTEEN. Street Smarts.

Your attitude

You can't sell something you don't believe in. Period.

Well, perhaps you can sell it once or twice to someone who really wants to buy. (And in that case, it's scarcely selling. It's more like just being there.)

But there's no way you can develop long-term relationships with clients, keep them interested, and keep talking about the same product over and over.

So, if you can't think of one single reason why anyone would benefit from advertising on radio, you can't sell radio. If you don't believe newspapers are a good buy for business, you shouldn't try to sell newspaper.

Selling can be very discouraging. Even when you are convinced that your product would be good for a client, he or she may not see it that way at all.

Just when you think you've got the sale in the bag, it can all fall apart. And you have to remind yourself how many calls it takes to make a successful sale.

Tips for keeping yourself up

Here are a few tips for keeping yourself up for the chase:

1. Review all the pertinent information about your client – the business itself, the strengths and problems, and the decision maker you are working with.

2. Work to match the strengths of your product with the client needs.

3. Talk it through to yourself as though you were discussing the problem-solving aspects directly with the client – or explaining to someone else how your medium can provide the solutions needed.

4. Think about other successes you have had. (Feel good about these.) What worked then that you could use now?

5. Convince yourself you can do it. You've done it before. But guard against arrogance.

Work hard.
Work smart.

14. PREPARING THE PRESENTATION.

A *good presentation takes a lot of preparation. First, you need mental preparation. Even if you've never sold media – or anything – you already know some of the basics about selling.*

SOME OF THE BASICS

Tapping into your own sales sense

You simply need to tap your own sales sense.

Think back to times you've convinced people of your point of view or convinced them to do something you proposed – even if it was as simple as a choice of movies.

Now, work back through the process and think through your strategy and reasoning.

Chances are, you connected with others first. Then, you offered them choices that were appealing and easy to agree with.

A Sales Presentation does pretty much the same thing.

You'll find that you're actually a pretty good salesperson – particularly when you know your customer and can offer appealing choices.

Your Ultimate Selling Tool

The client sales presentation is your ultimate selling tool.

In it, you will need to muster facts and figures about the market, about the competition, about the business itself.

And then you'll have to connect those market facts with facts about your own medium.

You'll need to know in detail how your medium stacks up against the many other choices available to your buyer.

Formal or Informal

For some clients (particularly new or larger clients), you'll use charts, graphs and a presentation book. You may use slides as well. This kind of presentation is the most formal.

For other clients, sitting down with a stack of ads run for the business and from the competition, along with a calendar, may be the best plan.

But big or small, one of the underlying ways you connect is by showing those clients you understand their business.

You should do this for all businesses – small or large, locally-owned or national.

Whatever size client you present to, the purpose of all of your sales presentations – and all of your sales conversations – is to show the client how your own medium can meet his or her advertising and marketing needs.

That's the essence of selling in any market with any medium – whether the presentation is formal or informal.

YOU NEED TO KNOW THESE THINGS:

The following should come together at this point – aspects of each of these factors will be referred to repeatedly in your presentation. All of them are key to Making the Sale:

- **Client needs and goals**
- **Client problems**
- **Target audience**
- **The competition**
- **Your medium**

Let's review them briefly.

Client needs and goals

This can include your own observations and the answers to your client's qualification questions. Essentially, you need to have a point of view on what should be accomplished.

Client Problems

Every client has them. Show your knowledge.

Show your sympathy. Show your understanding of "The Problem the Advertising Must Solve."

These problems (or challenges) will be a key part of the Marketer segment of your presentation and set up the Message segment of your presentation.

In general, this is the key to a marketing focus.

By addressing the marketing problem, your recommendation is now focused on solving that problem, rather than just spending advertising money.

You and the client get on the same side of the problem and work to solve it. This is selling as a marketing partner.

That's the key – but there's more.

The Target Audience

You should know who the client's Target should be and how the client's audience matches up with your medium's audience.

The Competition

This should include your understanding of both the competitive businesses and the market as a whole.

Competitive efforts are a primary reason to advertise and a powerful motivator.

In today's tougher-than-ever marketplace, sometimes you have to work harder-than-ever just to stay even.

Acknowledging competitive efforts can also help you to avoid over-promising on results.

Your Medium

You need to be able to tell your medium's story in an exciting and persuasive way.

You need to bring all the facts and all the factors together into **how your own medium can solve the client's marketing problem and meet advertising needs.**

Your presentation drives toward making this important point – your medium is the critical connection between the marketer and the market.

THE PRESENTATION – A PREVIEW

This section of the book will tell you what you need to do to get ready to talk to your clients and put that presentation together.

First, we'll give an overview of the broad categories.

Then, we'll talk about each section specifically – as you'll see, these sections or categories cover **"The 4 M's of Media Sales."**

This outline is for a major sales presentation – naturally, there will be many meetings and informal discussions which will not be as comprehensive.

FOURTEEN. Preparing The Presentation.

But for the purposes of this chapter, each sales presentation should contain sections on: Market, Marketer, Media and Message.

1. Market

Your presentation should contain market information for the local area – **this should include charts or graphs to illustrate major points.**

Each chart or graph should have a descriptive heading.

A summary statement at the bottom of each page can help the reader understand the major point being made.

Basic points to include might be:

- **Size of market**
- **Growth patterns**
- **Migration in and out of the market area**
- **Age distribution**
- **Number and average size of households**
- **Educational levels**
- **Average per capita and household income levels**
- **Spending for major retail categories such as food, automotive, furniture, appliances, etc.**

By beginning with the Market, your presentation will establish a business-like context for evaluating marketing decisions.

It will help to position you as a Marketing Partner, rather than as a Media Salesperson.

2. Marketer

This is the part of the presentation the client most wants to hear about. Because it's about him (or her).

You need to summarize the basic points you have learned about their business.

Whatever format you use, you should invest some time in getting to know the client and the business. You should do this before you make an actual sales call or presentation.

Problems and Solutions.

You may want to use a problem and solution format.

Don't just talk about a client's Problems – you should also indicate his Opportunities. And, just as important, you should be setting up the thought that your medium is one of the answers to his marketing problems.

Problems and Opportunities.

Many types of marketing plans have a Situation Analysis section which lists Problems and Opportunities.

This is another useful way to present marketer information.
"SWOT."
And still another form of this is the "SWOT" format.

This stands for Strengths, Weaknesses, Opportunities, and Threats. This is another good way to organize marketing problems and opportunities.

Whichever approach works best, this section of your presentation should feature marketing challenges.

Then, you can focus on solutions – many of which may feature messages in your medium.

More about the Marketer section

Your medium will not be the answer to every problem.
You should realize this and be realistic in your presentation.

But once you focus on the problem, you may be surprised at how many creative ways there are to use your medium.

For example, let's say a retailer has a service problem – with poorly motivated store personnel. At first, you may not see this as a problem your medium can solve.

But think again. You could use your medium to salute "A New Spirit of Service," or offer a promotion that features a "Customer Satisfaction Guarantee."

You're selling Opportunity, not just space and time.
Even if the business has severe problems (and many do!), you need to do more than recite them. You need to point out strengths and opportunities as well.

You need to be positive and hopeful. Otherwise, your client may feel attacked, defensive, or worse yet, depressed.

You want the client to begin to rely on you for marketing solutions and associate you with opportunities – not problems.

You're building a relationship.
This may be the client's very favorite part of your presentation. Why? Because it's about his favorite topic – his business.

People like people who share their interests and the fact that you demonstrate an interest in the business can be a tremendously important part of building a relationship.

And that's what you're doing – even though, at the time, you may feel like you're presenting to a suspicious stranger who doesn't want to be sold.

Even at the beginning, you are building a relationship.

Show that you're interested in your (potential) client's business, and that's an important step in that client wanting to be a part of your business.

FOURTEEN. Preparing The Presentation.

3. Message

In this part of the presentation, the client gets to see (or hear) his company associated with your medium.

As mentioned, we generally believe you should include some form of speculative ads for each client in a sales presentation.

Certainly, this is not always appropriate or possible and the format here will vary depending upon your own medium.

But we think it's critical that instead of just imagining being a part of your medium, your potential client should actually see or hear that message on your medium.

If possible, you should take at least three single ad ideas and at least one idea for an on-going campaign.

Naturally, one approach will be liked best, but that's part of the reason you want to present more than one approach.

By offering more than one solution, the potential client will be engaged and involved in comparing and considering rather than being put in a position of just saying "yes" or "no."

Every approach should answer needs and solve problems – they should help position the business to compete and have the kind of persuasion necessary to attract new customers.

As mentioned, you may also need to take past advertising into account when you're developing these ads – the message you present may be their existing campaign with ads appropriately modified (size, etc.) for your medium.

With the focus of your message clearly dramatized, you can then move on to the next stage of your presentation.

4. Medium

In addition to information about your medium, your presentation should contain a proposed rate plan and schedule.

Ideally, you should have three plans ready.

Even though we all hope for the biggest contract we can get, you should offer a range of options. They should offer choices of ways to get the message out to the audience.

They should each be as different in dollar amounts and approach as possible – to offer some real alternatives.

Your plans should also integrate your medium with others the client may use. By taking charge of this kind of integration, you'll come across as someone who is interested in the client and his business success. You'll be a marketing partner – not just someone who wants to sell something.

Showing the client how various media can work together is likely to bring you more business – now and later.

A PRESENTATION OUTLINE:

Now here are the sections of your Sales Presentation presented in more detail.

1. PRESENTING THE MARKET

Market Facts

You need to be aware of local market facts and be able to place both the individual client and the media (your own included) within the context of that market.

One good way to present the overall market is to develop charts and graphs that show the basic market facts.

This has an obvious advantage, it pulls together several different kinds of market facts for you and clarifies them.

By showing charts and graphs and discussing them during a sales presentation, you demonstrate to the client that you are knowledgeable about the market.

Going over basic market facts with the client means you both share and agree on the same information. This kind of agreement is an excellent prelude to sales.

Charts and Graphs

There are three basic types of charts and graphs:

- **Pie charts**
- **Bar charts**
- **Line graphs**

Each is best for certain kinds of information.

It is simple to create sales graphs that are clear, functional and easy to read with a computer graphing program.

Most graphing programs have a wide selection of features that create easy-to-read graphs. Generally, all you need to do is make your selection, put in the appropriate percentages and type in the title or headlines and labels.

Many popular computer programs are available to produce these materials. New programs and new options are being introduced every day – so check around for the system that will work best for you.

Pie charts

Pie charts look like a circle – individual "slices" represent various categories.

Each slice represents the proportion of the circle that is its percentage of the whole.

FOURTEEN. Preparing The Presentation.

A pie chart is an excellent way to organize information when there are several different categories to be compared.

Because it is easy to see the relationship between the different categories at a glance, a pie chart works very well for material that contains several different parts – such as age distribution within a community.

This kind of visual picture of the distribution makes it easy to see what is going on in the market with just a glance.

For example, age distribution can be very important in targeting potential customers within a market.

Since certain businesses (music stores, clothing stores, restaurants and others) may cater to certain age goups, it is important to see how large those target groups are and to place them in context with other age groups in the market.

Suppose your market has this distribution:

18-24	14%
25-34	23%
35-44	21%
45-54	15%
55-64	11%
65+	16%

At a glance, we can see that over one-third of the market is between 18 and 34 – a segment of the market with great opportunities for food, clothing and entertainment.

Other segments represent other opportunities.

Age Distribution of Mecklenburg County Adult Population

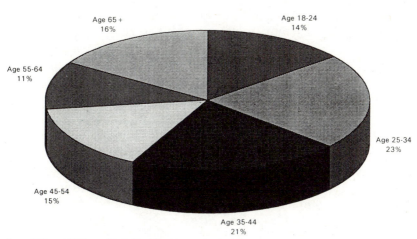

Age 65 + 16%

Age 18-24 14%

Age 55-64 11%

Age 25-34 23%

Age 45-54 15%

Age 35-44 21%

Source: KPC Research 1992 Survey of Readership and Shopping

Remember that some of the points you will make in this section need to be repeated when you present the facts about your medium.

So, if you have emphasized the 18-34 market in this section, you will want to refer to it later when you talk about your medium's audience.

Bar charts

Bar charts usually look like two thick lines next to one another. They may be constructed as vertical or horizontal charts. Here's a horizontal example…

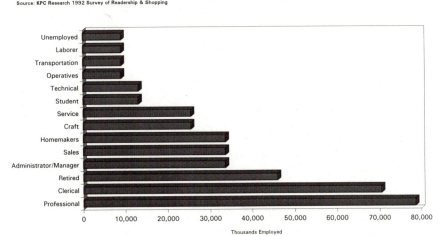

Mecklenburg County Employment Analysis

Source: KPC Research 1992 Survey of Readership & Shopping

This kind of chart provides an excellent way to compare two pieces of information at one point in time.

Of course, you could also show many categories within one bar chart. Before deciding whether to use a bar chart or a pie chart, ask yourself which one would make the information most clear.

For example, suppose that as of Summer 1995, 41% of the people in your city had graduated from college, while only 29% of those in a nearby market had finished college.

You could show this kind of information by using a bar chart – one bar would show your market, the second would show the other market.

Advertisers would see the difference as soon as they looked at your chart.

In constructing a bar chart, it is important that the length of the bars accurately reflects the percentages you're trying to illustrate.

It is very important that the length of the percentage categories remain consistent and evenly proportioned.

For example, suppose that the first 10 percent of the college graduate population in your city was represented by one inch of the bar on the chart.

If that is the case, all subsequent 10 percent increments must also be one inch in length. If not, your chart would be distorted and give an inaccurate picture of the percentages of college graduates in the two cities.

To prevent visual distortion, bars should be the same width.

You can gain more impact with more dramatic increments, but you must take care that you are portraying an accurate and clear picture of your facts and numbers.

Your charts should be both clear and accurate – it pays off in credibility.

The previous example uses education as a subject for a comparative chart. Knowing the education levels in a market can be very helpful – people with more education tend to make more money, so a market with a high level of education is usually one where there is a higher than average amount of discretionary income.

This can be very important for businesses such as upscale restaurants, book stores, theater, travel, certain kinds of car dealerships and the like.

A basic education measure is the percentage of people who have graduated from high school and the percentage who have graduated from college.

As the sample chart shows, if the education levels are higher in your market than in some surrounding markets, it is a good idea to make a comparison to show your market to the best advantage.

Line graphs

A line graph looks somewhat like a bar graph, but the line running through the graph often represents measurements of the same thing at different times.

A line graph is really a series of dots – each representing a fact in a time period – that are then connected by a line.

It's an excellent way to show growth and change over a number of years.

A line graph is the best way to show change over time.
Suppose you are using a line graph to illustrate advertising revenue spent by a client over the last five years.

You would put the range of dollar amounts on the x (vertical) axis of the graph and the individual years on the y (horizontal) axis of the graph. You would be able to track and compare the amount spent and see it easily.

The line chart below shows number of housing units – good for dramatizing the growing market in everything related to housing: furniture, real estate, hardware stores, appliances, etc.

Let's take another example: population growth.

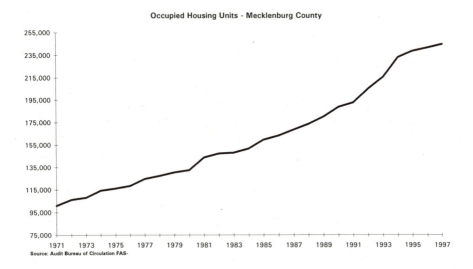

Occupied Housing Units - Mecklenburg County

Source: Audit Bureau of Circulation FAS-

It's often important to document market growth to show how vibrant the market can be for businesses.

Population growth in your market can also be an effective sales point – a client who has been in business for a long time may be unaware of the extent of the greater potential that has been developing.

Using the growth factor as part of a sales presentation allows you to point out advertising strategies designed to reach these potential new customers. By showing population growth, you are showing the client new business opportunity.

When constructing a line graph, the horizontal increments (years, months, etc.) must be the same width.

Make increments consistent – proportions dramatic

The vertical increments must be consistent with each other (i.e. the space between the 5000 to 9999 must be the same height as the space between 10,000 and 14,999.) Otherwise, you are distorting the facts you are trying to portray.

You can set the vertical and horizontal proportions independently of each other, but they must each be consistent within that dimension.

You should set the horizontal and vertical scales of your chart in such a way that your facts are portrayed accurately – but dramatically.

For example, in a city of 200,000 that had experienced growth of 2000 to 3500 each year, a chart with increments of 50,000 would not be very dramatic.

The growth would not show up at all.

But if you set the vertical dimension for increments of 1000, you would be making your point more dramatically – and the chart would still be accurate.

Which chart to choose

Charts are tools. They can help you sell your market and they can help you sell the importance of your medium in the market. They can help you customize presentations for each client and they can help you sell your ideas by dramatizing marketplace facts.

• Pie charts are best for comparing many categories.

• Bar charts are best for making a comparison of two or more categories at one point in time.

• Line graphs are best for showing change over time.

The right charts can help you show the client your knowledge of his market and the size of his marketing opportunity.

After you've covered the market, it's time to talk to the client about his or her business – it's time to talk marketing.

2. PRESENTING THE MARKETER

The primary objectives for this part of the presentation are:

• Establish that you understand the client's business.

• Present key marketing problems (or challenges) faced by that business.

• Set the stage for the opportunities your medium (and your message) represent in addressing those problems and meeting those challenges.

The Need for Custom Presentations

Every client is different.

So while you may have basic sales presentation formats for both new and established clients, you still have to customize a strategy for each individual client.

As you analyze each client's particular situation, try to be honest with yourself about each client.

Two Major Errors to Avoid

Here are two major errors to avoid:

1. Being unrealistic

Being unrealistic about how much advertising can do to change things quickly. Or being unrealistic about how much is reasonable for a client to place with you.

Unless you are honest with yourself about that client's business and needs, you may be engaging in wishful thinking when you plan on how you would like the market to behave – or how you would like that client to behave.

If the client senses you don't have a grip on reality, everything you've done to establish yourself as a marketing partner will go out the window.

2. Not recognizing real opportunities

Talking about problems can be unpleasant. And getting to the root of a problem can be tough work.

But here is where you can discover the opportunity – a problem that your advertising and marketing plan may be able to fix.

Understanding the Client's Business

Your understanding of the client's business will generally be based on the following resources:

• Category Research and Information

Your medium should have available research and information on the general retail category in which the client does business. You will also want to use other source materials – which we discussed in Chapter 5.

• Audience Information

A key factor here focuses on the Audience – you need to establish a match-up with customers (and potential customers) and the audience your medium delivers.

• Specific Information and Observations

You need to be able to talk about the client's favorite topic – the business. Naturally, you can't be expected to know as much about a business as the person who runs it, but you can demonstrate your interest and intelligence.

And, you may be able to offer some insights.

Most business people genuinely enjoy hearing others talk about their business – even if it's just recounting store visits.

The Importance of Store Visits

To get a realistic view and to find those opportunities, your presentation should be based on real world experience as well as information resources.

Generally, you should make at least two visits to the business before you make a sales presentation – an initial visit and a qualifying visit.

The purpose of the initial visit is to introduce yourself and get to know the manager or owner and the store itself.

Your own observation and what the manager tells you are important fact-finding tools that will give you information to make an appropriate and successful sales presentation on a subsequent visit.

You then need to make what is termed a qualifying visit.

Under some circumstances this can be one and the same as your initial visit. But, generally speaking, the manager cannot give you enough time on that first visit.

You also need to think about your initial impressions to formulate the right questions for the qualifying visit.

Experience has shown that two visits are best.

Initial Questions

Here are some questions to guide your thinking in analyzing individual client situations during your initial visit:

How is the business doing at this time?

Is there lots of traffic in the store?

Do customers seem to be buying?

Do they seem happy?

Are they being waited on?

Is there a good atmosphere within the business?

Do the people who work there seem busy but happy?

Both the initial and qualifying visits to the client will help identify client needs for you.

Qualifying Questions

The initial visit will probably lead to more questions for the qualifying visit. Some of these are questions you can appropriately ask the store manager, others you will ask yourself as you discuss and observe.

Would they like more store traffic on off-days? (Most would.)

Is there an untapped market that the client may be missing and should have? (If that is the case, you might want to show the size of that market in the previous section.)

Is present advertising too much like the competition's?

Does the client seem to be using the most effective media mix for the business? (If it's similar to the competition, you may have an opportunity based on differentiation.)

Who is the real competition for this business? Does the manager recognize all the competition there really is?

By thinking about the answers to questions like these, you can begin to develop your presentation as a problem-solving approach to sales. You can then position your medium and your package as the way to solve client problems.

As we said, this part of the presentation will vary based on the individual client situation.

But, in general, it should cover:
- **A look at the overall category**
- **A look at the local market**
- **The Target Audience**
- **The business itself**
- **Problems and Challenges** – both for the category and for the specific business.
- **Opportunities** – this sets the stage for your next section – messages that address problems and meet challenges.

3. PRESENTING THE MESSAGE

An Important Part of Your Presentation

Spec ads can be an important part of your presentation.

These ads are used to introduce ideas you have about possible selling messages for the client.

When presenting print, these ads should be fairly large – giving the client a good idea of what the graphic and copy will look like in a big size. (You may also want to paste an actual size copy of the ad in your publication.)

As mentioned, we believe it's best to present a range of ideas for discussion plus one or more campaign ideas.

For radio, it can be as simple as scripts or possible themes – or even examples of similar work done in other markets. Of course, it can be a commercial fully produced at your station.

Using Spec to Sell

Presenting your ad and campaign ideas to a client and using them to sell does several things:

1. It shows the client you are interested enough in the business to go to the trouble to develop ads specifically for that business. This also positions you as a professional who understands the importance of customer service.

2. It shows the client actual ads. It allows him to see (or hear) how his message might look (or sound) in your medium.

This can be powerful persuasion.

3. It gives you a great tool for talking. Now you can talk with the client about both the business and the ad messages he feels work best.

Even if the client does not like the actual ads, they provide concrete ideas to discuss.

In telling you what he or she does not like, the client is also telling you more about what might work.

Structured Presentation – Freeform Discussion

This section of the presentation will begin in a structured way – but should end with creative discussion.

You should let this part of the discussion take as long as the client wishes.

New ideas may be generated. React positively.

Your ad messages may be only a step on the way to developing the final message – don't be defensive. Involving the client is very good news indeed.

Your ad may inspire the client to talk about other ad ideas. You may find the client sharing thoughts with you they've never shared before.

In some cases, clients have agreed to schedules based on ideas generated during this part of the meeting.

Over time, you'll be able to recognize when to move to the final section of your presentation – featuring your medium and some proposed rate packages.

4. PRESENTING YOUR MEDIUM

In this final part of the presentation, you will need to be able to talk about your own medium and to point out its strengths in reaching the target.

You also need to be aware of any potential weaknesses – either points that may be seen as weaknesses by a potential client or ones pointed out by a competitor.

You also need to be aware of all the competing media in your market and identify those that may be most appealing to the client you are trying to sell.

Your Medium's Audience

For your own medium, you need to know everything about your medium's audience – numbers of readers, listeners or viewers, areas of the market reached or served.

And again, you must make the connection between your audience and the people that marketer needs to reach.

This is the reason to use your medium – to connect with your audience.

Your Medium's Benefits

You must identify the particular benefits your medium offers for this client and make sure the focus of your presentation emphasizes these benefits.

Focus on how your medium delivers the message that meets the client's marketing needs.

As you prepare this part of the presentation, analyze what you offer as opposed to your competitors. (You might want to refer back to the Local Media Checklist on page 69.)

You should also be leading up to the benefits of the creative material, placement, and rate packages you will offer the client.

Your Medium's Services

You may also want to discuss client services you offer – art, audio taping, music, video taping, etc.

You should mention whether they come with the basic rate package or carry a charge.

If appropriate, you should mention deadlines, graphic possibilities, any restrictions on size or time your medium imposes, any restrictions on competitive placement, and, of course, all price rate schedules available.

PROBLEMS AND OBJECTIONS

Solving Problems

Using this presentation structure, you can begin to develop your presentation as a problem-solving approach to sales.

You establish marketing challenges for the client.

You then position your medium and your proposed rate packages as ways to address these client problems – and meet the marketing challenges.

Remember, you can't convince a client to solve problems that aren't real or important.

Your whole presentation should be strategically planned to identify problems and solve them.

This is the underlying strategy for your presentation.

Preparing for Objections

Business people need to see the value in what they are buying. Until you establish yourself as an ally, most clients will try to put you off.

They will put off making the decision by objecting to something – the cost, the medium or the ads.

Rarely will there be a presentation where the client does not offer some objections.

As you prepare your presentation, you should also start preparations to answer objections and turn them into benefits. (We'll talk more about this a bit further on.)

DEVELOPING RATE PLANS

We've discussed how rate plans work in various local media.

Now it's time to think about pulling together three rate plan choices for your sales presentation.

Gathering Intelligence

In your initial visits, you should have found out about how much is spent per month and per year on local advertising.

If this client has advertised with you before, you will know that figure exactly.

If not, your own competitive intelligence should give you some idea – and sometimes the client will tell you.

Some clients plan to spend a certain percentage of sales. Others plan to spend a fixed amount. Most clients know about how much they can spend. Decide how much of this budget you would like to secure.

That is the figure you work from.

Presenting Three Different Rate Plans

The most effective approach is to develop three different rate packages for presentation.

Think of them as A, B, C or big, medium and small.

Usually, the middle plan reflects what you realistically think the client should buy from you.

The usual method for presenting cost is to talk about the biggest plan first, emphasizing its strong points in terms of coverage, size and impact.

Even if your client will eventually go for it, he will still ask about other options. (After all, everyone likes to comparison shop for big ticket/risk items.)

You generally show the middle plan next. It should differ from the bigger plan both in cost and opportunity.

In other words, it should not just be the bigger one cut down or cut apart.

Only show the smallest one if the client is still hesitating. Again, it should differ meaningfully from the other plans.

It should be clear that larger buys offer a greater impact and are a bargain for the coverage and flexibility, but the smallest one may be a way to get your sales foot in the door and would be better than nothing.

You do, after all, want to sell a contract.

Sell savings, too

Here's one way to emphasize what a bargain this is – show the cost at open rate at the bottom and figure the percentage savings by going on contract. That way, you can talk about savings and illustrate that point with figures.

Here are some ideas for making your three plans differ:
- **Size of ad**
- **Frequency of ad**
- **Timing**
- **Placement by day of week**
- **Type of ad in keeping with special timing**

Depending on the type of client, you should be able to think of other variations.

RATE PLAN DEVELOPMENT EXERCISE

Example

Budget of $20,000, based on last year's sales.

Manager is decision maker. Manager is interested in newspaper, but does some radio and some direct mail.

Your job: Present three rate plans for your paper.

Plan A

Budget: $19,000
Emphasis of your campaign:

Frequency:
At least one ad per week through the year.
Other ads to be determind by budget and special events.
In your plan, suggest specific times for the additional ads.
Placement by day of week:

Total cost of package:

Savings over open rate:

Plan B:
Budget $14,000
Emphasis of your campaign:

Frequency:
Placement each week, month, or season.

Total cost of package:

Savings over open rate:

Plan C
Budget: $10,000
Emphasis of your campaign:

Frequency:

Placement schedule:

Total cost of package:

Savings over open rate:

A FEW MORE THINGS...

As you put your presentation and rate plan together, there are a few other things you need to be doing.

Update your background information

Your own database should include information on each individual client and business. You should review this before every visit – particularly before this visit.

Remember, as you work with the client, you should be expanding the information you have.

If possible, indicate the best times of day, week and month to visit. Keep notes – what happened on your last visit, the correctly spelled name and title of the decision-maker, others you'll see on the visit, etc.

One last thing...

As you get ready to present to the client, remember...
Listen, don't argue.

SAMPLE PRESENTATION CHECKLIST:

For review purposes, here are some check points for each section of your presentation:

The Market

√ This part of the presentation should include salient facts about the market.

√ First, give general facts useful to any advertiser.

√ Then, focus on aspects of particular importance to this marketer – these are usually important facts about the market in terms of audience and opportunity.

√ Illustrate important points with charts and graphs.

The Marketer

√ Be certain to talk about the advertiser (this can be done here or at the start of your presentation).

√ State how you see the current business and opportunities for this advertiser (even if some judgments are wrong – in the opinion of the client – you'll be having a discussion on the topic with an opportunity to listen and learn).

√ Present as Problems/Challenges and Opportunities. Answer, as best you can, each problem or challenge with a statement of marketing opportunity – some, but probably not all, can be addressed with advertising in your medium. [Example: Problem – Existing customer base aging, dwindling, and moving out of area. Opportunity – Reach large number of potential customers entering target demographic.]

√ If possible, ask for agreement along the way, based on your previous conversations with this advertiser. [Example: When we met, you identified the young professional (22-34) market as one of your primary targets. Would you agree that this market offers opportunities if…]

√ Discuss how your medium can help to bring the important target audience to the business.

√ Include audience reach and profile material from your own medium's audience.

√ Show how these offer opportunity.

The Message

Here is where you show the spec ads, campaigns, promotions and other ideas you have for this advertiser.

√ You may want to begin by discussing the positioning of this advertiser in relation to the market and the competition.

√ Begin with some sort of strategy statement. Seek agreement in strategic direction before presenting spec work.

√ Stage the work. Set it up with discussion as to the problem/challenge this ad addresses. [NOTE: Consider showing pieces of the work – the theme, for example – before you show the whole ad.]

√ Contrast the message with competitive efforts – dramatize the differentiation.

√ Try to sell the work in terms of marketplace response – talk about how and why the audience will respond to this message.

√ Tie the message back to the marketing opportunity.

The Media Plan(s)

Here is where you discuss:

√ Rate plans – try to have three.

√ Overall costs – there may be other costs, like production – try to cover them, too.

√ Contract opportunities – show the added value that comes from larger schedules.

And More...

This is just a short checklist.

As you develop presentations for your market and your medium, you will have more points to add.

Remember, the more presentations you make, the better you'll do. And remember that, in media sales, the real rewards go to those few who make the extra effort.

PREPARING PROPOSALS

After you have established relationships, you will not have to make full presentations for every recommendation.

You will in the beginning, but after you have established important points about the market and your audience – and the way your medium is performing – you don't have to repeat all of that background material in every meeting.

By the way, every time you meet, you should ask about the client's business – every time.

(Thanks to John Fellows of Giraffe Marketing for providing some of this material.)

Shorter than a Presentation

Proposals are shorter than presentations – they can often be done on a few pieces of paper – sometimes on a single sheet.

They are usually used when you are presenting a new idea to

an existing client.

Since many of the points you have made about the market and your medium are now well-established – the message strategy may be agreed upon as well.

So, you can present new programs in a more abbreviated fashion. In many cases, you may not need to present alternate spending levels. In other cases, two levels, high and medium, will be very adequate.

A proposal might cover these areas:

Budget and Overview

Many recommend establishing this right away.

The first thing the buyer wants to know is cost and you may want to provide this information up front. Give the specific dollar amount.

For example, "This proposes a three-month traffic sponsorship for Nova Cellular including three daily billboards [morning, noon, and afternoon drive time] during the WXY Traffic Extra. It includes 32 sixty second ROS (run-of-station) spots per week every other week - plus bonus spots and bonus billboards – for a total of 200 billboards and 200 spots – for $20,000."

The client already has experience with your medium and you've proven your value. Or, if this is still in doubt, you may be bringing the client a program to establish that value.

Theme

Focus on the core message. Your theme should generally be seven words or less.

For example, "Cash Copiers Cost Less and Last Longer!"

Your medium is there to deliver the client's selling message – this helps to drive that fact home.

Objective

State the objective as succinctly as possible.

Focus on the end-results you expect the client to get by following your recommendations.

John Fellows recommends offering one tangible and one intangible objective. For example, "Increase phone inquiries from 25 to 35 per day. Continue building market position as the most prompt and reliable copier maintenance service."

Strategy

In one or two lines, describe the strategy for this proposal – this is not the overall communications strategy, it is the strategy for this program. It should be compatible with the overall strategy, but this is only the strategy for the program being proposed.

For example, "Reinforce Cash Copiers main theme during the prime selling season." "Radio provides cost-effective continuity to maintain name awareness." Or, "To reach potential Nova Cellular customers while they're driving." Or "Connect Nova, the #1 cellular reseller, with the #1 Traffic Report."

Tactics

State the specific actions to be taken to achieve the objective. Here, you can include an integrated multi-media suggestion, or simply state the role you believe your medium should play in the overall plan.

For example, "Consistently sponsor news or weather broadcasts on _____. Periodically run short-duration, high-frequency schedules."

Recommendation

This is where you make specific suggestions – such as the schedule.

For example, you might write the client's name on a calendar as many times as the ad runs on the days it runs and attach that to your proposal.

For newspaper, a typed schedule with a copy of the ad to be run can do a good job of communicating the recommendation.

Responsibilities

Appointment of responsibilities is particularly important when you're proposing a promotion.

Spell out, in detail, what each party is expected to do – and when. Deadlines and due dates may be critical.

Results

Here, you want to show the client how much "bang for the buck" you'll be delivering.

In radio, you may want a reach and frequency analysis for the entire schedule. In newspaper, readership numbers might help. In outdoor, gross impressions are often used.

Show how your medium is delivering for that client.

You may also wish to refer back to the initially stated objective. (Remember, it's an objective, not a guarantee.)

Rationale

This is the "why buy now" step.

Here, you build upon all the logic you've presented as well as appropriate emotional appeals, in order to bring your prospect to a buying decision.

This step is intentionally left for last.

For example, "By promoting the Cash Copier slogan, you strengthen your market position. By promoting during the peak season, you reach prospects when they're most ready to buy. By promoting Cash Copiers on WXY, you influence a significant number of your primary prospects."

Each of these sections should be short, organized and to the point. Each proposal should be presented as an effort to help the client with his marketing.

Whether or not the proposal is accepted, the result should be an increase in the perception that you are a marketing partner with the client's best business interests at heart.

Each proposal and each presentation is a step toward making the connections and building the relationships that result in a successful career.

Good luck.

15.
MAKING THE PRESENTATION.

Most clients are very busy. So are you.
If you can get a client to give you a full 20 minutes of attention, you're lucky.
You're also well on your way to making a sale.
First, let's review what you should have with you.

THINGS YOU NEED

A few things you should have with you when you go to the presentation are:
- Business cards
- A copy of your medium (if print)
- Tapes of good campaigns (if broadcast)
- A folder with the history of this client, client ads from your own or other medium, and competitive advertising
- And, last but not least, your presentation

You should also have a "book" version of that presentation.

PRESENTATION BOOKS

Many sales reps make up a special presentation book for each client – even for established clients – when they are trying to sell something new, such as a new plan or a new promotional program.

Often, the medium you work for already has a format established with binders or folder covers, letterhead and type format and the other mechanical things you may need to help you get the material organized.

You may want some of the presentation work, like slides or overheads, to be done by an outside supplier.

Table of Contents & Summary

If the presentation is in a booklet format, be sure there is both a table of contents and a summary. You might also consider short summary paragraphs for each section of your presentation.

Remember, the objective is to get the client to go through it with you and then to look at it later as well.

The Table of Contents will help the client go back to an area of interest. The summary pieces will help busy executives focus on your main selling points.

Leave a "Leave Behind"

If the presentation is with flip charts, slides, or tape, be particularly sure to also bring something along – and not just the rate package.

That thing you leave behind is a "leave behind."

For slides, you can get "Four-Ups," which have four slides on a page. These can also function as a handy script guide.

Whatever format you use, you should create some sort of "leave behind."

GETTING STARTED

"Opening the Sale"

As short as 20 minutes might seem, you need to spend the first few minutes building rapport with the client. This "warm up" is actually part of your presentation. We call it "opening the sale."

Business people are just like everyone else. And, since you're building a long-term relationship, spending just a brief bit of time reviewing and talking is a good investment for you. It gives you a further identity with the client. (Adjust this for individual client preferences. Some people will give you the time, but really want to get right down to business.)

The more individualized you can make this "getting into it" time, the stronger you'll be. In addition to keeping notes about the business, you might want to keep notes about children, hobbies, or interests.

You might want to spend a little time on that.

But remember, you're there for business.

Starting the Presentation

You're there. You're prepared with all the facts and figures. You're psyched up to sell. Watch out. You're probably also in danger of overwhelming the client.

Remember that one of the most important things you can do throughout your presentation is to *listen to the client.*

Remember that. One of the reasons you're presenting is so that you will have an opportunity to listen.

So introduce your presentation just as you planned, but also remember to pause and ask questions that can't be answered with a simple yes or no.

As you start your presentation you want to initiate involvement – keep that in mind throughout.

THE PRESENTATION

Next, let's review what's inside the book – the organization of your presentation.

Your presentation should cover the following areas.

1. Market
Market information for the local area.

Ideally, you will begin by presenting a general view of the market that the client agrees with and then, by your selection of charts, helping the client see aspects of the market in a new way – or with new importance.

This part of the presentation should include charts or graphs to illustrate major points. Each chart or graph should have a descriptive heading.

A summary statement at the bottom of each page can help the reader to understand the major point being made.

For initial presentations, basic points that should be covered are: size of market; growth patterns; migration in and out of the market area; age distribution; number and average size of households; educational levels; averages for per capita and household income levels; spending for major retail categories such as food, automotive, furniture, appliances, and the like.

2. Marketer
Summary of basic points you have learned about the client business.

Remember to humanize this section by recounting moments from some of your visits.

We recommend organizing this section with some sort of problem and solution format.

But don't just tell your client about his problems – be sure to point out strengths as well. Otherwise, he'll just feel attacked.

Remember, you're building a relationship.

Use the problems (or challenges) to set up your solutions
– the initial focus of the solution should be presented here
and the pay-off contained in the sections that feature your
message and your medium.

3. Message

Speculative ads for your client.

The format here will vary depending upon your own medium.

If possible, be sure to take at least three ad ideas and an
idea for an on-going campaign you can discuss as well.

At a minimum, you must have some representation of the
client on your medium – even if it is only a TV frame with the
client's logo and theme on it.

Since the ads themselves often communicate very quickly, be
sure to work in enough set-up time to stage them properly.

4. Medium

Audience information, rate plans, and rate sheets.

Remember, three different plans work best.

You should probably begin with a recap of your medium's
audience matched up against the client's target – or potential
target.

From there, make a transition to presenting your plans.

Start with the biggest plan first.

And more...

**End with ideas or plans for integrating your medium
with other media vehicles in the market.**

Show that you're a key part of the larger picture.

Remember, if you take charge of this kind of thinking,
you'll come across as someone who is interested in the client
and his business success – not just someone who wants to
make money.

Besides, showing the client how the various local media
can work together is very likely to bring you more business –
now and later – than you would otherwise have.

AS YOU PRESENT...

Here are some other important things to remember as you
make your presentation.

Let the client help you sell

The sales presentation is a discovery process.

The client should be considering what the business needs
and how what you offer can help solve problems.

Give facts. Then ask questions.

Get the client to agree with you about the business, about the market, and about the medium.

It's fine to solve the business problems together. It's even better to let the client talk himself into your presentation plan.

Clients have good ideas

Create an atmosphere where those ideas are shared with you. Be the person whose good questions prompt the client to think about the business in a new way.

Try to make your presentation interactive. The give and take you establish at the beginning will be particularly helpful when you run into... objections.

HANDLING OBJECTIONS

Be prepared for objections.

In most cases, you'll run into objections of some sort throughout your presentation.

Meeting and overcoming objections is part of your job.

Objections can help you sell

Most good businesspeople will not be comfortable with a decision unless it has been challenged.

Don't take it personally.

In fact, look at it as a potentially positive part of the selling process. You, yourself, debate the pros and cons in your purchase decisions – whether it's a large purchase like a car or just the best-looking produce at the grocery store.

It's the same thing with a media decision. The key is to make the client's natural challenging of your proposal a way to help build confidence and credibility in the decision.

Turn objections into benefits

The best way to overcome objections is to turn them into benefits – that's right, benefits.

For example, if your medium has coverage beyond the normal trading area, emphasize the potential benefit of drawing in new customers and making the store look bigger and more important by associating with your medium.

Just as every problem contains an opportunity, every objection contains a benefit.

In practice, turning objections into benefits can be a little hard, particularly if you're a beginner.

That's why a bit of rehearsal on the most probable objections should have been part of your preparation.

Objections are important

They may be real obstacles to your selling success – or they may be a natural reaction to spending a lot of money. Treat these concerns as the signs of smart business habits.

When you hear an objection, you need to repeat it and then confirm that it is the real objection. Confirming it will not make it more real. And you do need to deal with the real objection to overcome it.

You can do it if you believe in what you sell and you've done your homework well.

Answering the objection

Talk about it. Once it's raised, be as straightforward as possible. It won't go away if you ignore it.

And you won't have any chance to refute it.

Many times an objection is really a concern or a question. You need to listen carefully.

Sometimes, the client is not giving you the real objection or reason for hesitating.

What you hear may only be an excuse not to deal with the sale or to buy. You need to get down to the real objection.

Finding the real objection

The initial objection may not be the real objection.

For example, you may need to ask a number of questions (and listen) to get to the real objection.

Questioning may begin related to an objection about the effectiveness of your medium, but the real objection may be client concerns about the size of the budget.

You can even bring objections up yourself. Pam Lontos, a sales trainer, notes that, *"If you have been selling at least three months, you already have heard and know 99% of all objections for your format and Radio."*

Remember your street smarts. Listen carefully and ask good questions. Explain values in terms that mean something to that particular business.

Remember, people buy for their reasons, not yours.

Learn to use the positive benefit points you thought of to handle objections.

HANDLING OBJECTIONS - EXAMPLES

Here are some examples of ways to handle objections:

Client A. Try a New Strategy

Client A has a local pizza business.

FIFTEEN. Making The Presentation.

It's not a franchise and they don't deliver. What they have to offer is fresh ingredients, pizza made to order, woodburning ovens and a great sauce.

But Client A is sure all of his business comes from word-of-mouth. His claim is that he doesn't need advertising.

While it's true the restaurant is often busier than they can handle at noon, it's often empty at night. When the nearby offices and businesses close, much of the store traffic stops.

You've thought about this before the presentation.

You feel Client A has the potential to draw people to his location with the right advertising and that evening will be the time that new business can be generated.

You meet his objection that he doesn't need advertising with the down-time argument and propose advertising to address just that issue.

You just turned a problem into a benefit.

For something like pizza, you can use humor – or you could appeal to all those who want healthy food. Parking is easier at night, and the area is safe overall.

Your pitch to Client A is to use advertising to bring in evening business – right off, you recognize that he doesn't need it in the daytime.

A typical question here would be: "What if advertising could bring more business at night? Wouldn't that be worth some investment (note the word investment, not cost) to find out?"

Be sure to stress that there has to be enough investment to give it a chance. Implied here is the opportunity Client A has and the fact that you'll recognize it if it doesn't work.

You're now working as a team, as marketing partners, to try to solve the evening lack of business problem.

Client B. Try Again

Client B says he tried advertising with your medium, but he couldn't see any results at all.

Advertising is, after all, hard to measure.

Here's a case where you need to assess just how much effort has been made. If an all out and well-planned advertising effort has been mounted, perhaps B is right.

Or perhaps the ads themselves did not address the right problem or the right audience. Or, as is often the case, the price and the item were not a big enough draw.

When the purpose of the advertising is to recruit new

customers, it is often necessary to combine the advertising message with a very attractive promotional offer.

If it is the type of business that depends on repeat customers (most are), you need to emphasize the long-term value of that customer and the need to invest enough short-term to attract that customer.

In this case, you could suggest a different ad campaign, different placement, or a different offer – with very attractive pricing. Go back to the goals of the ad plan.

Try to get some kind of agreement about what the campaign was to achieve. Point out how hard it is to measure impact and suggest some kind of ads and offers that might make it easier. Point out all the competitive activity and suggest some kind of offer that meets the competition.

Go over the calendar and placement schedule.

Perhaps you and Client B need to work together to determine more effective times to advertise.

By analyzing root causes of the objections, you are able to address real business problems and work to solve them.

The objections have now been turned into tools for improving the program – with you and the client working to solve them.

Client C. Keep Trying

Client C tells you outright that he just doesn't advertise.

Or that he just doesn't advertise on radio – and that's what you're selling.

Each case is individual. In C's case, it may well be the best thing to pull back a bit.

You can keep going by to see Client C on a regular basis.

You can talk a bit, build rapport, suggest promotions for the business.

Two things can come from this approach:

1. You build trust with Client C and prove you're interested in his business – this may bring you some ad dollars eventually.

2. Client C may recommend you to friends who do advertise. Some time investment with C is very probably a good investment for you.

Overall, however, remember the job is to sell.

In Client C's case, you're going for the long-term gain.

One common objection is cost

A common way to try to address that objection is to stress that advertising dollars are an investment, not a cost.

FIFTEEN. Making The Presentation.

Better yet, show the value – to the individual business – that is returned by that advertising investment.

Talking about investment versus expenditure and value versus cost can be a powerful tool in getting the client to think positively about advertising expenditures.

CLOSING THE SALE

This is the area where most beginners fall down.

At this point, you've been through all the objections and the good points you needed to make.

The speculative ads have been discussed and dissected.

Now you need to ask for the order. The money.

That's hard for two reasons:

1. It feels awkward until you have experience.

2. This is the place where you'll really be turned down (you think). But if you've done a good job until now, you've laid all the foundation you need.

Here's what you've done to this point:
- **Built rapport**
- **Listened to the client**
- **Discussed the market**
- **Discussed the business**
- **Listened to the client**
- **Asked good questions**
- **Shown ads specific to the business**
- **Listened to the client**
- **Answered objections**
- **Listened to the client**
- **Laid strategy**
- **Explained rate plans**
- **Listened to the client**
- **Stressed value and investment over cost**
- **Shown yourself to be both professional and flexible**

Build on this.

Listen to the Client

Notice how many times "Listened to the client" is listed.

Ask: Which plan is best for you? When shall we start? How shall we modify (or improve) the ads? Do you want the Wednesday-Sunday or the Tuesday-Friday placement?

Never ask: Shall we do this? How do you feel about this? The how-do-you-feel questions should have come much earlier in the presentation.

If you've built your sales presentation well, the closing should be natural. If the client balks, backtrack and review.

AFTER THE SALE

Once you've closed, keep up the enthusiasm.

End on an upbeat note. Promise to return.

Give a promise of good customer satisfaction.

If you don't ask for the order, you won't sell anything. Learn to handle rejection.

If you didn't "Make The Sale"

A "no" is not the end of the line between you and the client.

You can come back with a new plan, new information and new ads.

Here's where the street smart instincts come into play.

In this kind of job, you're setting the agenda for the long-term relationship. You don't have to win every time – you just need to win over time.

Clients differ. Some will buy right away. Some will buy only after a period of time.

You need to be as flexible as possible.

Always remember that you need to talk with a lot of people for every sale.

Everyone has a different style. Be honest with yourself and evaluate yours. What works for you is something you need to adapt for all your clients – while customizing for each.

REVIEWING YOUR PERFORMANCE

After the presentation, you should work on evaluating and improving – particularly at the beginning of your career.

It takes a while to get it right, so you should spend a good amount of effort on reviewing and then "polishing" your performance.

Evaluating your presentation

Here are key points to review – be honest with yourself.

Did you open strongly with a clear statement of purpose?

Did you talk about benefits for the client's business?

Did you use your facts and market data well?

Did you make them relevant for the individual business?

Did you listen well?

Were the budget plans appropriate and relevant?

Had you rehearsed for the right objections? Were you able to meet them in a positive way?

FIFTEEN. Making The Presentation.

Did you close – ask for the order?

How was your presentation style?

Did you use your voice well? Make eye contact?

Did you have a smooth comfortable pace?

Did you manage to be both in control of the presentation and flexible to client needs?

Did you talk knowledgeably about your medium?

If you did all these things, you're on the right track – whether you made the sale or not. Keep trying.

OTHER TYPES OF PRESENTATIONS

Out-of-town decision-makers

Today, many local businesses are owned by companies that are outside the local market area. The advertising decision-makers do not live within the local area and are not a part of that community.

To reach the decision-makers for these kinds of businesses, you'll have to travel to them. Many of these kinds of regional or national businesses use advertising agencies, so your presentation may be to a regional office group, to an agency or to both.

Today, many locally owned businesses may use an agency as well. So even on the local market level, you may have to make an agency presentation.

A typical situation

Here's an example. Let's say you are a sales rep for one of the three top-rated radio stations.

The client is the local branch of a regional food store, and you have been asked to do a presentation about your station for an agency at their regional location.

So have two other radio stations – your main competitors.

Do your homework

You will be presenting to a very knowledgeable audience. You will need to know not only your local branch, but about the food store chain, its policies, its locations and its advertising patterns.

Your audience will already know much of this information.

When you deal with local decision makers, you get to build trust and confidence over time. When you make a presentation to non-local decision makers, you may only get one shot.

You're likely to have fifteen minutes to sell your station and yourself.

Realize that you're dealing with people who don't know what it is like to live and work in the area. More than ever, you'll be selling your local market and your own local medium.

They're looking for audience statistics and what looks like the best buy overall.

You need to anticipate the questions – both spoken and unspoken. You'll need to put your medium in context and develop extra value for it beyond the statistics and audience figures as well as you can.

For radio, they are likely to deal in cost per point and ratings as the decision variables. You need to be able to discuss the place your medium has in that market.

The Need for Planning

In planning this type of presentation, be aware that transitions are particularly important. This kind of presentation is more formal and there is much less chance for interaction.

Questions are likely to be posed at the end, so you'll also lose the advantage of asking for agreement throughout.

You may well be standing in front of a room, with your audience at a conference table. You'll have to project enthusiasm and warmth while selling. You'll have to plan and practice and be in control of the presentation.

You also know you have competition – and it's likely to be giving a presentation right after yours.

It's up to you to make your medium indispensable.

Point out all the ways in which your medium can really help the business to reach its customers.

Know the strengths and weaknesses of all the media in the marketplace. Stress the particular positive values of your own.

And remember, the reason they're asking you to present is that they are serious about spending money – so it's worth the extra effort.

Agency Presentations – the Message Section

Naturally, when presenting to an agency, the message part of the presentation is much reduced or eliminated.

But you should still be prepared to be helpful in suggesting what might work best for their client.

Showing or playing other successful approaches in that category – which worked in other markets – is another appropriate way to present messages when presenting to an agency.

When you show successful messages in your medium, the agency is challenged as well.

VI.
STAYING
ON THE
JOB.

"Keeping everlastingly at it."

N.W. Ayer

This final section is about staying on the job.
And it's about growing on the job.
It's about earning and learning.

As your presentation skills improve, as you build your client base, you'll also need to develop other abilities.

Here, we'll discuss some of the other important aspects of building a successful career in media sales – from the basics of getting paid to what it takes to get promoted.

We've asked other top professionals to share a little of their experience with you.

And we've provided some Resources to help you keep moving ahead.

16. SALES JOB FACTS.

When you work in sales, you work in many different jobs. You work in marketing. You work in idea and message development, media placement, new business development – an entire range of activities that create customer satisfaction and customer success.

The Media Rep is the person who helps build and develop that success for many different kinds of businesses and many different types of clients.

If you like variety, details, deadlines, problem solving, developing strategy and competition, you'll find it can be an exciting and rewarding career.

CONTINUING CLIENT SERVICE

The sale is only the beginning

Every client relationship must be nurtured.

Even after a winning presentation, your job continues.

It takes so much effort to develop a customer, you have to retain as high a percentage as possible for your overall business to grow. That's why customer satisfaction will always remain a top priority.

Beginning accounts – small clients

When you start in the business, you'll undoubtedly be given a client list with many smaller clients.

While each of them will only generate a fraction of your total commission, they are an important part of the success of any local medium.

And they may well be an important part of your early success.

Working with a small client list will teach you about many different types of businesses and people. You'll gain a feeling for the community. And you'll gain the experience you'll need as you add larger clients to your list.

So even though the big clients may pay the greatest share, the small client businesses are the ones that do the most to help you pay your dues.

Landing larger clients

As your career grows, so will your client list.

If a more senior salesperson leaves, you may be assigned some of those accounts – particularly if you've done a good job servicing your first accounts.

You'll also land a few larger clients on your own.

One of the best ways to learn to land those big fish comes from learning to land – and hold on to – the small ones.

Keeping track of the customer's business

When you're in advertising, you have to remember that the important issue isn't the advertising, it's the client's business.

When business is good, the ads are good.

When business is bad, the ads are bad.

Even if it's the same ad.

Though the advertising is often the only thing you have any control over, you need to stay in touch with the overall health of the client's business. And you need to do all you can to help make it healthier.

Good salespeople keep in touch even when there is nothing new to sell. They keep in touch with the client and they keep in touch with the business.

Good salespeople make a regular habit of doing things, like bringing clippings and information to clients.

Your job is to help the client's business grow. Think of yourself as part of the team.

If things get tough for a client (it happens all the time), look for ways to stay on that client's team. One way to do that is to have a game plan for customer crises.

Customer Crisis Game Plan:

First, identify the "crisis" by category.

It may be new competition, renewed competition from an old source, seasonal slump, weather, etc.

Even though it's a crisis, chances are it's neither unprecedented nor unexplainable.

The first step is to identify the problem.

Second, identify possible solutions.

Possible solutions may be increased advertising (your medium or another, like direct mail), change in advertising (minor adjustment or entirely new positioning), finding additional target markets (geographic or demographic), promotions, etc.

Remember that advertising is not always the answer.

If possible, decide with the client if new or different or more frequent advertising might be an answer to the problem.

If so, refer to your files of ads placed in your medium and those placed or run in other media – for this client and for the competition.

Third, formulate a strategy.

Of all the possibilities, which seems the best? (Remember, at this stage, a strategy is also an hypothesis.)

Ads? Promotions? In-store event? New positioning? (Note: Be sure to decide how to evaluate the new strategy before you implement it. Then do so after it has been executed.)

Or, you may have some alternate strategies to discuss with the client.

Finally, develop a recommended plan.

In addition, you also need a back-up or follow-up plan for your client presentation.

Each crisis is an opportunity to build your problem-solving skills and your client relationships.

You will neither solve every problem nor get every recommendation approved, but you'll solve some of them.

And, each time, you'll learn.

IBM had a saying which can be useful to all of us, *"Each problem is an opportunity to demonstrate service."*

Learn to love problems. If there weren't problems, they wouldn't need us.

Over time, you'll want to keep a running file of all your solutions for this and other clients.

Be flexible. Be available. Be ready to help.

By keeping up with the client on a regular basis, you'll have a better feel of how to deal with a crisis – in fact, you may even be able to sense one coming on before the client does.

MANAGING YOUR TIME

We are each given the same amount of time in a day.

How well you use that time will be a major determinant of how well you do – particularly at the start of your career.

You'll have to manage your time so that you give each business the attention it needs to grow.

You'll have to decide just how much time to spend with each to be effective, yet not waste time.

You'll be building relationships.

And, every day, managing your limited time will be a constant challenge.

You need to allow time for special clients, presentations, and cold call prospecting.

You'll need to set goals and divide your time to meet them.

To do that well, you'll need to set priorities.

Priorities: When, Who, Where

Because of the complexity of the tasks and the number of clients you serve, your time-management plan actually resembles a multi-dimensional grid – you need to include:

- Tasks organized by immediacy (when)
- Tasks organized by importance (who)
- Task organized by geography (where)

Let's review them.

Tasks organized by immediacy (when)

Review goals and client needs on a regular basis and tag them as "A," "B," and "C" priorities.

A. What must be done first because of deadlines (and in order to survive). This needs immediate attention.

B. What, while important, can wait until tomorrow – or at least until later in the afternoon.

C. Recurring tasks – long-term or monthly. Set deadlines for these and move them up the priority list as needed.

Tasks organized by importance (who) and context (what)

Some clients are more important at some times.

You need to put this in context, as it will vary.

Your calendar will help to guide you and approaching deadlines often help do the organizing for you.

Bigger (more productive) clients may take a disproportionate amount of your time because there are more ads to produce and because the campaigns are more complicated. But be sure to leave time for the many smaller clients as well.

As you service others, it can be easy to forget that you and your own career goals are important, too.

Factor in what you need to keep growing in your own career and what your business needs are long-term.

Otherwise, you'll keep putting out small fires and never get to the important long-term tasks.

Task organized by geography (where)

Plot time needed for each client by the map of your area.

Try to schedule routine appointments in a geographically sensible way. Keep prospecting.

Follow-up work in one part of town may allow you to squeeze in a few initial visits to nearby businesses.

Keep those antennae tuned and those "street smarts" working – particularly when you're out on the street.

A few more time-management tips:

• Keep a running assessment of your goals and time frame for each client.

• Keep a "futures" book which notes any upcoming needs for a client, including: end of contract year, seasonal slump or rush, special events, other deadlines, etc. Refer to this calendar when planning your weekly or monthly schedule.

• Try to find some time every week to plan – so you aren't spending all of your time responding to clients. (This can happen. You'll find yourself very busy without moving ahead on some of your important priorities.)

• Keep a running "collections" list.

Never stop prospecting

Small clients can help you to build networks of potential contacts and customers.

People all over the community want their goods and services and your medium is the way to bring information about them to the buying audience.

That puts you in contact with others you can help.

It's one more reason good salespeople need to become a part of the community.

You'll see your clients away from the business as well. The decision-makers need to see you out in the community.

Not only will it help you be a better salesperson, it just might help you be a better person, too.

SIXTEEN. Sales Job Facts.

A TYPICAL JOB DESCRIPTION

It's easy to see why time management is so critical. Here's the job description for a typical media sales job:

• Keep track of 60-80 on-going clients who are on the active schedule for your medium.

• Make sure all ad copy and tapes are in on time and have gone through production.

• Arrange to have proofs sent to all clients who need them.

• Make certain all scheduled ads have run and are correct.

• Call and meet with clients on a regular basis to talk about the advertising program, gather new information about the client and business, pass on information and news to the client and plan new schedules and new advertising in advance.

• Keep a file of all ads run by each of your clients in your own medium and competing media.

• Keep updating a file of ideas for each client.

• Prospect for new clients.

• Keep a list of all new or expanding businesses with a view to developing new advertising business for your own medium.

• Revisit former clients who have dropped your medium or changed their ad schedules in some way.

• Keep in touch with all your contacts.

• Have a schedule for making cold calls to generate new information and new business.

• Continue to gather information for presentations to these new prospects and inactive customers.

• Attend community and business trade functions in your area and your region.

• Keep up with the research data for your area and update your own information files regularly.

• Attend meetings of your own professional organizations in the area – sometimes a national or regional meeting – and keep on the lookout for new ideas and new contacts.

• Volunteer to be a program chairman, membership chair, or other officer in your professional organization.

• Keep track of the competition.

• Keep alert – for new clients, for new ads from your own clients, for new services, and for other competitive developments.

- Keep up with all your own paperwork and telephone calls. Stay organized. Being able to answer client questions quickly is a great competitive advantage.
- Keep all the records regarding your work in order.

If all the above sounds interesting, you may be ready for the challenge.

All media sales jobs have essentially this job description.

Remember, in many ways you can make your own success, help clients with their businesses and help your own career at the same time. It all goes together.

COMPENSATION

Here are a few other questions you might have.

This section isn't about checklists, it's about paychecks.

How do you get paid?

Most media firms pay a base salary plus commission.

Some pay on commission only. While that commission rate is higher, it also means that you won't get paid at all if you don't make any sales.

To even things out, sometimes you are paid a "draw" against future commissions.

Some firms start you out with a salary for a few months and then go to a heavier commission schedule once you have a start working with a few clients.

How does it work?

You'll be given a goal – a certain dollar amount of billings or sales to get every month. This is your base, and you must achieve that to survive on the job.

Goals are set according to expectations – in a seasonal market, for example, you'll be expected to bring in a greater percentage of the annual goal in the peak months – same thing for the Christmas season when merchants and services advertise more.

Your goal for every month will depend upon the types of businesses you have on your own list and upon the area in which you are working.

Once you make the base billing goal for each month, you will begin to earn commission on additional sales.

Commissions

Generally, there is a different commission rate for different categories of business.

SIXTEEN. Sales Job Facts.

So you'll probably earn different rates of commission on different types of accounts – for example, you may earn less on political ads than on new department store business.

You may earn a different percentage on agency business or national business than on local business.

Basically, higher commission is generally earned on new business and for those accounts with a higher level of difficulty. If your paper or radio station has had the same account for years and you never sell any additional advertising, your commission rate may be lower on that account.

The commission rate for each type of business on your list is something that you and your boss agree on when you sign your contract.

An Example:

Here is a typical example of a commission rate schedule for one medium billing radio station in a seasonal market of 35,000 year-round residents and a seasonal average of 140,000:

Base sales = $7500 a month

Commission beyond base sales:

New business development = 18% commission
Agency ads = 12% commission
Political ads = 10% commission
Regular clients = 14% commission

Collections

One important thing you should know – *many media only pay the commission on your sales once the bill is paid.*

If the check from the business does not reach the bank by a certain date, you'll get paid from that sale in the next month.

This can be a bit tough on you if you sold an ad in the early part of the month and were counting on the sale to come through as a commission for you.

Some clients do not pay right away. You may be asked to help collect accounts by either calling your client or going there in person.

Collections can be an adventure.

To illustrate the book, we considered using a cartoon of me leaping over a farmyard fence. I ran into a farmer with a shotgun during an attempt to collect on some media bills.

Once you've had a collection adventure or two, you'll find it easy to understand the reason for the qualification questions we covered earlier.

Sad to say, there will always be a small group of so-called

business people who consider paying media bills as optional.

Usually, a bit of asking around will give you ample warning.

These people leave a trail, and even your competitors are glad to warn you.

TRADE ACCOUNTS

The broadcast media use "trade" with clients as well as cash. Here's how it works:

If a client wants a trade account, the sales rep will sell some ads – but there is no cash exchanged.

Instead, the client receives free time on the air in exchange for goods or services the business offers.

For example, a restaurant may "trade" air time at market price for the equal price of dinners at the restaurant.

Some radio stations trade for gasoline or other automotive services for the sales reps. As a part of the "perks" or "bonus," the rep may use the dinners for clients and sometimes for personal business. Trade may also be given to a sales rep as a reward for good work – a sort of bonus.

Stations also trade with clients in regional markets.

For example, a hotel in Atlanta may trade with a radio station in Jacksonville, Florida. The hotel hopes to lure people from the Jacksonville area for a weekend.

The radio station personnel may get to use the hotel trade for a trip of their own. Or a listener promotion may be developed – win a weekend in Atlanta.

Sometimes trade is used in addition to cash for "added value" promotions. Let's say that, in addition to a cash buy for radio time, you agree with a local pizza chain to feature their products as part of a listener phone-in program. The pizza chain gets additional free mentions on your station for the cost of a pizza.

While most stations would prefer to have cash accounts, the trade practice keeps clients on the air and generates business neither party would have otherwise. Most stations will only allow a certain percentage of business from any client to be in trade. Some clients do not do any trade at all – it depends upon the station and upon the nature of the advertiser's business.

Growing your business

After you've been in the business a year or two, your commission and salary schedule will usually depend upon your previous year's performance.

You may gain a higher base salary, but you'll also have new numbers (your own!) in sales to match. Your success should all work out to your benefit, however.

Sometimes, if your geographic area grows, some of your accounts may be taken away and given to someone else. While this seems very unfair to some sales reps, you need to be sure you have received some kind of commission reward for generating the new business in the first place.

If you become a sales manager, you will often have to make these kinds of adjustments. For example, some reps are great at landing new accounts, but not as good at service.

Others are the opposite – superb at ongoing support, but not the best in landing new accounts. While you always want someone who does both well, it doesn't always work that way.

You also need to realize that new business does not stay that way long. Some media pay a new business commission for the first few months and then move that account to regular business – at a regular commission rate.

As you work to grow your business, management will work with you to provide incentives.

Then, as you grow, they will keep your base rising (even though they may trim a bit here and there) as they raise your goals. It's usually a process of discussion and negotiation.

That's how you can, as one of my former students described it, "decide how big a raise to give yourself every year."

The way it works out is that your efforts reward both your medium (your employer) and you. And your efforts help the client as well.

So it should be a win-win-win situation.

Commission-only jobs

Should you decide to join a medium on a commission-only basis, you will be paid a higher commission for all you sell, but you will not receive any benefits or salary.

Some media use commission-only sales people just to generate new business; these may pay quite handsomely – 25 percent or more.

Commonly, you only get to keep these new clients for six to twelve months before they're turned over to a regular rep.

Selling additional products

Newspapers and broadcast media today often offer other subsidiary and supplemental products to clients.

In the newspaper business, virtually everyone offers a range of special sections and supplements.

These may be regular sections, such as auto or jobs, or they may be annual or one time only sections such as gardening or special event coverage.

The sales reps may sell space in these as well as the main newspaper product – or there may be a special sales staff to sell these other products.

There is often a special commission schedule for these products. To receive this commision you must usually sell new space and not just move old accounts from the regular pages.

For broadcast media, you are often selling promotions or special packages in addition to the regular air time.

Again, there may be special commissions or incentives for these sales.

Other combinations

Many media companies have more than one media outlet in a market. There may be a radio station and a TV station. Or more than one radio station.

Newspapers, for example, often own broadcast properties in their markets.

There are almost as many combinations as there are markets.

In each case, there are additional opportunities to practice "integration" and extend your campaign across local media – some of these opportunities may be commissionable – others will raise your profile with upper management.

A TYPICAL DAY

An important component in deciding on a career is discovering what a job would really be like on a day by day basis.

Here's a look at a Media Rep job.

Exciting and routine

As with nearly all jobs, sales has a combination of exciting and routine tasks. Most sales people love the visible parts of the job – talking with clients, meeting deadlines, developing and presenting strategy and ideas.

And, most sales people put up with the routine paperwork – filling out orders, checking proofs, following up on ads that are running and making several calls to check on future ad campaigns and client plans.

Generally speaking, the best time of the day for sales calls is between 9 AM and 4 PM although some clients prefer to meet early in the morning or at the close of the business day.

A typical day (if such a thing exists) might be like the following. In this case, we'll pick a rep for a newspaper.

8 AM - 9 AM

Check on ads that ran last night and this morning. Check all phone calls. Return all possible calls.

Look over plans for the day, confirming some appointments and making sure files and take-along items are ready and in order for the day. Perhaps you'll meet with someone from your art or production department.

Meet with supervisor (sometimes there are early morning sales meetings).

Work with sales assistant (if you have one) to outline and confirm work for that day.

9 AM - Noon

Meet with several regular clients. For some, this will be a routine call, perhaps picking up new ads or bringing proofs by to discuss.

Perhaps proofs have been faxed to the client and the two of you meet to discuss a schedule using these new ads.

As usual, you will plan your day for maximum client hours and minimum driving – and, as always, some clients will have conflicts and you'll spend time driving routes that are less efficient. But you'll use this time on your cellular phone to confirm appointments, make others, and check back with the office.

If you find yourself with an extra half-hour, you may make a cold call on a business in the area that is on your list.

Noon - 1 PM

Some days you'll have a business lunch or a professional meeting. Other days you'll grab something to eat on the way to other meetings.

1 PM - 4 PM

More client meetings. Perhaps you'll have a presentation for a new campaign or new spec ads for a client.

Maybe you'll spend some of the time prospecting a new client on a second or third visit. Or perhaps you'll have an agency presentation – either in town or away.

4 PM - 6 PM

Back to the office sometime in this time frame to check on the day, production, art and calls that weren't forwarded.

Check in with your sales assistant, art or production departments, your boss or all of these.

Organize the next day.

Evening

Meet with a client for a drink or at their office for a late presentation. Even if you go out on your own, you're likely to see people who are clients – or who could be.

You're always making contacts. If you take someone out for a business dinner, you'll no doubt see one of your clients – who manages or owns the restaurant you choose.

Work can be fun

Sound busy? It is.

The advantages of this kind of out-of-the-office busy schedule is that you know everyone in town.

It's an active schedule – and it's fun.

And, as time goes on, some of the relationships may grow to become genuine friendships.

[Note: Work can be fun, but we were also asked to mention that, sad to say, some of these occasions can still be an opportunity to experience a less enlightened view of proper business behavior.

Women still have to be on guard – clients, and potential clients, have been known to harass – and worse.]

PROFESSIONAL ORGANIZATIONS

As a part of your professional development – and as a part of becoming a member of the professional community – you'll belong to several professional organizations.

Your local Ad Club

First of all, you'll belong to your local ad club, which is likely to be a member of the American Advertising Federation, and meet once a month – at lunch or dinner. It will also hold a variety of public service, professional development, and fund-raising activities every year.

Local community groups

You are also likely to belong to the Chamber of Commerce and other community organizations.

This means that you and your newspaper, radio station or television station will be involved in any number of charitable and community activities.

For example, you may be the liaison person for the drive to help poor children at Christmas.

On a Saturday in December, you may find yourself helping underpriviledged children pick out clothing for themselves and presents for their families.

Or you may be involved in a community literacy effort and find yourself teaching reading once a week in the early evening.

You might also find yourself helping to organize a town meeting on some important local issue like water quality or crime. And you may find that you'll become a better salesperson at the same time you become a better person.

Regional and national groups

In addition, you'll want to belong to one or more of the regional and national organizations related to your medium.

These include your state Press Association, the National Newspaper Association, or the Newspaper Association of America (depending upon the size of your newspaper), the International Newspaper Marketing Association, the Radio Advertising Bureau, Cable Advertising Bureau, the Outdoor Association, and others.

For a listing of national associations and addresses, see the Resource Guide in the back of this book. (Note to students: many local, regional and national organizations, such as the American Advertising Federation, also have student chapters.)

17. IMPROVING PERFORMANCE.

*I*n this section, we'll talk about getting better at doing your job. We'll talk about what your clients want from you, and some top professionals will serve up a few words to the wise.

WHAT CLIENTS WANT FROM YOU

What do advertisers want?

Naturally, they want the best package for the best price – but that package has to be tailored to their individual and specific needs.

Matching up their business against target groups and purchase cycles is key.

So the first thing they want is for you to understand their needs and their business.

Advertising rates and packages for a medium are effective only when they are perceived to represent a cost effective alternative to other advertising media.

You have to recognize that each individual medium offers some audience advantage but also some constraints.

Advertisers want some assurance that the allocation of budget to each medium is their best possible investment.

As marketing problems get more difficult, media weight alone will not solve today's problems – it has to be part of an effective marketing program.

From the sales viewpoint, this means it is no longer acceptable to push one's own medium as the panacea for all client problems. Sales reps must think in terms of marketing and media packages.

SEVENTEEN. Improving Performance.

That means that you should always be looking for clients that you can do a good job for.

Perceived cost effectiveness, efficiency in reaching the target audience, control over placement and timing, and quality and reliability of service provided are the key factors swaying decisions about how an advertiser will spend his money.

Today, advertisers demand service. A big part of that service is making their businesses successful – and building not only immediate business, but repeat business.

Good business people deliver good service to *their* clients – people who spend money with them. They spend money with you – so it's not unreasonable that they should expect service, too.

You sell potential and opportunity, but you must sell results and service as well. The challenge, as we've said from the beginning, is to make the critical connection between media, message, and client needs.

You must be the facilitator to motivate customers and bring seller and buyer together.

Advertisers want value

Advertisers don't want the cheapest medium. They don't want deals if the deals don't work. What they want today – and have always wanted – is value for the money. It's your job to make sure they see that that is what you can offer.

Advertisers also want placement of ads to be easy. If they have to do all of their own work, why do they need you?

They want deadlines, specifications, discounts, and placement to be clear. They want to be able to get clear answers from you, and they want those answers to make sense in terms of value.

They know you're in business, too. They respect that.

So, if you must have rules to run your business (like deadlines and color charges), they can understand that if you explain it in a business-like way.

Advertisers want service

Advertisers want you to be available when they need to ask questions. You and your clients may come to like one another, but yours is still a business relationship.

You need to keep appointments, return calls, and answer questions. You need to be responsible to ask questions as well – once you know the client and the business, you'll notice ads or buys that do not seem to fit with the overall plan.

You need to ask the client about these.

Advertisers want good information

Both client businesses and your business – the media – operate in an increasingly competitive arena.

Advertisers need detailed information about readers, viewers and listeners. They want facts and figures about the market, about competition, and about your business.

They want rate structures that make sense in the competitive environment.

And, whether they know it or not, they want you to be a marketing partner.

Advertisers want you to understand how they think.

They want – and need – you to put yourself in their place. Let's illustrate that with a story.

I know a 12-year old who moved from Charlotte, North Carolina to Anchorage, Alaska when she was eight.

Now, as we all know, there are many striking differences betwen Anchorage and Charlotte. If I asked you to point them out, you might come up with many different answers.

I think most of us would come up with something to do with the differences in climate, in terrain, in lifestyle or in opportunities.

For example, in Alaska, there are mountains, water, glaciers and a whole culture based upon the Northland: adventure, survival, independence, and the like.

Charlotte is flat, has hardly any winter, lots of trees, is a large banking center and has many people who are relatively conservative and lead traditional lives.

So, I asked this child, "Addie, what do you think is the biggest difference between Charlotte and Anchorage?"

She thought for a while and finally said, "Well, there aren't any Hardees restaurants in Anchorage. There are McDonald's, but no Hardees."

Not the answer you'd expect. But what this 12-year old said has a lot to do with marketing and sales. To her, this was the big difference that counted. What we think is obvious may not be obvious to the client at all.

Yet, we often make the mistake of assuming the customer thinks the way we do – same issues, same relevance, and same understandings.

What you need to do instead is to think about client needs and add benefits from the client's view.

We must be prepared to do a reality check on that view in relation to the target audience, the competition and the resources of the businesses – that's the beginning of problem-solving necessary for success on all sides.

What advertisers want is for you to listen to them. They want the best package for the money.

And, most of all, they want it to work.

TIPS FROM TOP SALES PROFESSIONALS.

This is the very first version of this book.

So this section is a little shorter than it will be in later editions. It will contain good advice from people who have already succeeded in the world of media.

Our first contribution is some excellent advice from Chris Lytle of The AdVisory Board.

First, Three Secrets of Success, and then the Four Stages of a successful career in media sales..

THREE SECRETS OF SUCCESS

There are 3 secrets of success:
1. You've got to know what you're doing.
2. You've got to know you know what you're doing
3. You've got to be known for what you know.

If your client knows you don't know what you're doing, all he or she needs from you is your lowest price.

The most important thing you can do is to quit selling your medium and start selling what your client sells.

Your clients get better when you get better.

Chris Lytle
The AdVisory Board

FOUR STAGES OF SUCCESS

What kind of sales person do you want to be?

That's a conscious choice that you make every day.

Jim Holden is president of the Chicago-based Holden Group.

Holden's view on the Four Stages of Competitive Readiness appeared in a recent issue of *Sales and Marketing Manager Canada*.

His Four Stages are a great way to think about where you are in selling and where you want to be.

Stage One – The Emerging Salesperson

Stage One is the Emerging Salesperson. The aim of an Emerging Salesperson is to be considered, to get in on the buy.

In Stage One, it's "Here's my business card. If you need anything just give me a call."

Stage One sellers focus on their own station.

"We're country. We're strong with adults 25-54. We skew slightly toward women."

Their relationship with clients is casual. "Let's do lunch sometime," "I was in the neighborhood and wanted to drop this off."

And they provide customers with product or service options. "Here's our media kit. We have news, sports, and weather sponsorships available." "Here's a special package for you to consider." That's the Stage One or Emerging Salesperson.

Stage Two – The Salesperson

Stage Two is the Salesperson. The aim: to make the sale.

Stage Two focuses on the customer.

"Here's how this will help you. Here are three reasons to act now." The relationship is trusting.

The salesperson has knowledge and credibility, and provides the client with application solutions. "Here's a way to build traffic." "Here's a way to position yourself." "Here's a plan to help you beat your competitor."

Stage Three – The Competitive Salesperson

Now let's go to Stage Three, the Competitive Salesperson.

The aim here is to get repeat orders, not just a sale. This ties into what Harvey MacKay says, "A good salesperson is one who can get the order and the reorder from a customer who is doing business with someone else."

In Stage Three, the focus is on the competition.

"I can beat that guy." "I can undercut that guy." "I can be more creative than that guy."

The relationship with the client is one of mutual understanding. "I know your needs, you know my needs."

And the Competitive Salesperson provides the client with

information on business issues.

This is the clipper and sender – someone actively concerned about the client's business.

This is a person who is going the extra mile.

Stage Four – The Competitive Sales Consultant

But not as far as the Stage Four Salesperson.

According to Holden, Stage Four is the Competitive Sales Consultant. At Stage Four, the aim is to "own" the account – to be a sustaining resource may be another way to look at it.

To be of such service that you get invited to the client's Christmas party. To be thought of as an unpaid employee of the client's business.

The focus is on the customer's markets.

You are actually worried about your prospect's prospects' problems or your customer's customer rather than simply concerned about your competitors.

The relationship with clients is *symbiotic.*

(I looked up symbiosis in the dictionary. Let me read you the definition. "Symbiosis – association of two different organisms which live attached to each other and contribute to each other's support.")

It's the ultimate win-win – a wonderful state to be in with a client. Competitive Sales Consultants provide the clients with strategic direction.

Wow. That's a long way from Herb Tarlek (Sales Manager on the TV show *WKRP in Cincinnati*), who would probably be classified as a Stage One or, on his best days, a Stage Two salesperson.

This evolution is very important because, if you don't know that there are different stages of salespeople, you cannot consciously decide what kind of salesperson you want to be.

"The reality," says Holden, "is you can do only two things in selling. You can service demand like 100 other competitors, or you can create demand. When we talk about Stage Three and Stage Four selling we are talking about demand creation. That's where the action is.

That's where the profits are, too.

Chris Lytle
The AdVisory Board

THE BEGINNING...

This book is over. For now.

But we want it to grow – as we want your career to grow.

So we'll keep on updating it with more good advice from media professionals and more new information from the fast-changing world of media.

WE WANT TO HEAR FROM YOU

Whether you're a fresh newcomer or an experienced pro, a Sales Manager or a Trainee, we'd like to know more about your career as a Media Person.

If you have good advice, or an interesting story, or a new observation, we'd like you to share it with us.

You'll be helping many others who are just entering the world of Media Sales.

And we'll finish by thanking you in advance.

The Next Edition

You can send a short article or a long letter.

Send an example of an ad campaign that really helped one of your clients. Tell us what happened.

Tell us whatever you think would be helpful to those who read the next edition of this book.

Send your materials to:

Prof. Mary Alice Shaver
c/o The Copy Workshop
2144 N. Hudson
Chicago, IL 60614
☎ 312-871-1179 FX 312-281-4643
e-mail CopyWork@aol.com

18. RESOURCES:

We've put together a list of some of the things you really need to know as a Media Rep – Names, Addresses, Books, Reference Materials, Checklists, and Worksheets.

They'll come in handy as you build your career.

PROFESSIONAL ORGANIZATIONS:

American Advertising Federation (AAF)
Serves local ad clubs, runs ADDY Awards, and AAF/NSAC College World Series of Advertising
(Use them to find your local ad club.)
1400 K St. NW • Washington, DC 20005
202-898-0089 FX: 202-898-0159

National Newspaper Publishers Association
Supports smaller daily newspapers and weeklies
3200 13th St. NW • Washington DC 20010
202-588-8764 FX: 202-588-5029

Newspaper Association of America
Organization for daily newspapers – provides services in advertising, circulation, production, and research
1160 Sunrise Valley Dr. • Reston, VA 22091-1412
703-648-1000 FX: 703-620-4557

Suburban Newspapers of America
401 N. Michigan Ave. • Chicago, IL 60611
312-644-6610

The Canadian Daily Newspaper Association
890 Yonge St. #1100 • Toronto, ONT M4W 3P4
416-923-3567

The Canadian Community Newspapers Association
90 Eglinton Ave. East #206 • Toronto, ONT M4W 2Y3
416-482-1090

The Newspaper Marketing Bureau, Inc.
10 Bay St. #201 • Toronto, ONT M5J 2R8
416-364-3744

National Association of Broadcasters
1771 N St. NW • Washington DC 20036
800-368-5644 FX: 202-775-3515

Cable Television Advertising Bureau (CAB)
Serves sales departments of cable television industry
757 Third Ave. • New York, NY 10017
212-751-7770 FX: 212-832-3268

Television Bureau of Canada (TVB)
Serves Canadian television industry
890 Yonge St. #700 • Toronto, ONT M4W 3P4
416-923-8813 FX: 416-923-8279

Radio Advertising Bureau (RAB)
Supports radio stations and radio sales departments
304 Park Ave. S. • New York, NY 10010
800-232-3131

Radio Marketing Bureau
Serves Canadian radio industry
146 Yorkville Ave. • Toronto, ONT M5R 1C2
1-800-ON-RADIO 416-922-5757 FX: 416-922-6542

City Regional Magazine Association
355 Commerce St. • Washington DC 22314
703-548-5016

Outdoor Advertising Association of America (OAAA)
Represents the outdoor industry
1212 New York Ave. NW #1210 • Washington DC 20005
202-371-5566

Institute of Outdoor Advertising (IOA)
Marketing and creative center for OAAA – OBIE Awards
324 Madison Avenue, NW #702 • New York, NY 10173
212-986-5920

Outdoor Advertising Association of Canada (OAAC)
Serves Canadian outdoor industry
21 St. Claire Ave. East #100 • Toronto, ONT M4T 1L9
416-968-3435 FX: 416-968-0154

Yellow Pages Publishers Association (YPPA)
National trade association for the Yellow Pages industry
820 Kirts Blvd. #100 • Troy, MI 48084
810-244-6200/810-244-0703 FX: 810-244-0872

18. Resources:

Association of Directory Marketing (ADM)
Organization of Certified Marketing Representatives, agencies, and directory publishers
1187 Thorn Run Road – One Thorn Run Center #202
Moon Township, PA 15108 • 412-269-0663

MAGAZINES:

Advertising Age
National advertising weekly
740 N. Rush • Chicago, IL 60611 • 312-649-5200

AdWeek
Weekly – has regional editions with more localized coverage
1515 Broadway • New York, NY 10036 • 212-536-5336

Marketing
Weekly – serves Canadian advertising community
777 Bay St. • Toronto, ONT M5W 1A7

Strategy
Semi-monthly – serves Canadian advertising community
366 Adelaide St. W. #500 • Toronto, ONT M5V 1R9

Broadcasting
1705 DeSales St. NW • Washington, DC 20036
202-659-2340

Media Market Guide
Serves Radio industry with marketing information
PO Box 119 • Bethlehem, NH 03574
603-832-7170 FX: 603-869-3135

MediaWeek
1515 Broadway • New York, NY 10036 • 212-536-5336

Editor & Publisher
Weekly magazine for the newspaper industry
119 W. 19th St. • New York, NY 10011-4234
212-675-4380

The Publisher
Published by Canadian Community Newspapers Association
90 Eglinton Ave. East #206 • Toronto, ONT M4W 2Y3
416-482-1090

Radio Ink
Weekly magazine for the radio industry
1501 Corporate Dr. • Boynton Beach, FL 33426-6654
407-736-4416 FX: 407-736-6134

Presstime
Monthly magazine of Newspaper Association of America
11060 Sunrise Valley Drive • Reston, VA 22091
703-648-1286

Sales & Marketing Management
Provides semi-annual updated information on demographics and sales data for all counties and major metro areas
355 Park Avenue South, 4th Floor • New York, NY 10010
212-592-6200 FX: 212-592-6309

Standard Rate and Data Service (SRDS)
Provides rates and demographic data for newspaper, radio, TV, magazines and business periodicals
1700 Higgins Road • Des Plaines, IL 60018
708-375-5000 FX: 708-375-5501

Broadcasting and Cable Yearbook
Published by R R Bowker • A Reed Reference Company
800-521-8110 FX: 908-464-3553

Link Magazine
Magazine of Yellow Pages Directory Advertising
820 Kirts Blvd. Suite 100 • Troy, MI 48084-4826
810-244-6211 FX: 810-244-6230

BOOKS AND REFERENCES:

Local Media

Newspaper Advertising Sales. The Complete Guide to Job Finding, Facts and Forecasts
Harry Chin
Newspaper Research Press
16135 NE 85th St. PO Box 2381
Redmond, WA 98073-2381

How to Get Rewarding Results with Radio
John Fellows, "Mr. Radio™" • Giraffe Marketing, Inc.
PO Box 66838 • Falmouth, ME 04105-6838
1-800-587-5756 FX: 207-781-5755

Effective Radio Advertising. Winning Customers with Targeted Campaigns and Creative Commercials
Weinberger, Campbell, Brody
Lexington Books • New York

How to Get Results from
Your Yellow Pages Advertising
Kathleen M. Murtagh
Business Services of Meriden • Dept. BR

PO Box 2745 • Meriden, CT 06450-1745
[$9.95 + $2 handling from the publisher]
René Gnam's Direct Mail Workshop
1001 Ideas, Tips, Rule Breakers & Brainstorms for
Improving Profits Fast
René Gnam
Prentice-Hall • Englewood Cliffs, New Jersey 07632
Successful Direct Marketing Methods
Bob Stone
NTC Business Books • Lincolnwood, IL

Marketing
Positioning: The Battle for Your Mind
Jack Trout & Al Ries
McGraw-Hill - Hardcover
Warner Books - Paperback
The 22 Immutable Laws of Marketing
Jack Trout & Al Ries
HarperBusiness/Harper Collins
10 E. 53rd St. New York, NY 10022
Advertising Campaign Planning: Developing an
Advertising-based Marketing Plan
Jim Avery
Published by The Copy Workshop
2144 N. Hudson • Chicago, IL 60614
312-871-1179 FX: 312-281-4643
AMA Complete Guide to
Small Business Advertising
Joe Vitale
NTC Business Books • Lincolnwood, IL

Research
Journal of Advertising Research
641 Lexington Ave. • New York, NY 10022-3108
212-751-5656 FX: 212-319-5265
Journal of Advertising
Published by the American Academy of Advertising
Dr. Les Carlson, Editor • Department of Marketing
245 Sirrine Hall • College of Commerce and Industry
Clemson University • Clemson, SC 29634-1325
American Demographics
P.O. Box 68 • Ithaca, NY 14851 • 607-273-6343
Accuratings
180 N. Wabash • Chicago, IL 60601 • 312-726-8300

Arbitron
142 W. 57th St. • New York, NY 10019
212-887-1300
Research Methods in Mass Communication
Guido H.Stempel III and Bruce H. Westley
Prentice-Hall • Englewod Cliffs, NJ
Marketing Research/Marketing Environment
William Dillon, Thomas Madden, and Neil Firtle
Irwin 1994 • Burr Ridge, IL
**Hitting The Sweet Spot. How Consumer Insights
Can Inspire Better Marketing and Advertising.**
by Dr. Lisa Fortini-Campbell, Ph.D.
The Copy Workshop
2144 N. Hudson • Chicago, IL 60614
312-871-1179 FX: 312-281-4643

Message Development
The Copy Workshop Workbook
by Bruce Bendinger
The Copy Workshop
2144 N. Hudson • Chicago, IL 60614
312-871-1179 FX: 312-281-4643
**The Non-Designer's Design Book. Design and
Typographic Principles for the Visual Novice**
Robin Williams
Peachpit Press • Berkeley, CA
Copy Chasers on Creating Business-to-Business Ads
Edmund O. Lawler
NTC Business Books • Lincolnwood, IL
Tested Advertising Methods
John Caples
Prentice Hall • Englewood Cliffs, NJ 07632
How to Make Your Advertising Make Money
John Caples
Prentice Hall • Englewood Cliffs, NJ 07632
The Copywriter's Handbook
Robert W. Bly
Dodd Mead & Co • New York, NY
Successful Direct Marketing Methods
Bob Stone
NTC Business Books • Lincolnwood, IL
Herschell Gordon Lewis on the Art of Writing Copy
Herschell Gordon Lewis

18. Resources:

Prentice Hall • Englewood Cliffs, NJ 07632

Presentations

I Can See You Naked
by Ron Hoff
Andrews MacNeel

Sales and Sales Management

The Radio Book
Radio Ink Magazine/Streamline Publishing
8000 North Federal Highway • Boca Raton, FL 33487
1-800-226-7857

High Performance Selling
Ken Greenwood
Streamline Press
224 Datura St. • W. Palm Beach, FL 33401

Guerrilla Selling. Unconventional Weapons & Tactics for Increasing Your Sales
Jay Conrad Levenson, Bill Gallagher, Orvel Ray Wilson
Published by Houghton Mifflin

Sales & Sales Training

The AdVisory Board, Inc. Chris Lytle & Associates
Trains sales departments, managers and business owners
700 Regent St. #200 • Madison, WI 53715
1-800-255-9853 FX: 608-284-1184

Giraffe Marketing, Inc.
Sales and advertising training for sales departments, associations and business groups
PO Box 66838 • Falmouth, ME 04105-6838
1-800-587-5756 FX: 207-781-5755
email: MrRadio01@aol.com

Lontos Sales & Motivation
Trains radio sales departments
PO Box 2874 • Laguna Hills, CA 92654
714-831-8861